Essential Articles 12

What is Essential Articles?

Essential Articles 12 is a collection of **the year's most important and topical** news and editorial pieces brought together for **teachers, students and librarians.** It comes to you both as a printed book and online PDF (also on cd)

We've read through thou
of newspapers, magaz
material which is not ea
pieces from well known

We have selected the
thought-provoking piec
**not just news, so t
valuable over time.**

Organised into convenie
to use and one of the mo

Online ace

With Essential Articles 1
to the whole book. Just
your password. You can
the contents always avail
anytime!

How do yo

You probably won't be able to resist just browsing through Essential Articles, but it should also be your first stop when researching almost any subject. Whether you want to raise an issue in the classroom, or find information for a project, Essential Articles is almost certain to have something for you. And, if you want to copy an article, feel free. We've already taken care of the copyright, as long as you're using it within your own institution.

By using either the contents, index or our new online Quicksearch you will be able to find articles on related topics.

Header pages

There is a header page at the beginning of each
ating questions, points of
liscuss within articles.

, you can easily find **personal
with opposing points of**
king for lesson ideas, ways to
esearching one of the topical
der pages are a great place to

ection between **Essential
publication, Fact File.**
ct File support and illuminate
al Articles, while those same
life. You can find them using
eed to waste hours on fruitless

.uk/quicksearch

antly generate a list of
a topic, searching current and
act File and Essential Articles.
Just type the word you want to find into the search box.

Essential Articles 12

CAREL PRESS
www.carelpress.com

Editors: Christine Shepherd & Chas White

Essential Articles 12

Published by Carel Press Ltd
4 Hewson St, Carlisle CA2 5AU
Tel +44 (0)1228 538928, Fax 591816
info@carelpress.com
www.carelpress.com
This collection © 2010 Christine A Shepherd
& Chas White

Acknowledgements
Additional illustrations: Adrian Burrows
Designers: Adrian Burrows, Anne Louise
Kershaw, Debbie Maxwell

Editorial team: Anne Louise Kershaw, Debbie
Maxwell, Christine A Shepherd, Chas White,
Jack Gregory
Subscriptions: Ann Batey (Manager), Brenda
Hughes, Anne Maclagan

We wish to thank all those writers, editors,
photographers, cartoonists, artists, press
agencies and wire services who have given
permission to reproduce copyright material.
Every effort has been made to trace copyright
holders of material but in a few cases this has
not been possible. The publishers would be
glad to hear from anyone who has not been
consulted.

We are particularly grateful to Kezia Storr of
PA for her helpfulness and efficiency.

Cover design: Anne Louise Kershaw
Front cover cartoon by Christian Adams

**British Library
Cataloguing in Publication Data**
Essential Articles 12: The articles you need
on the issues that matter   1. Social
problems – Study and teaching (Secondary)
– Great Britain 2. Social sciences – Study
and teaching (Secondary) – Great Britain
    I. Shepherd, Christine A   II. White, C
    361.00712 41
    ISBN 978-1-905600-19-9

Printed by Finemark, Poland

Contents

“ *I think people are seduced by the project and the fact that a little kid could produce something so gorgeous* ”
page 23

Contents

> *I am convinced that it is a grave misfortune for babies to be born with Down's ... It's a misfortune for their parents and their siblings as well*
> *page 48*

" *She described the birth as a 'miraculous experience' – but many see the babies as mere 'users of resources', money-grubbing, nappy-requiring, food-scoffing cling-ons*
page 80 "

Contents

> *It's the social worker's assessment and the network that protect the child. But it's a judgment call and sometimes the call is wrong*
> page 92

> *The human soap opera continues even as the plot turns dark*
> *page 128*

Contents

> *I came here to be closer to the Prophet, but I am witnessing extreme intolerance*
> *page 163*

Poverty ... puts women and girls at higher risk of being targeted by traffickers
page 190

Animals

Issues to think about and discuss

Of all the species in all the world, which would we miss the most? - Animals plants and insects are disappearing at an alarming rate. Is there a single type of plant or animal which we really can't afford to lose? If you could save only one species would it be the primates - our nearest relative? Or should we save the tiny, but vital, plankton? And are there some species that we would actually be better off without?

A pet prescription – Companion animals can bring a sense of purpose to the lives of elderly people, argues this writer. And they give children a sense of responsibility. But can you agree with him that it is a good thing for a child to sob in distress as a pet is put to sleep?

Michelito – Marvel or murderer? – Is an eleven year old bullfighter astonishingly brave and skilled? A child prodigy, just like Mozart? Is he just cruel? Or perhaps he is a victim of his parents' ambitions.

Animals

Environment

Tradition

Blood sport

Childhood pet

Animals

Bullfighting

Eco-systems

Heartbreak

Of all the species in all the world, which would we miss most?

By Richard Gray, Science Correspondent

From the Amazon rainforests to the frozen ice fields of the Arctic, animals, plants and insects are disappearing at alarming rates from pollution, habitat loss, climate change and hunting.

Nearly 17,000 species are now considered to be threatened with extinction and 869 species are classed as extinct or extinct in the wild on the International Union for Conservation of Nature's Red List. In the last year alone 183 species became more endangered.

Now, in the face of the growing threat posed by environmental changes around the globe, five leading scientists are to argue whether there is a single type of plant or animal which the planet really cannot afford to lose. The debate, titled Irreplaceable – The World's Most Invaluable Species, will see five experts present the case for the world's most important animals and plants from a shortlist of five: primates, bats, bees, fungi and plankton.

Primates, which are among the most threatened of animals, are likely to win hearts due to their cuddly exterior while those with a sweet tooth for honey will doubtless sympathise with the bees, which are suffering near catastrophic declines.

Fungi are among the most abundant organisms on the planet and include amongst their numbers the Earth's biggest living organism, a giant fungus known as Armillaria ostoyae which stretches for 2,384 acres in Oregon's Blue Mountains.

Bats are the biggest family of mammals and the only one that can fly, but are threatened by habitat loss and persecution by humans.

Plankton provides food for some of the smallest and biggest animals on the planet, including the Blue Whale.

Here we examine the contenders in detail and asks if we can afford to lose any of them at all.

The big five:
Life just wouldn't be the same without them

PLANKTON

SIZE: 10 micrometres (0.0004 inches) to 1 millimetre (0.04 inches)

NUMBER OF DIFFERENT SPECIES: 50,000 in the light zone of the ocean alone

STRENGTH IN NUMBERS: Billions of trillions

THREATS: Pesticides and pollution can damage plankton blooms

It is hard to feel too attached to plankton. A drifting soup of microscopic algae, creatures and bacteria, they are not even one group of species but bridge entire taxonomic kingdoms. Plankton is essentially anything living in water that is too small to swim against the current.

But despite its small size, blooms of plankton are visible from space and can sustain billions of marine creatures. The plant-like organisms in plankton, known as phytoplankton, are found close to the surface of the water where there is sufficient light to allow photosynthesis.

"Half of the world's oxygen is produced by these organisms," explained Professor David Thomas, from the school of ocean sciences at the University of Bangor. "If you took that away you would lose the basis of life on the globe."

Professor Thomas said: "If you go back far enough in time, life started in the plankton, so we owe it a remarkable debt."

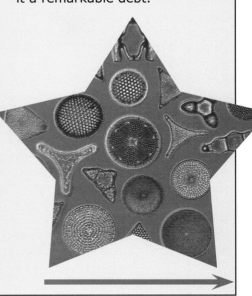

BATS

SIZE: 2 grams (0.07 ounces) to 1.5kg (3 pounds)

NUMBER OF DIFFERENT SPECIES: 1,100

STRENGTH IN NUMBERS: billions

THREATS: One in five species are threatened by habitat loss and persecution

Bats are the only mammal capable of flying and are so highly evolved to be capable of pinpointing a single insect flying in the pitch black and plucking it out of the air using echo location.

They are a major predator of insects and play a key role in controlling insect numbers. They are also the most abundant mammal on the planet – one in five mammals is a bat.

"Bats have an extraordinary diversity, which makes them an essential part of the ecosystem," said Dr Kate Jones, a bat expert from the Zoological Society of London. "Most crucially, bats are major agents of pollination and seed dispersal. Without them many crops would fail because they play such an essential part of the ecosystem."

BEES

SIZE: Around 12.7mm

NUMBER OF DIFFERENT SPECIES: 20,000 known species of bee

STRENGTH IN NUMBERS: Billions of individuals – a single honey bee hive can contain 40,000 bees

THREATS: Disease and climate change have seen populations plummet by up to 80%

Without bees, humans would starve. These industrious little insects are the world's greatest pollinators. Millions of years of evolution has seen many plants become almost entirely reliant upon bees to help them breed.

Crops such as almonds, peaches, avocados and apricots are totally reliant upon bee pollination.

The total worldwide economic value of pollination has been estimated to be around £130 billion a year, and that is without the honey and wax that bees also produce.

Bee numbers have, however, fallen by up to 80% in some parts of the world due to disease, climate change and pesticide use. The situation has grown so critical that beekeepers are warning there will be no British honey left in the shops by Christmas.

George McGavin, an honorary research associate at Oxford University's Museum of Natural History, said: "The planet could go on functioning quite happily without any large animals such as primates.

"We rely upon bees for just about every vegetable, flower and fruit around. They are a crucial terrestrial group and we would face mass starvation without them."

FUNGI

SIZE: a single cell to 2,300 acres

NUMBER OF DIFFERENT SPECIES: Up to 1.5 million

STRENGTH IN NUMBERS: millions of billions

THREATS: Probably the least threatened group and the cause of threat to many other species in the form of disease

Fungi are a much maligned group of species. They include pests that can kill gardeners' plants, diseases that are responsible for ailments such as athlete's foot and moulds that leave unsightly stains in our houses.

But without fungi we would not have gardens, houses or even feet at all. It was fungi that first allowed plants to move out of the oceans and on to land by establishing a symbiotic relationship that still exists today.

"It was fungi that allowed plants to move onto land around 600 million years ago," explained Professor Lynn Boddy, a mycologist at the Cardiff School of Biosciences. "Without fungi we would still be living in the ocean."

The other main role that fungi perform is as nature's recyclers. They clean up remains of dead plants and animals by decomposing them and returning the nutrients they hold back to the environment to be used again. Professor Boddy said fungi were also vital in the production of foods – such as bread, cheese and beer and chocolate – and medicines such as penicillin."

PRIMATES

NUMBER OF DIFFERENT SPECIES: 394

WEIGHT: 28g to 200kg

STRENGTH IN NUMBERS: 400,000 great apes, around a billion other primates

THREATS: 114 species are threatened with extinction. Bushmeat hunters and habitat loss are the main threats

Primates are our closest cousins and share more than 90% of our DNA.

Ian Redmond, chairman of Ape Alliance, an international coalition of organisations and individuals working for the conservation and welfare of apes, said: "Primates are a keystone species in tropical rainforests. They are major dispersers of seeds as they eat fruits and then dispense the seeds in little packets of fertiliser around the forest.

"We need to protect primates today in order to have forests tomorrow that can absorb carbon dioxide from the atmosphere and prevent the erosion of soil."

And here are a few species we may be happy to do without

Feral Pigeons

Known as the rats of the sky, they are considered pests in most city centres around Britain.

Wasps

Capable of injecting venom from the end of their sting even after they have died, it is a popular question faced by entomologists - what are wasps actually good for?

Rats

They carry plague and live in the sewers. Even Sir David Attenborough, the wildlife presenter, does not like them.

Stinging Nettles

The bane of all schoolboys who have ever been forced to wear short trousers. Although nettle soup is a known delicacy.

Woodlice

These scuttling crustaceans thrive in the warm damp corners of houses and are reputed to be a good substitute for prawns in seafood sauces.

The Sunday Telegraph 12 November 2008
© Telegraph Group Ltd 2008

A pet prescription

Des Spence

He lay curled up in a filthy box at the back of the cattle shed with his six brothers and sisters. As we approached he yelped loudly and wagged his tail – and thus he chose us and we chose him.

He herded the chickens, tagged along on marches through the fields, waited for the school bus, ate titbits under the table, danced with us to The Cure, and licked my sleeping face in the mornings. One day he was killed by a car.

His mother was a working border collie, and the farmer disapproved of his becoming a "pet." He grew up with us. He herded the chickens, tagged along on marches through the fields, waited for the school bus, ate titbits under the table, danced with us to The Cure, and licked my sleeping face in the mornings. One day he was killed by a car. My now grown brother sobbed quietly as we buried Gem in the back garden. He was the first of the family to die.

Is keeping a pet good for your health? I have strong misgivings about caged pets: reptiles that wake every two weeks to eat a rat, the rodents that become so fat that they almost explode, or the forlorn birds in cages that live for 80 years repeating

the same expletive. But the traditional companion pets such as dogs and cats are very important to people. (I wonder, however, about the dogs that live in handbags, the child eating breeds, and the inbred royalty of the Kennel Club.) These once wild animals are now tamed by the sofa and open fires.

Indeed, the elderly pet owner seems both happier and fitter than the average. Pets offer elderly people friendship, a substitute for those long gone and ungrateful children, an exercise routine, but above all a sense of purpose. None of these is in the gift of our medication. But it's in childhood that companion pets are most important.

I despair of virtual electronic pets – children reduced to cooing over yet another disposable object or flickering image. For it is only real pets that can

nurture a sense of responsibility, caring, and duty, thus preparing children for the reality of adulthood and parenthood. It is an opportunity often denied to our "have it all" but "have nothing" children. And ultimately pets convey an understanding of the cycle of life and death in a sanitised and medicalised world.

Only real pets can nurture a sense of responsibility, caring, and duty, thus preparing children for the reality of adulthood and parenthood.

So when I find my 3 year old asleep in the dog's bed, the dog asleep in my 7 year old's bed, and the dead mouse left on my daughter's bed by the cat, I am happy. And when my 10 year old son recounted how he had sobbed as he held our old dog while he was euthanased recently, all I said was, "Good."

Des Spence is a general practitioner, Glasgow

*BMJ
13 September 2008
Volume 337; a1616*

MICHELITO – MARVEL OR MURDERER?

Photo: Russel Chan/AP/Press Association Images

Strong passions are aroused by an 11 year old who has been achieving astonishing results in the controversial world of bullfighting.

Michel Lagravère, a chubby faced youngster, is a star in his native Mexico after setting a record by killing six young bulls in one weekend – apparently the youngest matador to achieve such a feat.

He started training at the age of four at his father's bullfighting school. He was only six when he first faced a bull and first made a kill. In Mexico there are no limitations on age, while in other bullfighting strongholds, such as southern France and Spain, youngsters are banned from killing bulls, even though they can appear in the ring.

"How can one accept that children see blood flowing and that men are torturing animals in full view without anyone stopping them?"

However Michelito, as he is known, and his phenomenal, if gory, success does not go unchallenged. In summer 2008, several of Michelito's fights in Southern France were banned and there has been opposition from both child welfare and animal welfare groups. Child protection agencies tried unsuccessfully to ban him from fighting on the grounds that he should not be allowed to put his life in danger. His mother, Diana Peniche, saw no problem: "I have no reason to forbid him from his passion and I think people will understand me. People who've followed my son's career have seen that the boy has special qualities." Certainly in his many fights the boy has never had a serious accident, but he has always faced young bulls not adult animals.

PETA – People for the Ethical Treatment of Animals – argues: "This was calf-killing. Like the child "bullfighter" these animals were still youngsters, but, unlike him, they didn't choose to be there and they didn't want to hurt anyone. They just wanted to prance and play."

"I wonder if we haven't got better things to do than pitting a baby animal against a baby human".

Jean-Claude Laborde, head of the main anti-bullfighting group in Southern France, said: "I wonder if we haven't got better things to do than pitting a baby animal against a baby human". Groups opposed to bullfighting were also outraged that young children were taken to witness the spectacle. One activist wrote to President Sarkozy, "How can one accept that children see blood flowing and that men are torturing animals in full view without anyone stopping them?" Michelito is a particular target for opposition because of his star status and because, unlike other apprentices, he always prefers to end his fights with a kill.

His father, also named Michel Lagravère, and himself a former bullfighter, refers to other prodigiously talented youngsters in defending his son: "I have never seen anyone so gifted. No-one ever stopped Mozart playing the piano or Maradona kicking a football – so they should just leave him alone." And Michelito himself is as defiant, "No-one can stop me fighting," he told local newspaper Diario de Yucatan. "I was born a bull fighter and I will die one."

Sources: Various

Art & culture
Issues to think about and discuss

Che Obama: The new cult of personality – Is it strange that Barack Obama's image is suddenly everywhere? Is this a celebration or a cult of personality? Do the people wearing the t-shirts really know what the president stands for?

Art & minds – Are the arts just an indulgence for the rich, or a necessity in even the most turmoil-filled lives? Are we what we eat and drink, or what we love, feel and get inspired by? Danny Boyle argues children need more than the basics if they are going to rebuild their lives.

A two-year-old could do that... and in fact she has! – A gallery owner loved the bold abstract work of this artist – and so did the paying public. So does it matter that she's only two? At what age can you be considered an artist? What makes a piece of art worthy of praise? Does it matter what the artist intended or is art only in the eye of the beholder?

Art & culture

Intention

Necessity

Appreciation

Inspiration

Personality

Art & culture

Icons

Image

Tragedy

Che Obama: the new cult of personality

Why does no one else find it creepy that Obama's image now adorns everything from t-shirts to hats to train tickets?
Helen Searls

Standing on the National Mall in the cold, waiting for the inauguration ceremony to begin, it was hard to escape the feeling that something very new was afoot. Not only were we all about to witness a slice of history – the swearing in of the nation's first black president – we were also about to witness the inauguration of the first truly iconic superstar into the office of US president.

It is hard to convey the scale on which Obama the icon has gripped the country and its capital in particular. The new president is not merely popular, nor is he even just a superstar politician. President Obama has become something else in the eyes of the nation and perhaps even the world. He is now an icon. And like all true icons, the man's image is everywhere.

The Obama cult started fairly modestly with the usual campaign buttons, yard signs and bumper stickers. But from early on, this was more than a traditional display of political support. The Obama image became a central feature of his own political campaign. The slogan 'Yes we can' and a pop art image of Obama captured more of a mood than an old-fashioned political campaign could. Gradually the now famous pop art image, created by a Los Angeles graffiti artist, Shepard Fairey, started to appear on t-shirts and on posters. It is doubtful that anyone ever thought to wear a t-shirt with George Bush's image splashed across it, except to deride him. Now, wearing the image of the president is not only popular, it has become almost obligatory in some circles.

It is doubtful that anyone ever thought to wear a t-shirt with George Bush's image splashed across it, except to deride him

Obama's image is not just appearing on t-shirts. There are Obama hats, Obama pencil cases, Obama hoodies, Obama screen savers, Obama jewellery, Obama coffee cups and Obama street murals. And Obamamania has gone mainstream

Obama's image is not just appearing on t-shirts. There are Obama hats, Obama pencil cases, Obama hoodies, Obama screen savers, Obama jewellery, Obama coffee cups and Obama street murals. And Obamamania has gone mainstream. Today in DC we can buy metro tickets sporting Obama's image. Numerous buildings are decorated with huge banners welcoming the new president. Even the National Portrait Galley has got in on the act, snapping up Shepard Fairey's original collage for the gallery walls long before the new president's official portrait will be commissioned.

Such is the strength of the cult surrounding Obama's image that vendors at the inauguration were hard pushed to find new ways to commemorate the day. Many tried, of course. On my own walk into the city I saw Ben's Chili Bowl on U Street, a local landmark, displaying a huge red, white and blue ice sculpture of the letters OBAMA. A church on 16th Street offered hot cocoa and a chance to be photographed with a life-sized Obama cut-out. On the Mall itself everything from Obama special inauguration bandanas to Obama dollar bills (with President Lincoln's image replaced with President Obama's) to my own personal favourite, Obama water, was on offer.

The pervasive nature of President Obama's image is something new and quite different in American presidential politics. When President George W Bush came to office you could maybe get a mug, a commemorative coin or a button, but even his most ardent supporters did not adorn themselves with his image. True, some did sport Stetsons, but that was about the extent of the personality cult around the previous occupant of the White House.

In contrast, today our new president's image is everywhere and yet no one seems to find this strange or creepy. During the Cold War, American politicians used to vilify communist countries for the cult of personality that surrounded their leaders. But Maoist China and Stalin's Russia have nothing on Obama's America when it comes to the cult now surrounding the new US president.

It could be argued that one explanation

Photo by Alex Barth

Few who owned the poster knew very much about Che Guevara the politician, but having it on your wall signalled that you were somehow progressive and radical

for Obamamania is simply that people want to take with them a little bit of history. Coming just 40 years after Martin Luther King's 'I have a dream' speech on the same mall, many elderly Americans shed tears of joy, disbelief and triumph as the first black president took the presidential oath. This was a moving occasion and it is not surprising that many want a memento or a souvenir of the moment that most thought could never happen.

But the cult around Obama the person goes way beyond souvenir hunting. Normally if you buy a souvenir you put it on a shelf somewhere and move on. This is something different. The image of Obama is not merely something to collect. It is something to wear and show off. It marks or labels those who wear it and as such it is a symbol, not just an image. Moreover, as a symbol it means something different than President Obama the real-life politician.

President Obama the politician has political goals and aspirations just like other politicians. In contrast, the Iconic Obama is not tied to or associated with any real or specific goals. To imagine that all the people wearing the t-shirts and putting up Obama posters are fervent supporters of Obama's programme or policies misses the point of what has happened here.

That face now represents a sense of hope and faith about the future. It is a hope that many share and want to identify with. And when businesses or individuals display Obama's image they are expressing their faith and identification with such a sentiment. It is not hope for a very specific goal, but that does not diminish its appeal. People want to be part of the Obama nation. It is a nation built on sentiment – more akin to the Red Sox Nation than any real political entity.

Or maybe a better analogy is the poster child of the sixties, Che Guevara, whose simple image was again just a face decoupled from a political message, used to decorate the bedrooms of the youth of America and Europe. Few who owned the poster knew very much about Che Guevara the politician, but having it on your wall signalled that you were somehow progressive and radical. Today, though, progress and radicalism have been replaced by hope and faith. And it is not simply teenagers who want to identify with this message.

Helen Searls is executive producer at Feature Story News in Washington, DC.

Spiked 21 January 2009
http://www.spiked-online.com

Prospect Magazine

"Don't jump just yet, let's wait to see what Obama does."

That face now represents a sense of hope and faith about the future

In the wake of catastrophe, food and shelter is not all that children need argues **Danny Boyle** director of the award winning film *Slumdog Millionaire* – they also need the creative means to express what has happened in their lives.

"'Art for art's sake' is another piece of deoderised dog *****", Nigerian novelist Chinua Achebe famously fulminated.

Whilst Achebe went too far in my view – art for art's sake can be great fun, I'm in the movie business after all – it's lamentable that art in the West is too often straight-jacketed into purposelessness. As a result, the arts can be dismissed as a decorative frill or a recreational distraction – an escapist and ultimately impotent indulgence to transport us from the doldrums of our comfortable Western existence.

But not in Africa, where ravaged by war, famine, disease and domestic violence, the arts are being invoked to help child victims of rape, AIDS and war to cope with and confront conditions no human was designed to endure.

Of course, as aid agencies struggle to help people caught up in rebel-held areas of the Republic of Congo, it's impossible to deny that what's needed most in crisis-stricken Southern Africa is hardly film, music and theatre but water, food and medicine.

But in the wake of a catastrophe, these essential staples of life are not enough to fully restore it. Through the arts, the humanities, young children living in catastrophic circumstances need to be given something to live for and something to express their lives through.

For the past three years, I've helped to nurture a new arts-led voluntary initiative called Dramatic Need, which works with children living in abysmal conditions in sub-Saharan Africa.

Last year, the organisation encountered four year-old Bongani, an orphan whose mum had died of AIDS when he was three. In some ways, he was typical, as more than a third of all young South African mothers are HIV positive. This little boy, along with 30 others, was being cared for in a crèche in a squatter camp in the North West Province of South Africa. With pitiful resources, their teacher and carer struggled to provide these kids with anything that engaged their attention. They were not learning, or behaving. The teacher told of four year olds violently attacking each other, and on one occasion, her.

Because these kids were so young, volunteers focused on basic things like helping them to make coloured playdough and paint murals on the corrugated iron walls outside their school. One day, they helped the children to make papier-mache masks. "Make your mask as scary as possible" was the brief. At the end of the day, as the teacher began to collect thirty-four Cubist masterpieces – eyes askew, noses where the ears should be – Bongani, this small, typically placid four year old, went beserk, screaming, shouting, lashing out, repeating the same sentence in Tswana over and over again. His teacher translated: "He's saying 'Don't take her away, don't take my mum away again'."

Bongani had shaped his grief into a mask of newspaper, paint and wallpaper paste. I am neither ▶

Main photo: Seboko Phillemo Morobi: his instinctive talent and determinati transcend his background and disability.
© Dramatic Need

art &
minds

dramatic need

Dramatic Need dance workshop for troubled teenagers in Viljoenskroon, Free State, South Africa – hosted by Oumaki Lekgetho (foreground).
© Dramatic Need

clairvoyant nor therapist, but I was told about the effect it had on him when he was allowed to take it home. They said the kid practically flew.

For children – and for many adults – art plays a vital role in helping them to express feelings and difficulties that they aren't otherwise able to articulate. Its importance is never greater than in post-conflict conditions. Of course, water, food, and first aid are essential to deliver during a crisis, but in recovering from conflict, none of these things can restore human dignity to a person dying from disease or help a rape victim to cope with their outrage.

To suggest that the only things that maintain our humanity are those that serve our biological needs, our basic needs, seems to me palpably incorrect. We are not just what we eat. We are also what we feel, what we fear, what we love and what we hate. Unexpressed tensions find their strength in violence. I look at the Congo now; if there is not a means to move beyond the hatreds and resentments of the past, then we will never move past violence.

I am not suggesting that a bunch of paint-brushes dropped in Goma will help anyone. But I am suggesting that post-conflict relief should look to means of coping with and expressing individual trauma, and that the arts

– used for millennia as a method of self-expression – can play a vital role. Whether visual or performance-based, they can be psychotherapeutic. They allow people to participate in their own recovery, help them to relocate and resuscitate their sense of self. It's not for nothing that the arts are called the humanities; they humanise us.

Often the arts can help children to confront – as well as comprehend – deep-seated, community-held taboos, such as HIV and domestic violence, which, in some rural areas where Dramatic Need works, affect around 80% of women. In May this year, we ran a drama workshop with a group of teenagers in South Africa, encouraging them to pick a challenging topic, an issue that mattered to them. One of the girls chose domestic violence, or "anger at home" as she called it. Not unusual given its prevalence, but what was striking to the Dramatic Need volunteers was the fact that emerged later: this 14 year-old girl had chosen to use her play to dramatise her own rape, a secret she confided in a volunteer afterwards.

It was clear that she'd invested a huge part of herself emotionally, and despite breaking down several times during rehearsals, she was determined to carry on. After performing the

play to her unsuspecting peers, she thanked the volunteer for giving her the chance to "make people know" the horrific things to which she'd been subjected. Whilst she'd not revealed its autobiographical dimension, her drama had helped to exorcise a demon that had thrived on silence.

But the escape that artistic self-expression provides African children is not only imaginary or psychological. For the extremely talented, it provides a way of getting out of the ghetto, of fulfilling unimagined ambitions, and unlocking unknown creative potential.

Seboko Phillemon Morobi (see main picture on page 21) an 18-year-old boy from Viljoenskroon, Northern Free State, South Africa lost his right hand in an accident and his parents to HIV when he was very young. Despite being highly intelligent and having taught himself to speak English, in a dominant agricultural community with high unemployment, being disabled would mean he had little chance of finding work and would be destined to lead a life in abject poverty. When they found Seboko, he was sleeping in a neighbour's barn, and walking six miles each day to school.

He showed an extraordinary interest to get involved in a film-making workshop Dramatic Need was running, using mobile phones to capture and cut mini documentaries about things the children cared about. This young guy – who'd never seen, let alone edited a film before – displayed an instinctive genius for shaping narrative. Dramatic Need has now secured him an internship at Design Republic, Johannesburg's leading media agency. We are currently fundraising to help him get there.

For these African children, then, art is not an adjunct to life but truly capable of transforming it. It has an educative, enhancing, restorative, reorienting power, not despite – but precisely because – of the desperate circumstances in which its practitioners find themselves.

My film *Slumdog Millionaire*, tells the story of a child who escapes the slums of Mumbai. During the filming I saw plenty of what the world's poorest children endure and, frankly, anything that lightens their load or brightens their day is important. In these rural and township parts of Southern Africa – where tragedy is the rule, not the exception – the essential, humanitarian relevance of the arts is unequivocal.

Danny Boyle is the director of the film *Slumdog Millionaire*, and a trustee of Dramatic Need.

We are not just what we eat. We are also what we feel, fear, love and hate.

MORE INFORMATION

http://www.dramaticneed.org

Developments magazine Issue 44 2009

A two-year-old could do that... and in fact she has!

Critics of abstract art often like to belittle it by stating that the painting could easily have been created by a child. Melbourne gallery director Mark Jamieson has more reason than most to know the truth in this. When Nikka Kalashnikova, a Russian-born photographer whom he represents showed Jamieson some paintings, he liked them so much he decided to include them in a group exhibition at the Brunswick Street gallery, where he is a director. Jamieson was told the artists name was Aelita Andre, what he wasn't told is that Aelita is Kalashnikova's two-year-old daughter.

It was only after he publicised the show that he discovered Aelita's real age. Shocked, slightly embarrassed and admitting it is 'difficult to judge

chinos and at age one, completed all the works in her first show. "She does all the same kid things that other kids do" explains Michael – painting being one of them. The difference however is that rather than sticking Aelita's latest creation up on the fridge, Nikka took it to an art gallery.

It all began, as with most kids, by painting on large sheets of paper in her play-group. However one day her father placed one of his canvases on the floor to paint. Aelita responded by crawling onto her father's canvas and dabbing and smearing paint with such passion and enjoyment

Aelita Andre painting, photograph by Nikka Kalashnikova

> *"There was something different in the way Aelita painted, the way she was working, her interest in the paints and the brush strokes and her concentration"*

abstract art', still he decided to 'Give it a go'.

Aelita whose father, Michael Andre and mother Nikka both paint as a hobby, began painting before she could walk. She speaks both English and Russian, likes chocolate and baby-

that her father just let her continue. Then he placed another canvas beside his on the floor and let her paint on her own. And on it went.

Aelita's parents allowed her to continue doing what she clearly enjoyed doing. Michael explains "Maybe,

being artistically inclined we paid more attention to what she was doing. But I liked the way she was concentrating on the brush strokes and getting colours." Nikka continues "There was something different in the way Aelita painted, the way she was working, her interest in the paints and the brush strokes and her concentration, it was something different." Many people have been suspicious of exactly how much control Aelita has over the painting but her parents insist they only do what she herself can't. She picks the colour for the background and they will prepare the canvas. She

chooses the colours she wants to paint with, they simply remove the lids for her. Aelita is constantly looking at new ways to use the paint using her hands, feet, even walking on the canvas and sometimes actually falling onto it, nappy and all.

Her parents say that her work is so vivid, expressive and energetic and depicts such amazing subjects that "As soon as she finished her first acrylic on canvas, I saw the MIR Russian Space Station surrounded by cherry blossoms. It was just so poignant and evocative". The old issue of intention in art is

MIR Space Station in Cherry Blossoms by Aelita Andre, photograph by Nikka Kalashnikova

Michael replies "There is nothing that could make Aelita paint, she does it all of her own free will. She's enjoying it and we're having fun." Aelita seems blissfully unaware of the global attention she has attracted, "She has no idea what is happening and so she'll go on producing regardless of the attention she's receiving which is good for us as she's not fussed by that," Nikka continues, "a lot of parents push, but this is like a game for her."

Asked why she originally kept the artist's age a secret, Nikka replies, "I didn't want it to have discrimination, you know, this is Aelita, she is two years old and this is her painting, I'm sure she can't be good if she's two and so on. I think just hang it up on the wall and have a look at it." Which is exactly what people seeing the exhibition did, and it seems a lot of them liked what they saw. Nearly half of Aelita's pieces sold on the first night of the exhibition, one larger three canvas piece for £3,200. "All of the money goes into a trust fund" explains Michael, "so it's all towards her future."

And will she have a future in art? "Maybe she'll be the next Picasso, I doubt it," says Robert Nelson, "but at the moment I think people are seduced by the project and the fact that a little kid could produce something so gorgeous." And Aelita is showing no signs of stopping producing such bright, bold and thought-provoking pieces. Although she's still not weaned off the bottle, her work has already sold for thousands, and continues to ignite heated debates about art around the world.

Sources: Various

again raised here; is that what Aelita meant to paint? Not everyone believes that the artist's intention is the most important consideration when it comes to appreciating a piece of art. What really matters, and some believe can only matter to the viewer, is what they themselves perceive in the art – what you see, enjoy and appreciate when you look at a painting.

For those who do appreciate it, Aelita is producing plenty of work. Her parents say she is obsessed with painting, running around demanding "painting, painting!" and "kist, kist!" (the Russian word for 'paintbrush'). They say that when people see her paintings they can't believe a toddler painted them. Indeed when her work was shown to art critic Robert Nelson, who was not given any of the artist's background information, he said his first impression was of "credible abstractions, maybe playing on Asian screens with their reds." On learning that the artist was a child he said that 'credible' art can be found at any primary school. "The fact that they're done by a two year old doesn't mean they're not good, in fact they possess something quite magical by virtue of the fact that a child has been involved."

Now a worldwide sensation, Aelita's rise began from simultaneous front page articles in both leading Australian newspapers: The Sydney Morning Herald and The Age. She has since had TV crews from China, Japan, Australia and the UK to view her work and her exhibitions. While you'd have to pay £230 million to get a painting signed by Jackson Pollock, buyers will receive the painting with Aelita's full palm print on the reverse of the canvas.

Asked whether her parents are simply living their dreams through their daughter,

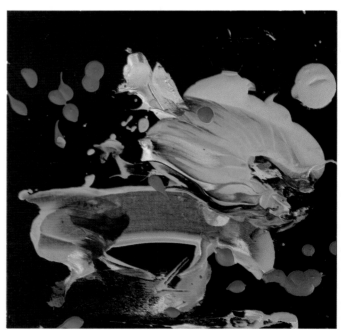

Sausage dog by Aelita Andre, photograph by Nikka Kalashnikova

For more about Aelita and to see more of her art go to:
http://aelitaandreart.com

Body image

Issues to think about and discuss

Think before you ink? & I hate my lizard – Why do celebrities feel the need to cover themselves in slogans and designs? What does a tattoo say about you? When is a good time to have a tattoo? One writer thinks they are "the cheap plumage of the attention-seeker". The lizard tattoo was supposed to demonstrate "a new-found right to self-expression" but it wasn't even a successful act of rebellion.

"My daughter begged me to eat, but all I wanted was to lose weight" – Do all anorexia sufferers fit the same profile? What brings it on and what can be done? For a time, anorexia proved to be stronger even than a mother's love for her daughter.

Dear Graham – Why might someone's friends undermine her attempts to get slim? Is it just jealousy? Graham Norton's answer is inventive, but is it accurate?

Bikini or bingo wings? – Why is there so much pressure on women and their bodies? Is it better to age gracefully, or keep your independence and wear what you like? Should you wear shorts when you're fifty or is it time to conform?

Body image

Media attention

Diets

Anorexia

Friends

Body image

Tattoos

Celebrities

Pressure

Fashion

Think before you ink?

'Body graffiti' may be popular among celebrities such as Angelina Jolie and Amy Winehouse, but that doesn't make it classy, attractive or wise, says Simon Mills

'Tattoos; not just for losers any more." So declared an article celebrating the art of body graffiti last weekend. It went on to reference a bunch of winning celebrities, all covered in badly drawn cod-philosophical/faux-tribal/cloyingly sentimental illustrations, to show just how

Tattoos are in Vogue this month (which presumably means they won't be in vogue in a few months' time).

gentrified tattoos have become. They included such aspirational figureheads as Pete Doherty (branded with his son's name), Amy Winehouse (adorned with 1950s pin-ups and playing cards, among many others) and Peaches Geldof (a bow and a cross). Or, if you like, crackhead, car crash and airhead.

Tattoos not for losers any more? Hmmm.

Tattoos are in Vogue this month, too (which presumably means they won't be in vogue in a few months' time). The fashion glossy applauds the widespread cult of the illustrated woman by citing Angelina Jolie, Sienna Miller, Kate Moss and even Samantha Cameron (who has a dolphin on her ankle) as beautiful,

classy examples of artfully needled ladies. But here's the thing. It is hard to argue that any of these irrefutably beautiful women has been anything but blighted - rather than enhanced - by her rash decision to become graffitied.

Angelina is a particularly interesting case. Her body, indelibly violated from the neck down, looks like a more shapely version of that fellow in Christopher Nolan's thriller Memento, who couldn't remember anything and had to have notes inked into his skin. I'm sure every single dermal artwork has meant something to Angelina on her life "journey", but in among the elaborate tiger "tramp stamp" on her back and a laborious series of map references (don't ask) is surely the most boring tattoo ever: the legend "Know Your Rights". Why would

Badly drawn girl: have Angelina Jolie's tattoos enhanced or blighted her looks?

anyone have something that you might find on the noticeboard of a small claims court etched between her shoulderblades?

Then there's Amy Winehouse. To my eyes, the daily tragedy of the staggering beehive is only made more wretched by the ugly marks that cover her emaciated body - tattoos that are modish, apparently ("old school" sailor-style designs being particularly in), but look to me as if some hyperactive five-year-old has been let loose with a rainbow pack of Sharpies.

Victoria Beckham probably thinks her tattoos are classier than Amy's because they are, you know, dead spiritual... like scented candles and Madonna albums. Her body is a holy war of Hindi Sanskrit, Hebrew, Latin and Roman numerals, which represent her children's birth dates. One doubts that Victoria (who once admitted she never had time to finish a book) has ploughed through the Zohar or four Vedas, or can confidently count to 100 in Roman (who can?), so why does she feel the need to cover herself in ciphers and foreign languages?

For that matter, why does anybody need to prove commitment to children and spouse and, most commonly, dead relatives, via some ill-conceived body modification? My wife would be horrified if I etched my thigh with some facsimile of her face and my mother, God rest her soul, would spin in her plot if I inked my arm with a mawkish tribute. What's wrong with carrying around a photo?

Surely the most boring tattoo ever: the legend 'Know Your Rights'. Why would anyone have something that you might find on the noticeboard of a small claims court etched between her shoulderblades?

scary or alternative any more. Now that they have been co-opted by the masses - the squares, the mortgaged, the Volvo drivers, the wusses and the girls - we have come to accept their fairground aesthetic in much the same way we have decided to allow Gordon Ramsay's pointless swearing.

"If a client wanted to give up a City job to become a rock star, I would be supportive of them getting a tattoo," says Lisa Bathurst, an image consultant. "Generally, though, I think a devil's advocate approach might be better and I'd advise someone to think very carefully. A tattoo might look cool and sexy when you are in your twenties and thirties, but there comes a point when things start to fill out and stretch and then it might not look so good.

Victoria Beckham probably thinks her tattoos are classier than Amy's because they are, you know, dead spiritual... like scented candles and Madonna albums.

Most tattoos are the cheap plumage of the attention-seeker, visual ice breakers for last-chance barflies and aspiring reality TV show contestants. They certainly aren't

"Circumstances and lifestyles change. Our culture is now fairly accepting of tattoos, but others aren't," Bathurst adds. "I lived in Japan for five years, and over there

you have to cover up all tattoos when you go to the gym."

Statistically speaking, tattoos are a craze of epidemic proportions - and a ghastly cliché. One in five Brits has one, and one in two Americans. May I quote the much-tattooed Ozzy Osbourne here? "If you want to be f***ing individual," he once said, "don't get a tattoo. Every f***er's got one these days."

Tattoos are an all-pain-no-gain, self-inflicted suffering. They take a couple of hours to get, a lifetime to regret, and a heck of lot of money to erase. Studies show that about 10 million people in the US will have them removed this year, mostly through laser surgery. Shortly after breaking up with Billy Bob Thornton, a Rolling Stone journalist pointed out the "Billy Bob" tattoo on Angelina Jolie's arm. "Where does that leave you?" asked the hack. "With a lot of dermatology appointments," she replied.

Hip-hop producer Pharrell Williams, who has an entire shoulder inked in tribal designs, will soon undergo a removal procedure, which involves applying new skin over old art. "These guys actually grow the skin for you," he explained to Vogue.co.uk.

"First you have to give them a sample of your skin, which they then replicate. Once that's been done, they sew it on - and it's seamless." Ewww.

The conservative response to youngsters, especially females, thinking of getting tattooed has always been: "Imagine what it will look like when you are old." But I don't buy that. When you're old, you wear woolly tights and long-sleeved cardies. No one sees your flesh when you are pensionable, and your outdated, embarrassing tattoo will be hidden.

No, much better to think about what your beautiful, clean, firm and healthy body looks like right now, kid.

The Daily Telegraph 16 July 2008
© Telegraph Group Ltd 2008

'I HATE MY LIZARD'

Je ne regrette rien... except my tattoo – Becky Pugh

My friend and I had them done while travelling in New Zealand. The way we saw it, people on their gap years did wacky stuff — they grew dreadlocks, took drugs, lost their virginity. We spent hours weighing up the ways to deface our bodies, but had reached no firm conclusions. Then one day we dropped into an internet café and read an email from a friend in Australia who'd taken the plunge and had a butterfly tattooed on her wrist. The gauntlet had been thrown down.

We were 19 years old and believed we had no choice but to respond. I suppose we wanted to flaunt a new-found right to self-expression. Why we couldn't express ourselves through our clothes or some angst-ridden poetry, I'll never know.

The fateful act occurred in a "body art parlour" on the North Island. The skinhead bruiser who created it was covered in tattoos and his salon stank of cigarettes and fried food. The tattoo hurt like hell, cost a fortune and, worst of all, looks truly hideous. I had envisaged an oriental dragon nestling discreetly on my hip bone. But skinhead bruiser man spent three torturous hours inking a big, fat, blotchy lizard, on the edge of my belly. I am thankful that my clothes cover it up, but I live in fear of the way it will deform if I get pregnant.

Worst of all, it wasn't even a successful act of rebellion. My mother didn't give a damn when she saw it and my father still believes it's temporary. When I ask my husband what he thinks, he says: "I love it because it's part of you." What he means is: "I hate it, but what can I do?"

I never loved it, not even for a second. It's about as unfeminine as a hairy beard and as cool as a cappuccino. The moment I can afford to have it lasered off, it's a gonner.

The Daily Telegraph 16 July 2008
© Telegraph Group Ltd 2008

"My daughter begged me to eat, but all I wanted was to lose weight"

Anorexia has been seen as something that just affects teenagers. But, as **Annette Smith** tells **Emma Shrimsley,** it's an illness that can strike at any age...

There was a time when I used to think there was nothing stronger than a mother's bond with her child. But I was wrong. For me, anorexia was stronger. It is a guilt I will always live with – that my love for my daughter Lauren could not override my compulsion to be thin, and that, no matter how much she begged, I couldn't eat for her.

Like many women, I'd always loved food and was never one to hold back when the cakes came round. By my late 30s, I was a size 14–16 and weighed around 11 stone – which is quite heavy for me, as I'm only 5ft 4½in. But despite my generous proportions, I didn't feel unattractive at all. I took pride in my appearance and loved clothes shopping.

Life was good; I had a great husband, Steve, who I'd been with since I was 19, and a wonderful, close relationship with Lauren. But then six years ago, when I was 37, things started to unravel. My periods had always been heavy, but the constant bleeding became so bad that I needed to have a hysterectomy. Even though Steve and I had previously made the decision to have only one child, I felt surprisingly bereft. It was also a difficult recuperation and I lost 10lbs in the process.

I still felt weak three months later when I returned to work, but straight away colleagues started telling me how great I looked. Spurred on by the compliments, I joined a gym and cut out eating snacks. I lost more weight and my perception started to shift – suddenly my new weight of 10 stone seemed huge and I vowed to keep slimming.

By the spring of 2004, I was a size 12 and the compliments kept on coming. What people didn't know was that by now I was skipping breakfast, eating fruit and yogurt for lunch and my only proper meal was in the evening with Lauren and Steve.

Perhaps my weight would have stabilised there, but a series of tragedies caused things to spiral further out of control. My mother suddenly developed Lupus – a disease where the body's immune system turns on itself – and died within three months. Dad and I clung to each other for support and it became increasingly apparent that I didn't want to turn to Steve. His initial support wavered as I constantly pushed him away, and soon we just didn't know how to speak to each other. In hindsight, our marriage had been deteriorating for a while – Mum's death just highlighted our problems. We decided to separate.

In some ways it was a relief, but also another loss. One thing, however, remained constant and within my control – my weight. By now, I was a size 8. Friends and family began to comment that I was 'a little on the skinny side', but all I could see was my flabby stomach and big thighs. I wanted to cut down on my food even more, but hunger still got the better of me.

It was in January 2007 that I started to use laxatives. Afterwards I felt so much better and, within three or four weeks, I was taking a pack a night and visiting half a dozen different chemists to maintain my supplies. Once a pharmacist stopped me and said: 'You seem to buy a lot of these.' I walked out, mortified that I'd been rumbled and anxious that I now had one less supplier to call upon.

I was also cutting down drastically on food. On a 'good' day I might eat a bit of bread, a low-calorie soup, a low-fat yogurt and a satsuma. Some days I would exist on black coffee alone. I was exhausted all the time but could barely sleep due to the crippling stomach pains caused by so many laxatives.

The dieting took its toll on my personality as well. Previously I had been very sociable – now I was constantly on a short fuse, either crying or snapping at friends and family. I managed to drag myself to work each day but I completely avoided social situations, to the point of being reclusive. By March I had dropped to a size 6. Then the size 6 clothes became so big that I had to buy trousers from the children's section.

I continued to cook for Lauren but made excuses to avoid eating, telling her I'd had something at work or would eat later. When she did nag me, I forced food down and then took extra laxatives. Shamefully, I also started finding reasons to cancel our shopping trips because I knew it would be impossible to avoid going for lunch together.

I had been surprised at first that Lauren had let me off the hook, but I soon found out she was as desperate to avoid our outings as I was. 'I am ashamed of you,' she told me one evening. 'I used to be proud of you, but now you look so old and haggard.' She tried every approach she could think of to make me eat – begging, anger, emotional blackmail. She would offer to cook for me again and again until she could take it no more and scream: 'Why can't you just eat?' before storming out of the room telling me how selfish I was.

Our whole relationship changed and every conversation became about my eating. On one occasion we were discussing her school prom. It was usually a subject of great excitement, but all she could say now was: 'You probably won't even be around then.' I should have felt horrified that my 15-year-old daughter thought I was going to die, but the anorexia had taken over and I felt emotionally detached from the consequences of my actions. Furthermore, I didn't even contemplate how dangerous my eating habits could be to Lauren's own self image and attitude to food. 'How do you think I feel when you say you're fat even though you are wearing smaller clothes than me?' she once said.

Everyone around me tried to persuade me to eat. Colleagues would constantly invite me to the canteen; friends would ▶

Below left: Annette in 2003, when she was a size 16. Below right: in a photograph taken during her therapy sessions in an attempt to show her how thin she had become

'One thing remained constant and within my control – my weight loss. By now I was a size 8'

Annette is now in recovery and, having finished her counselling course, is happy with her size

trauma of the past few years. Even I now realised I was barely functioning. Lauren was the only good thing in my life – my only reason to exist.

Still, each time my counsellor weighed me I would be thrilled if I had lost more weight. If I gained, I would take extra laxatives. Eventually she gave up weighing me. When I talked to her I felt more positive, but the feeling evaporated almost as soon as the session ended. Countless times I would leave her and buy a sandwich on the way to work, only to sit with it uneaten in front of me.

I probably would have gone on like that had it not been for one weekend in November 2007. When I looked in the mirror as I put on my make-up, I saw how dark and sunken my eyes had become. I looked grey and ill. Later that day, I bumped into someone I hadn't

'Even I now realised I was barely functioning. Lauren was the only good thing in my life '

seen for months. When she saw me, she immediately started crying and sobbed: 'What are you doing to yourself?'

The next day I had planned to paint my lounge, but I felt so ill I had to keep stopping to sit down. It had been the same when I'd tried to do the housework the afternoon before. Sooner or later I was going to collapse or end up in hospital – I finally realised I couldn't do that to Lauren.

I went to the kitchen, made myself two pieces of toast and ate them. I waited for the guilt to hit me but it didn't. That night, for the first time in nearly a year, I went to bed without taking laxatives. The next morning I had a small bit of breakfast and a salad for lunch.

Each day I ate a bit more, but it wasn't an instant cure. A couple of weeks later when my clothes started getting tighter I was straight back on the laxatives, but the difference now was that I felt I wanted to get better. I knew I couldn't

give them up completely, but I made a concerted effort to cut down.

Lauren was so supportive and, amazingly, she had no residual anger – our relationship improved as soon as I started eating again. We resumed our evening meals together in November, starting with small portions for me at first. By January 2008, I had stopped taking the laxatives altogether and was back up to a size 6. I made sure I ate three times a day, even if they were small meals.

By February, Lauren and I decided we should go shopping together – our first trip out in months. We got ready just as we always had, deciding what to wear and chatting as we did our make-up. As we drove into town, I glanced over at Lauren and saw she was beaming. I felt the same way. Four months before, it had seemed unimaginable that we would be doing this again. We pottered around the shops before the big milestone – lunch. When I finished my meal of chicken and rice, she grinned at me and said: 'Well done, Mum. You're amazing.'

'I'm so sorry,' I told her. 'I don't think I'll ever be able to forgive myself.' My wonderful, understanding daughter refused to hold a grudge even if I couldn't let myself off the hook. 'You're OK now. That's all I care about,' she said.

From then on it was a nerve-wracking process going up through the dress sizes – but I kept telling myself it was a good thing. I am now a size 8–10 and happy with it. I don't know how much I actually weigh and I don't want to.

I had my last counselling session in June last year. It was scary letting go, but I know I can go back if I ever feel myself wavering and that reassures me hugely. It's still hard to deal with the guilt I have about Lauren, who is now 17, but remarkably she seems to have emerged from this a very wise young woman. I am immensely proud of her.

offer to cook. Thankfully, my oldest friend Debs refused to be put off. I had told her not to call me any more but she ignored me and finally, in August 2007 when I was too weak to protest, she dragged me to the GP. I remember feeling shocked because she was crying and, in the 32 years I've known her, I've rarely seen her cry. She told the GP she felt she was going to lose me and that I had gone from being gregarious and optimistic to aggressive and disinterested.

My doctor prescribed a course of anti-depressants and set up an appointment with a counsellor at a local NHS eating disorders clinic. I agreed to it because I feared they might try to hospitalise me otherwise. I thought I would completely clam up, but I spent the first session pouring out all the

For more information contact The British Dietetic Association, 0121 200 8080; bda.uk.com, or The Eating Disorders Association, 0845 634 1414; www.b-eat.co.uk.

Good Housekeeping, February 2009

Graham Norton

The TV presenter and comedian gives advice

Dear Graham

When my weight shot up to 14 stone, I was mocked so cruelly by a gang of schoolchildren at the bus stop that I decided there and then to do something about it. It's been a long and arduous slog and I still have some way to go, but the hardest thing is the lack of support from friends and family. It seems everyone prefers me fat and cuddly.

When I invite friends over, they bring boxes of chocolate, even though I ask them not to. "Oh, go on. One won't do you any harm," they say. People - my slimmer friends, especially - make me feel I'm being controlling and obsessive by dieting. And some days it seems as if all the world is conspiring to make me the obese, self-loathing 33-year-old woman I once was.

I sometimes wonder if it's jealousy that makes them behave this way. Most of my friends are still single and perhaps their biggest fear is that I will meet someone and leave them behind.

What do you think?
Debbie S, Swansea

Dear Debbie

Congratulations and hurrah for bored schoolchildren. I'm sorry you aren't getting the level of support you'd like, but you must understand that your strength of character reflects badly on the rest of us. Am I the only one who has breathed a sigh of relief when a friend who has been on the wagon picks up the wine bottle once more? Don't we all feel like pigs when someone refuses the offer of bread in a restaurant while we've already started slapping the butter on ours?

We can all sympathise with short bursts of self-discipline - such as losing weight for a wedding or not drinking because of antibiotics - but any encounter with pure unmitigated self-control leaves most of us feeling very unsettled and slightly judged, even if it is only by ourselves.

I hope for your sake that these are the reasons your friends are less than enthusiastic and that, by giving you tempting foods, they're not trying to cut down the competition for the cream of Swansea manhood. People are also very resistant to change and in their eyes you are Fat Debbie. You must admit it has a certain ring to it and rolls off the tongue faster than Debbie Who Lost all the Weight or, worse still, Gorgeous Debbie.

Joke about your diet when you are around family and friends and don't let them see how seriously you are taking it. Accept the boxes of chocolates with a smile, but then give them away to the schoolchildren at the bus stop. Revenge can be very sweet indeed.

Graham

The Daily Telegraph 12 November 2008
© Telegraph Group Ltd 2008

It seems everyone prefers me fat and cuddly.

Bikinis or bingo wings?

Bikinis or bingo wings? You'll never please the body police, so put the boot in to a fashion taboo before it's too late

Miranda Sawyer

Summer has arrived, prompting even the most modest of ladies to get, if not their ya-yas, their upper arms out in celebration. Let your wings flap free! And feel happy that you're not likely to have your photograph splashed across the papers accompanied by a thought-provoking headline such as: 'She spent £9,000 on a face lift, but why hasn't Anne Robinson done anything about her bingo wings?' Yes - why, Anne, why? Who are you to wear a short-sleeved T-shirt in a built-up area? Why can't you go burka until you've coughed up for an all-over hoik-back-and-staple? Or at least until your body looks like Helen Mirren's and the world is happy to letch and/or discuss it seriously on Woman's Hour.

If it's not Anne's upper arms, it's Madonna's hands, Demi's calves, Goldie's neck, Sarah Jessica's everything. And women are now so used to this bullying, boring norm that revealing any part of your body that's not taut, tanned and free of fuzz has become nothing short of revolutionary. Forget shackling yourself to a railing or hurling yourself headlong at the Queen's racehorse, just reveal your knees once you're over 30 and watch the status quo crumble like a stale cake.

When I was at the Latitude festival recently, I saw a very good-looking woman in her fifties dressed in up-to-the-minute festival attire. Namely, Hunter wellies, rock-band T-shirt and short-shorts: denim cut-offs chopped high enough to reveal her thighs. Said thighs were fine, in that they formed a vital section of a pair of working legs. The woman could walk and everything. But they were also shocking, because they weren't of Mirren standard. The skin was saggy, there were visible veins and blotches and puckers. Those thighs looked their age. And so the lady in the shorts caused much comment. Was it great that she was dressed like that at her age? Or was it utterly sad?

Many women don't like it if they feel an older woman is playing the sexy card. Their disapproval is competitive. Who does she think she is, poncing around in a miniskirt/with her cleavage on display/thinking she's attractive when she's not all that? Mixed up with that is a protective element: she'll get the piss taken out of her, she's showing too much flesh. She's doing it wrong.

Trinny and Susannah are mistresses of this twisted concern, as is the fashion writer Liz Jones. It's actually just a desire for females to conform, suburban convention at its most extreme. Forget dressing for a laugh, or because it reminds you of the Eighties, or because you've always loved those jeans. Once you're over 40, it is your duty to look acceptably lovely at all times. Celebrate your inner beauty, but only in bias-cut over-the-knee skirts.

Or am I wrong? Perhaps such style gurus have a point. Maybe their advice is needed. Perhaps Anne Robinson is grateful to the person who gave the nation a 'close-up of her crinkly arms'. After all, it can be hard to dress appropriately in these age-conscious, body-conscious and really quite warm times. Too much flesh is distracting, whether you're young or old. Vest tops and batty riders can put everyone off their commute, and it would be nice if builders took note.

Women are now so used to this bullying, boring norm that revealing any part of your body that's not taut, tanned and free of fuzz has become nothing short of revolutionary.

But, but, but... Who wants to be appropriate anyway? What if you like wearing earmuffs? Or bovver boots? Or even short-sleeved T-shirts? 'When I am an old woman, I shall wear purple ...' But that's playing the eccentric card, the asexual batty old bird. Is that all that's left to us as we age? The choice of pretty coordinates or I'm-old-keep-away bobbly coats? When we feel happy or formidable or, God forbid, sexy, how are we to express that in such tedious outfits?

Plus, you know what: if we don't dress in celebration now, we'll lose confidence later. A fortysomething woman said to me recently that she looked at pictures of herself 10 years ago and thought: 'Why was I worried about my appearance back then? I looked great.' So now she feels like wearing a bikini all the time, at work and parties and everything. Because, a decade hence, she'll look back at photos and think: 'God, I looked absolutely amazing.' It's an idea, anyway.

Observer Magazine 27 July 2008
© Guardian News & Media Ltd 2008

Britain & its citizens

Issues to think about and discuss

'A nasty little piece of class warfare' – Are there some people you just wouldn't want to mix with on holiday? Is eco-tourism a cover up for snobbery? A travel agency offers 'Chav-free' holidays – saying you won't meet anyone called Britney or Kylie-Lianne on their trips.

Let's hear it for mad monarchy – Is having a monarchy better than having a president as head of state? Is the system charming or absurd? According to comedian David Mitchell, the monarchy is unfair and eccentric but better than any alternative.

Why I threw green custard over the business secretary – What is the right or wrong way to protest? How far should you go to make your point? Is it fair to attack someone to defend the environment? How else could you protest if the government was doing something you strongly disagreed with? Leila Deen defends her actions but some say she is just childish.

All together now – A portrait of race in Britain & **A recent history of British race relations** – Pete Turner never found race an issue when he was growing up. Is he right to say that these days people who are racist know they should be embarrassed? Would race affect someone's experience of growing up in this country? Does the recent history of race relations suggest that we should share his optimistic views?

Britain &
its citizens

Protest

Class

Race

Attack

Monarchy

Tradition

Eco-tourism

Politics

Britain & its citizens

'a nasty little piece of smug class warfare'

Brendan O'Neill

A green holiday firm's promise of 'chav-free holidays' for the middle classes exposes the snobbery that underpins radical eco-tourism.

Activities Abroad, a green-leaning travel firm based in Northumberland, England, has caused a tink by guaranteeing its clients 'chav-free holidays'.

For the benefit of non-British readers, 'chav' is a derogatory term for working-class British youth, the tracksuit-wearing, blinged-up, lager-willing kind, who are said to populate areas such as Croydon, Bermondsey and Birmingham, but who are most frequently found hanging around in the minds of panicked middle-class, Middle England hacks. In a promo mail sent to 24,000 subscribers at the end of last week, Activities Abroad (AA) promised that no such despicable, lovely people will ever be found on one of its trips overseas.

Under the heading 'Chav-Free Activity Holidays', AA said: '...Children with middle-class names such as Duncan and Catherine are eight times more likely to pass their GCSEs than children with names such as Wayne and Dwayne. This got us thinking. Are there names you are likely to encounter and not encounter on an Activities Abroad holiday?' It did some quickfire research and discovered that on an AA trip you are unlikely to encounter people called 'Britney, Kylie-Lianne, Dazza, Chardonnay, Chantelle and Candice' (in short, thugs and slags), and are far more likely to run into people called Sarah, Alice, Lucy, Charlotte, James and Joseph' (in short, middle class and mild).

11 of AA's email subscribers complained; one denounced the mailshot as 'a nasty little piece of smug class warfare' and promised never to patronise AA again. The Guardian seemed especially miffed by the embarrassing mailout, conscious, perhaps, that AA is the kind of trendy, liberal, eco-aware holiday firm that it normally advertises in its pages. AA's holidays include husky safaris in the Canadian wilderness and volcano hiking in Costa Rica, which can set travellers back £2,000, and last year it won a silver award for 'most environmentally responsible small tour operator' at the British Travel Awards. Yet its managing director, Alistair McLean, was unapologetic about the email, telling one complaining customer: 'I make no apology for proclaiming myself to be middle class and a genuine contributor to our society.' Unlike those Waynes, Dwaynes, Chantelles and Candices, who of course contribute nothing.

AA's anti-chav advertising tactics are disturbing, and more than a little dumb, but are they really so shocking?

Poisonous snobbery towards 'chavvy' and working-class holidaymakers is rife today – only it tends to be expressed in code, in underhand concerns about CO2 emissions, trails of noxious gases in the blue sky, the dangers of cheap flights, and the denigration of foreign cultures by unthinking Brits. AA's mistake was to forget the coded lingo and state out loud the prejudices that underpin new forms of oh-so-superior eco-travel. Perhaps it has done us a crude service, then, by revealing for all to see the naked loathing of the young and horizon-exploring working classes that motivates much of the contemporary debate on tourism.

Much of what AA's Alistair McLean said in response to the 11 complaints about his email went entirely unreported in the Guardian's article, or anywhere else in the British press. This scion of Green travel – hailed by ethical columnists, decorated by the British Travel Awards, and a member of the Responsible Travel coalition ('holidays that give the world a break') – let rip against the Great Unwashed in one online discussion forum. To

> **On an AA trip you are unlikely to encounter people called 'Britney, Kylie-Lianne, Dazza, Chardonnay, Chantelle and Candice' (in short, thugs and slags), and are far more likely to run into people called 'Sarah, Alice, Lucy, Charlotte, James and Joseph' (in short, middle class and mild).**

AA's anti-chav advertising tactics are disturbing, and more than a little dumb, but are they really so shocking? Poisonous snobbery towards 'chavvy' and working-class holidaymakers is rife today.

one complainant, he spat: 'Do you encourage your children to go off and play with the shell-suited, Lambert and Butler sucking teenagers who hang around our shopping centres at night?' He laid into the 'shell-suited urchins who haunt our street corners'. And he pointed out that where his travel firm makes 'a positive contribution to our economy' – by paying 'corporation tax, income tax, PAYE… and [making contributions] to AIDS projects in South Africa and other charitable organisations' – he is tired of watching economic resources being 'frittered away by people who simply can't be bothered ("bovvered")'.

It's nasty stuff, fuelled by hysterical images of feral working-class kids running riot and old-style prejudices about the poor sponging off decent society. Yet the idea that lower-income communities – these 'urchins', these cigarette-sucking teenagers – are destructive, especially when they go on holiday, is widespread. In recent years, 'cheap flights' has become a thinly-disguised codeword for 'cheap people', for those Dwaynes and Waynes who apparently only go overseas in order to drink, puke and fornicate. Eco-activists and commentators try their best to present their opposition to cheap flights as being driven by concern for the environment or even,

laughably, as a radical anti-capitalist stance against 'the toffs' who allegedly populate Ryanair's £5 flights to Riga. Yet their mask of eco-respectability frequently slips to reveal a sneering snobbery underneath.

Caroline Lucas, leader of the UK Green Party, has written of the 'stratospheric cost of cheap flights' and demanded 'an end to cheap stag nights in Riga'. She fails to explain why a flight for a stag night in the Latvian capital is more destructive than, say, a flight to one of AA's husky safaris in the Canadian wilderness. Plane Stupid poses as an edgy campaign group that wants to ground the cheap flights of 'second home owners'. Yet in their more unguarded moments, its members spout bile about one kind of travel only. Its founder says: 'Our ability to live on Earth is at stake, and for what? So people can have a stag do in Prague.' In another statement, Plane Stupid said: 'There's been an enormous growth in binge-flying with the proliferation of stag and hen nights to Eastern

'…and would you and your family be travelling middle or upper middle class?'

European destinations chosen not for their architecture or culture but because people can fly there for 99p and get loaded for a tenner.' That's not edgy – it's the age-old middle-class prejudice against pointless, wasteful working-class tourism dressed up in a little bit of environmental garb.

Whether they're dissing 'cheap flights' (the correct code), 'stag night attendees' (the code starts to slip), or vile 'shell-suited urchins' called 'Dwayne and Wayne' (the code completely falls apart), the target of the eco-aware is always the kind of hedonistic travel indulged by youthful members of lower-income communities. Beneath their environmental concerns there lurks the long-standing prejudice that some forms of travel, involving huskies and volcanos, are worthwhile, and other forms, involving kicking back, relaxing, having unadulterated fun, are low, coarse, destructive and literally 'noxious'.

Tourism and travel have long been the targets of vicious snootiness. When

'My God, Wilkins, we're not the first. Chav culture is already here!'

centipedes'. In more recent times, from the 1980s onwards, commentators have attacked 'the vile behaviour of British tourists' in places like southern Spain, the 'disgusting inebriation, oral sex and other beachside practices [that would] startle a Blackpool donkey'. The image of the 'Blackpool donkey' is telling: the sentiment is that 'these people', these

noxious, whether metaphorically, as described by that Victorian observer, or literally, in the way that they are now described by today's snobs as being 'harmful to the environment'. AA's fantastically crude reduction of entire sections of the population to 'chavs', 'urchins', 'cigarette-suckers', all instantly recognisable by their ridiculous first names, reveals the deep snobbery that still underpins the tourism debate. Because it is about betterment and exploration, about escaping the local and dipping a foot into the global, about having ideas way, way above one's station, travel invites the undiluted snobbery of those who consider themselves 'superior by reason of intellect' like no other single issue.

> **Beneath their environmental concerns there lurks the long-standing prejudice that some forms of travel, involving huskies and volcanos, are worthwhile, and other forms, involving kicking back, relaxing, having unadulterated fun, are low, coarse, destructive and literally 'noxious'.**

in the Victorian era British workers first started venturing to the seaside, thanks to one Thomas Cook, snobbish commentators complained that 'of all noxious animals, the most noxious is a tourist'. Later, in the modern era of the 1920s and 30s, the middle classes who had long been travelling to places like Italy and Greece were alarmed to see the lower middle-classes, and even Americans, following in their wake. The British literary snob Osbert Sitwell described American tourists as a 'swarm of very noisy transatlantic locusts'. His sister, the poet Edith, said tourists were 'the most awful people with legs like flies, who come in to lunch in bathing costumes - flies,

destructive urchins, should really stay put in places like Blackpool rather than fouling the sophisticated world with their filthy habits as they get 'loaded for a tenner'.

Paul Fussell argued in his 1982 book Abroad: British Literary Travelling Between the Wars that: 'From the outset, mass tourism attracted the class-contempt of killjoys who conceived themselves... superior by reason of intellect, education, curiosity and spirit.' The language changes over the years – from 'animals' to 'locusts', 'centipedes' to 'yobs' and 'drunks' – but the sentiment remains remarkably similar: these people are

We should challenge the fake distinction made between 'enlightening travel' and 'filthy travel', and insist that travel is in itself a positive thing. Whether people go abroad to hang out with huskies or to chat up girls, to donkey-trek in Peru or to sunbathe in Magaluf, it's all about escaping, exploring and experiencing, and urchins who smoke and sponge off society (allegedly) should be as free to do that as the kids named Lucy, Charlotte and Alice.

Brendan O'Neill is editor of spiked. His satire on the green movement – Can I Recycle My Granny and 39 Other Eco-Dilemmas – is published by Hodder & Stoughton

Spiked 26 January 2009
http://www.spiked-online.com

Let's hear it for

mad monarchy

David Mitchell

Who can fail to have been impressed by the spectacle of President Obama's inauguration last week? I'll tell you who - the Queen. I bet she sat there watching it on an unpretentious four-by-three portable, while she sorted dog biscuits into separate Tupperwares, muttering: "It's bullshit, Philip! No carriages, no horses, no crown - it just looks like a bunch of businesspeople getting in and out of cars. It's as if the Rotary Club's taken over a whole country. And the new one's not even the son of one of the previous ones, unlike last time. I thought they were coming round to our way of thinking at last."

And she'd have a point. It might have been considerably grander than a new prime minister pulling up outside Number 10 and waving but, compared to the coronation, it looked like someone signing for their security pass and being shown where to hang their mug. And that's what comes of having an elected head of state. There's always got to be some fudge between the dignity and status of the office and the politician's desire to seem humbled by the occasion.

In fact, it's one of the most startling examples of politicians' self-belief that, as they assume offices of massive power for which they have striven, to the exclusion of all other activities, for decades, they'll still back their chances of coming across as humble. Now, there's an insight into the megalomaniac's mindset: "Not only can I get to be in charge of everything, I bet I can make people believe that I'm not really enjoying it so that, thanks to reverse psychology, they'll want me to stay in power longer!"

Whereas the Queen didn't have to pretend she wasn't enjoying the coronation; from the little bits of grainy footage I've seen, it's hilariously evident. A poor, terrified slip of a girl, the fluttering eye of a storm of pageantry, hesitantly mewing her lines, while thousands of incredibly important people in fancy dress behave as if she's the Almighty made flesh. That's what I call a show.

I don't envy the Americans their political system. I envy them their success, money, inner belief that everything isn't doomed to failure, attitude to breakfast,

"A poor, terrified slip of a girl... hesitantly mewing her lines, while thousands of incredibly important people in fancy dress behave as if she's the Almighty made flesh. That's what I call a show"

and teeth, but not their constitution. The fact that their figurehead and political leader is the same person gives them a terrible dilemma, especially when it was George W Bush. The man's clearly a prick (he says he'll wait for the judgment of history but, if the jury's out, it's only because they're deciding between personable incompetent and evil moron) but even his political enemies were squeamish about calling him one.

They had to respect the dignity of the office and couldn't come to terms with the American people having bestowed it on someone who can't string a sentence together and would only make the world worse if he could. To completely let rip in slagging off Bush would have caused collateral damage to national prestige, not

"Don't mistake me for a republican. I genuinely like this system. It means the most powerful man in the country still has to kowtow to someone (other than the president of the United States)"

only by undermining the office of president but, more important, by openly admitting how far America is from being the classless meritocracy it claims.

We in Britain have no illusions about being a classless meritocracy and it's therefore thoroughly appropriate that our head of state should be chosen by a method dominated by class and utterly and openly devoid of regard for merit. Separated from the nitty-gritty of politics and power, our monarchy can be a focus for both national pride and self-loathing, the latter being much more archetypally British than the former. A harmless little old lady dutifully going about various tasks she finds stressful seems about right for our national figurehead - neither better nor worse than we deserve.

Don't mistake me for a republican. I genuinely like this system. It means the most powerful man in the country still has to kowtow to someone (other than the president of the United States). It encourages tourism. The royal family, while nominally our betters, are in fact our captives and an interesting and profitable focus for media attention. It's as unfair as life; the royals can't escape and if you want to become royal, you basically can't. It's a more or less functional arrangement

that no one would ever have had the wit to devise deliberately.

Which is why Liberal Democrat MP Evan Harris's attempt to fiddle with it is so enervating. He wants to change the Act of Settlement whereby Catholics can't marry the sovereign and end the discrimination against female heirs to the throne. He thinks this will make the monarchy more fair. I suppose it will, in the same way that throwing some bread into the Grand Canyon will make it more a sandwich.

The monarchy is overwhelmingly, gloriously, intentionally unfair - that's the point. The defining unfairness is that you have to be a member of that family to be king or queen; fringe unfairnesses like their not being able to marry Catholics or men having priority in the line of succession are irrelevant in that context. And what's so fair about primogeniture, which Harris is not planning to touch, or the sovereign having to be Anglican, which is also apparently fine? He wants to spend parliamentary time, mid-credit crunch, on a law aimed primarily at helping Princesses Anne and Michael of Kent.

When will people get the message? If you want a fair system, have a republic, elect a president and live with some arsehole like David Cameron giving a speech every Christmas Day afternoon, bitter in the knowledge that you asked for it. Otherwise, we should stick with what we've got, rather than trying to tinker. No abdicating, no skipping Charles, no changing weird ancient laws. We get who we get because we'd rather live with the inadequacies of a random ancient structure than the inadequacies of one designed by Brown and Cameron.

The monarchy's not perfect, but it's also not harmful, powerful or, and this is the clincher, our fault. The inevitable imperfections of anything we replaced it with would be.

The Observer 25 January 2009
© Guardian News & Media Ltd 2009

Photo: Plane Stupid

WHY I THREW GREEN CUSTARD OVER THE BUSINESS SECRETARY
Leila Deen

Peter Mandelson epitomises all that is wrong with our democratic system. His CV is a reason for us to give up on democracy and take direct action. After several disgraces and resignations, Mandelson is back from exile in Europe to be shoe-horned into government as an unelected minister, via an archaic loophole which allows the Prime Minister to create peers and place them in power for his own political ends. This is what democracy in the UK looks like.

Mandy is charged with representing the interests of the British people on matters of business and industry. He has enormous influence over the decisions of government. All of this is reason enough to throw green slime over him, but here comes the real outrage. The third runway at Heathrow, a pantomime of unpopular decision-making, is supported by no one apart from a few in the aviation industry

– namely BAA, British Airways and their various stooges. In the past two years, the people of west London, the mayoral candidates, environmental and development organisations, the public, opposition parties, the Labour Party and finally the Cabinet, have all reportedly expressed overwhelming concerns about the runway, not least because – if it is built – our promise to reduce carbon emissions by 80 per cent will be totally out of reach. If we build a third runway, every other industry in Britain will have to cut its emissions to zero, which is obviously impossible. Yet the Government said yes to the runway. Why?

Well, Mandy rode back into town with his best mate Roland Rudd, who has been appointed as BAA's senior lobbyist. They met several times before Mandelson steam-rollered his colleagues into accepting this ridiculous plan (bashing his head on the cabinet

table in frustration, apparently). Is Mandy's close friendship with Rudd behind the green light for the runway? We are facing the catastrophic and irreversible devastation of our planet. We have five years to stabilise carbon emissions and start driving them down – firstly, by not expanding high-carbon industries. Aviation is the fastest-growing cause of climate change, and is responsible for about 13 per cent of Britain's total warming impact.

As a responsible person, I will not stand by while corrupt hypocrites like Peter Mandelson are allowed to schmooze away any chance we have of stopping this impending nightmare.

The Independent 7 March 2009,
© 2009 Independent
News and Media Limited

THE PEOPLE INVOLVED:

Lord Peter Mandelson

Was appointed Secretary of State for Business, Enterprise and Regulatory Reform in October 2008.

Always a controversial figure, his nicknames in the press include "Prince of Darkness", "Lord Voldemort" and, more usually, "Mandy".

In 1997 he was appointed Minister without Portfolio – coordinating departments and with responsibility for the Millennium Dome. Later he became Secretary of State for Trade and Industry.

In 1998 he resigned because he had taken an interest-free loan from another Labour MP who was actually being investigated by his department.

Ten months later he was appointed Secretary of State for Northern Ireland.

His second resignation came in 2001 after he had phoned the Home Office on behalf of an Indian businessman who was seeking British citizenship but was under investigation by the Indian government.

He resigned his seat as an MP to take up the post of European Commissioner. It was thought that this was the end of his career in UK politics.

On 3 October 2008, Gordon Brown surprisingly announced Mandelson's appointment as Business Secretary. Because he was no longer a Member of Parliament, Mandelson had to be given a seat in the House of Lords.

In January 2009 newspapers reported that he was strenuously supporting a third runway at Heathrow airport despite the objections of many of his cabinet colleagues.

Leila Deen

Is a member of Plane Stupid, a direct action group opposed to airport expansion and dedicated to 'bringing the aviation industry down to earth'.

The group mounts inventive protests such as setting up a golf course on an airport taxiway or blasting music at 110 decibels – the equivalent of a jumbo jet taking off – into the home of Scotland's First Minister.

Leila Deen herself has appeared at Heathrow dressed as a Suffragette and glued herself to the doors of the Department of Transport. She holds a Masters degree in International Studies and works for the World Development Movement, specialising in water issues. She has been quoted as saying: "Democracy has failed us... direct action historically has been a major way that we have got change."

The event

On 6 March 2009. Peter Mandelson was leaving a meeting about the Government's carbon strategy. Leila Deen approached him and threw a cup of green slime over him.

HOW DID READERS RESPOND?

As a result of your actions, a responsible person such as myself may now be unable to go up to Mandy and express my opinions to him, or hand him a petition etc because of increased security. Therefore you have infringed upon my democratic rights through your cheap publicity stunt to get on the telly, which is clearly what it was. Your little speech afterwards was pompous and cringeworthy. You seem to have this idea that it's your democratic right to go around assaulting people. You can't, it's against the law, and even you are not above it. And the "slime coursing through his veins" comment just epitomised the whole childish nature of this stunt.

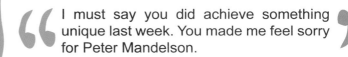

I must say you did achieve something unique last week. You made me feel sorry for Peter Mandelson.

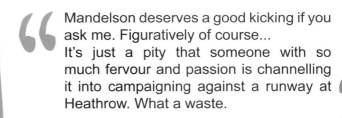

Mandelson deserves a good kicking if you ask me. Figuratively of course...
It's just a pity that someone with so much fervour and passion is channelling it into campaigning against a runway at Heathrow. What a waste.

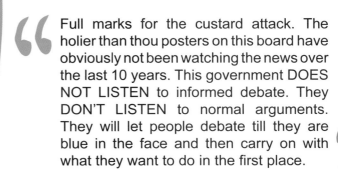

Full marks for the custard attack. The holier than thou posters on this board have obviously not been watching the news over the last 10 years. This government DOES NOT LISTEN to informed debate. They DON'T LISTEN to normal arguments. They will let people debate till they are blue in the face and then carry on with what they want to do in the first place.

Sources: Various

All together now – A portrait of race in Britain

PETE TURNER
BASS PLAYER IN ELBOW

Pete Turner is the bassist for the band, Elbow, who won the Mercury Music Prize. He grew up near Manchester and was adopted by a white British couple. He is not in touch with his birth parents, but he knows that his father was black and from Kenya and his mother was white

I was about four or five months old when I was adopted, and it's the best thing that ever happened to me. My parents are white, and from a very early age I've known they weren't my

"If people have racist views in this day and age I think they keep them to themselves, because they know they should be embarrassed"

birth parents – it's not like they could have hidden it! I think adopting a black child in the 70s was quite a thing, really, and I'm proud of my mum and dad for that. It's funny – I've got three or four friends who are adopted and, if you're not, you assume that you'd need to find out about your natural parents, but none of us do. I know that my natural father was a Kenyan and my natural mother was a white lady, but that's all I need to know.

I was always aware that I was the only black kid in school, but I just got on with it. Looking back on that period of time, I know that in certain areas of the country it must have been horrible, but for me it was never really an issue.

I remember when I was dead little, though, about the first time that I was allowed to walk into the village and get some sweets. I was walking in with my sister and I remember a guy sitting on the other side of the road who looked a proper skinhead. I remember him shouting "nigger", but not loud enough that my sister could hear properly, and she asked me whether he was talking to us. Even though she was two years older I didn't want her to know that someone had said that to me – I thought it would hurt her as much as it would hurt me, so I just said: "Oh it's all right, I know him."

When I was about 15, a mate of mine called Chris – who isn't black but used to think he was – moved up to near where I lived. He introduced me to Public Enemy and my life changed completely: that really was a massive, defining moment. It was so important for me hearing that music because it made me really aware of black culture; it made me aware of being a black person. I used to sit and look at Chuck D's lyrics and it took me to Martin Luther King and Malcolm X and hip-hop music, and the whole of black history.

Since then I don't think a band has made such an impact on my life. Me and Chris used to walk round this little village north of Bury with an absolutely massive ghetto blaster, playing "Fight the Power" really loud. We must have looked ridiculous.

These days there's a lot of black people in indie bands – it's changed enormously over the last few years. But a lot of the bands that I've always liked, such as the Specials, have had black members in them, so it's never really been a thing. In the band everything is fair game with us, so someone will say something and I'll kill myself laughing. Like recently, there was a picture of TV On The Radio – they're a band with four black guys and one white guy. One of the guys in the band pointed to the one white guy and said: "Pete, that's you."

On one hand I think there's been a lot of progress, but then I remember my mum being absolutely horrified and gutted when she got a leaflet from the

BNP through the door recently. It's people's fears: if you watch the news or you read the Mail you're going to panic about things. Maybe it's there as much as it ever was, but if people have racist views in this day and age I think they keep them to themselves because they know they should be embarrassed. I've gone to places where I've been very aware that I'm the only black person in town – but not in this country. I'm a Mancunian before I'm British, though. Manchester is a very cosmopolitan, liberal place and it's got a lot to do the way I am: it's a good place, full of good people. I don't walk round telling people how black I am – unlike my friend Chris!

But I know that when I walk into a room the first thing someone's going to see is a black man. I'm a black Mancunian man, but before that I'm Pete, and that's it.

Interview by Hermione Buckland-Hoby Observer Magazine 18 January 2009 © Guardian News & Media Ltd 2009

For more information and other personal accounts go to:
`http://www.equalityhumanrights. com/raceinbritain`

Photo: Roy Catherall/Roy Catherall/Press Association Images

A recent history of British race relations

1971 – Immigration Bill, Commonwealth citizens lose their automatic right to stay in the UK

1972 – Sir Trevor McDonald becomes Britain's first black TV news reporter

1976 – New Race Relations Act makes it illegal for employers to discriminate on racial ground. The Commission for Racial Equality is created

1978 – Viv Anderson becomes the first black footballer to be selected to play for England

1981 – Brixton riots

1982 – The Voice, a weekly newspaper aimed at Britain's Afro-Caribbean community is launched

1985 – Tottenham riots

1987 – The General Election sees four black MPs win Labour seats.

1987 – Naomi Campbell becomes the first black model to appear on the cover of British Vogue

1991 – Bill Morris is elected as the first black leader of a British trade union

1993 – Black teenager Stephen Lawrence is murdered in Eltham, southeast London by a group of white men

1993 – The BNP wins its first council seat in Millwall

1993 – Paul Ince becomes the first black football player to captain the England team

1997 – Mohammad Sarwar becomes Britain's first Pakistan-born Muslim MP

1999 – Macpherson report into the Stephen Lawrence case declares the police force to be "institutionally racist"

1999 – Indian-born Nasser Hussain becomes the first non-white captain of England's cricket side

2001 – Bradford riots

2001 – Tarique Ghaffur is promoted to Assistant Commissioner in the Met police. In 2008 he accuses the Met of racial discrimination

2001 – David Oyelowo is the first black actor to play an English king in a

Shakespeare play – Henry VI for the RSC

2002 – Love Music Hate Racism is launched with a concert in Manchester

2003 – Baroness Valerie Amos becomes the first black leader of the House of Lords

2004 – Linda Dobbs becomes the first non-white person to be appointed a High Court judge

2008 – Paul Ince becomes the first black footballer to be appointed manager of a Premier League team

2009 – Prince Harry apologises when a newspaper website runs a video of him calling army colleagues "Paki" and "rag head"

Disability

Issues to think about and discuss

A drama that never ends & **Parents of a Down's child must make painful choices** – The pros and cons of having a Down's syndrome child and the issues parents face. Sandy Lewis speaks about the realities of life and her fears for the future of her Down's Syndrome son. Minette Marrin argues that women who have opted for abortion are quite right: "a damaged baby is a damaged family".

If we screen out autism we run the risk of losing genius too – Whose decision is it to abort a damaged foetus? Should society have a say as well as those most closely involved? Does screening mean we are discarding human beings and human potential? This article suggests that we must not risk destroying a future genius: "even at the expense of suffering families."

'My mother once thought of killing us both, life was so hard' – Why are so few disabled people in work? Why don't we see more of them in the media? Can disability actually be an asset? Gary O'Donoghue thinks that it sometimes can – provided we don't wrap people in cotton wool. He gives a personal account of growing up blind yet succeeding as a broadcaster.

Not childsplay - What reaction would you expect these days to a disabled children's presenter? Did parents have a point when they said that she shouldn't have been on TV 'at nine o'clock in the morning and in front of two year olds'?

Disability

Prenatal screening

Acting

Disability

Prejudice

Broadcasting

Television

Down's syndrome

A drama that never ends

He is a successful actor, but his Down's syndrome has led to battles with doctors, teachers and councils. Max Lewis and his mum Sandy talk to Cassandra Jardine

Snogging is 15-year-old Max Lewis's favourite pastime. Fortunately for him, his mother Sandy is a liberal type. "We let him have supper parties," she says. "I put out the food and drink and give them a bell to ring if they need something. I always knock before I enter."

Despite his tender age, Max is already on to his sixth girlfriend and it sounds as if his eye is roving yet again.

"I might grow out of Hannah when I'm older," he says, curled up on a sofa at the family home in Finchley, north London. "I'm always trying to find a blonde girl like Mum. And Sarah dumped me."

But there is something special about Max: he has a passion, and a talent, for acting.

Most teenagers would rather die than make such uncool admissions, but Max is unusual.

He has Down's syndrome, a chromosomal abnormality with a host of physical and mental problems - but these pale before the insensitive treatment he has encountered. "I hate it when people look at me all the time," he says. "They think I'm stupid and can't do anything."

Compared with other people with Down's, Sandy says, Max is not particularly gifted. His IQ is well below 100. "Academic" stuff he finds very hard - though he managed to disguise his poor reading for years by learning his favourite books off by heart.

But there is something special about Max: he has a passion, and a talent, for acting. At his acting group, Chickenshed, he made such a mark that he was cast as Cate Blanchett and Bill Nighy's child

Sandy has had to put up with crass behaviour from doctors, teachers, classmates' parents and erstwhile friends... Max is a complete human being, not a misfortune

in the 2006 Oscar-nominated film *Notes on a Scandal*.

His favourite line, "Up your bum", was cut, he says - perhaps because he proved such a scene-stealer - but there was enough left of his gleeful dancing, eating and chatting on screen to land him a part in Lynda LaPlante's police drama *Trial and Retribution*, and for him to be interviewed on Breakfast TV. His fame has now landed him a new role as a poster boy for disability.

This month the charity National Children's Homes (NCH) is relaunching itself under the new name Action for Children (AFC) and Max has become one of its celebrity spokesmen.

Chief executive Clare Tickell explains that the change of the 140-year-old name was necessary because the charity no longer provides homes for children, but aims to give a voice to children who are vulnerable, either because their parents can't look after them or because - as in Max's case - they have a disability.

"We must find ways of letting them feel we are hearing what they have to say," Clare Tickell says. "Max is remarkable because of the courage and tenacity he shows, despite the challenges he has had to face."

Some of those challenges were physical. Max was born with club feet, which have been remedied, and

a hole in the heart that may require an operation.

His condition also means he has a tendency to poor muscle tone, which makes it difficult for him to walk further than the corner shop, and a low metabolism so he tends to put on weight. The latter is a big issue, as food is his second greatest pleasure in life after performing.

But many other obstacles have been put in Max's and his parents' way.

From the moment her son was born in March 1993, Sandy has had to put up with crass behaviour

from doctors, teachers, classmates' parents and erstwhile friends who, she says, didn't seem to realise that Max is a complete human being, not a misfortune. Instead of pity or ostracism, she wants support and understanding.

The long struggle for help placed a strain on the whole family. Bottled-up rage and frustration led Sandy, who has recently written a book about life with Max, to suffer bouts of depression.

She gave up work to care for him and her husband Paul, who used to work in marketing for Warner

Brothers, had to go freelance to ensure enough flexibility in his hours.

For 15 years they have had no respite care. "Even now we can never go out with our younger son, Charlie [who's 12], for more than a few minutes because Max can't walk, won't sit in a wheelchair and won't be left alone," says Sandy. "It has never been possible to go to the playground or for a walk in the woods.

"Max also has phobias of dogs, clowns and metal detectors," she adds. "He is usually continent, but if he gets excited he can have accidents. And he says what comes into his head.

When we went on a family holiday to Dubai he addressed all the men in Arab dress as 'shepherds', because they reminded him of his school nativity play. Charlie has always suffered from Max being the centre of attention - and sometimes he can be really embarrassing."

Added to that are the battles with authority that are the lot of a parent with a disabled child. "When Max's special needs were assessed," Sandy says, "speech therapy was described as a fundamental necessity.

Although the borough was obliged to provide it, he got none. We had to pay for it ourselves and take Barnet [Council] to court, which cost thousands."

Then there are the constant changes of policy that make it hard to know what kind of help or education is available for a disabled

Bottled-up rage and frustration led Sandy, who has recently written a book about life with Max, to suffer bouts of depression.

child. Action for Children has totted up the changes over the past 21 years (the notional childhood of a disabled child).

"Even we were surprised by what we found," says Clare Tickell. "There have been 98 Acts of Parliament, 82 different strategies, 77 initiatives and 50 new funding streams affecting children's services during that time.

I'm not saying that they aren't well-intentioned, but the culture of uncertainty does not help vulnerable children. They and their parents need consistency and reliability."

Max is one of those who has suffered from changes in education policy. In line with past ideas about inclusion, he originally started in a mainstream school. But as the educational and social gap between him and his classmates widened, problems developed.

"Parents complained that he was holding their children back," says Sandy. "Most children were kind, but they never invited him round to tea. Max doesn't want kindness, he wants mates."

He then moved to a special school – but that was not the end of the story. "There, because all kinds of difficulties are lumped together, he was put beside a child of normal intelligence who was violent. Max was picking up that behaviour."

Sandy Lewis can talk calmly now about such problems largely because she has offloaded her 15 years of hurt and irritation into her book. "My anger has evaporated," she says, but the family's battles are not over yet. They want to find Max a college course in theatre studies.

One day he will also need a safe place where he can live independently. And, of course, entertain his girlfriends.

The Daily Telegraph 9 November 2008
© Telegraph Group Ltd 2008

"My anger has evaporated," she says, but the family's battles are not over yet. One day he will also need a safe place where he can live independently. And, of course, entertain his girlfriends.

Living with Max

'A delightful book about a funny, adorable boy'
Judi Dench

'Having a son with Down's syndrome was, and still is, the best thing that has ever happened to me. It is also the worst.'

SANDY LEWIS

Parents of a Down's child must make painful choices

Minette Marrin

Eugenics is one of those knock-down words used to silence argument. It was used several times last week, in radio discussions and articles about women choosing to give birth to babies with Down's syndrome.

The subject came up partly as advance publicity for a Sky Real Lives television documentary about a heroic young woman who adopted seven babies with Down's, whose mothers had rejected them. There was also a BBC news story suggesting that more women these days are knowingly choosing to give birth to babies with Down's.

In fact the news story was misleading.

Actually, the proportion of pregnant women who choose to abort their foetuses when antenatal screening has detected Down's syndrome has remained constant since screening started, at about 91%. Also the number of Down's abortions has tripled since 1989. The total number of babies born with Down's each year has indeed increased since then, but not by much. This small increase may be due in part to the fact that many women have children when they are much older these days, and some of them refuse antenatal screening.

This misleading news story provoked an impassioned response. Several parents of babies and children with Down's, and representatives of pressure groups, said publicly how much love and happiness such children bring, despite any "challenges", and how they can, with support, live happy, independent lives.

More or less disguised was a strong tone of moral disapproval of anyone who feels that the birth of a Down's baby is a misfortune, to be avoided if possible. Hardly anyone now dares to say so. The word "eugenics" is often used by Down's lobbyists to make the nasty suggestion that people who think it is right to abort a foetus with a Down's diagnosis are as bad as Nazis. This is argument by abuse.

I protest out of long personal experience.

Someone close to me in our family has a learning disability, which has been a handicap and a sorrow to her, and my lifelong experience of children and adults with learning disabilities, including many with Down's, as they have grown older has given me a different perspective. I am convinced that it is a grave misfortune for babies to be born with Down's or any comparably serious syndrome. It's a misfortune for their parents and their siblings as well. Sad observations over decades have convinced me: a damaged baby is a damaged family, even now.

I resent the moral condescension of those who claim that people who think like me are not only wrong but hateful; there have been vicious attacks on me in the blogosphere by disability-lobby extremists. My point of view does not make me a heartless eugenicist.

For one thing I do not think that any woman should be pressed, for any reason, to have an abortion. To do so would be wrong. She must be free to choose and free to make a bad choice. What's more, I firmly believe that people with disabilities should get all possible help and understanding to lead fulfilling lives, from society in general and from the taxpayer.

My belief that certain foetuses would be better not coming to term has nothing, logically, to do with my belief that everything possible should be done to help babies who do come to term and are born among us to share our imperfect world.

There are some strange contradictions surrounding the question of abortion. People who reject abortion as always wrong are consistent and one cannot argue with them. But anyone who thinks abortion is acceptable under some circumstances, and who yet disapproves of what's emotionally seen as "eugenic" abortion, is in an untenable position. After all, people accept abortion for certain "social reasons", and what more powerful "social reason" could there be for an abortion than the virtual certainty that the foetus would be condemned to a life of frustration, disappointment, dependence, serious illness and poverty, to the great sorrow and hardship of its family?

I listen with amazement and sadness to new parents of Down's babies describing a rosy future of love, acceptance and independence (with "support", of course).

The truth is, though people are too compassionate to point it out, that support is in short supply and is expensive. With or without it, Down's children face a future blighted by low or very low intelligence and by a high risk of heart defects (30%-50%), intestinal malformation, leukaemia, kidney and thyroid disease, poor hearing and vision and early-onset Alzheimer's (25% as opposed to the normal 6%), as well as increased chances of diabetes and seizure disorders, including impaired executive function.

In a hyper-sexualised culture that worships

Down's children face a future of low intelligence and a high risk of heart defects

bodily perfection, beauty and sexual success, adult life is also bound to be painful for people with Down's.

When they are babies and children, that may not be a problem. What happens, though, when the Down's child becomes a teenager, interested in how he or she looks and keen to discover love and sex? It is all too predictable – a growing sense of sexual rejection. Any babies born will be taken away, probably rightly. It is heartrending.

In every other way the doors to adult life will seem all but closed, despite everyone's best efforts to push them open. Without a great deal of help, a person with Down's will find it hard to get and keep a job. At a time of recession, with social services understaffed and underfunded, there will be little money for social care. Even now there is nowhere near enough money to help everyone with learning disabilities lead a full and semi-independent life.

Then comes the hardest question of all – what happens when the parents die? The best of social services can do only so much, and it is never enough. Loving brothers and sisters may help, and help a lot; they may well have to, until they die, though they themselves did not choose to take on such a time-consuming, lifelong responsibility.

Most pregnant women instinctively understand all this. That's why nearly all choose abortion. Those who choose differently should understand they are choosing hardship, perhaps great hardship, for their child and for their other children. This has nothing to do with eugenics and everything to do with the painful complexity of moral choices.

*The Sunday Times
30 November
2008*

*Photos
posed
by
models*

If we screen out autism we run the risk of losing genius too

Magnus Linklater

As the number of disorders identifiable by prenatal testing grows, the debate about how to handle them is intensifying

Robin was sitting in the classroom, giving me an exact account of the Russian Revolution. It was his specialist subject and he knew every date, every manoeuvre, the names of the Bolshevik leaders, and where they were when the Winter Palace was stormed. Robin was 16.

"So, what do you think of Lenin?" I asked. He looked at me blankly. "I don't think anything of Lenin," he said. Robin was autistic.

He had an extraordinary grasp of facts, meticulously arranged in his mind. He had no concept of analysis or interpretation. The idea of forming an opinion was alien to him. With that incapacity came social isolation, an inability to form friendships or any lasting relationship. He was stranded, with his brilliant but disabled mind. Bringing him up had been a constant strain for his parents.

Quite how he would fare in the wider world was not yet clear.

Robin, and thousands like him, are at the centre of an ethical debate with far-reaching consequences. Within a few years it may become possible for expectant mothers to have prenatal tests to determine if their child is likely to be autistic.

These may be genetic, to see whether the characteristics of autism have been inherited, or tests of amniotic fluid in the womb to detect high levels of testosterone that have been found to be associated with the condition - mainly in boys.

As the parents of the first British baby screened to be free of a breast cancer gene celebrate the birth of a healthy daughter, this must seem yet another miraculous step in the advance of science. For any family that has experienced the anguish of living with an autistic child, the prospect of being able to determine if another is about to be born would be invaluable. It would offer that most precious commodity - a choice.

Just as with Down's syndrome, cystic fibrosis or spina bifida, a mother-to-be could decide whether she can cope with the strain of bringing up a disabled child. With an autistic child, it may mean a lifetime of rejection - living with someone unlikely ever to fit into the family, who responds with blank incomprehension to affection, whose behaviour may be erratic and disturbing, whose condition is permanent. Autism, and its associated condition, Asperger's syndrome, can range from virtual incapacity at one end of the spectrum to the merely strange at the

"He was stranded, with his brilliant but disabled mind"

other. To bring up one autistic child is a challenge to the sanity of an entire family. To bring up two might destroy it.

The evidence of Down's syndrome suggests that very high numbers of mothers-to-be opt for an abortion if pre-natal tests show that their child has the condition. In America it is as high as 90 per cent. In Britain, it is not so high and may be reversing - as knowledge grows, perhaps more mothers elect to keep their babies. There is, however, a critical difference between Down's and autism, highlighted by Professor Simon Baron-Cohen, director of the Autism Research Centre at Cambridge. He points out that autistic males often turn out to be skilled at mathematics and engineering - some reaching near-genius level. Almost all the mathematical giants of the past have been male. He says that Newton and Einstein were almost certainly autistic, finding relationships difficult. Artists, too, have suffered from autism or Asperger's - including the blind pianist Derek Paravicini, the artist Peter Howson and, reportedly, the film director Steven Spielberg. So if we found a test for autism, and gave parents the opportunity of aborting the foetus, we might eliminate not just an unwanted and difficult child but a potential genius.

Here lies the dilemma. Should medical science offer the opportunity to eliminate a child who may turn out to be, not only a valuable member of society, but an important contributor to its future? And here lies a further twist in the moral maze. If that were the decision, what would be the justification for deciding that only the most intelligent members of society should be protected, while the less able were judged expendable. Does not that come close to Nazi-style eugenics, the one aspect of genetic engineering we have all determined will never again be contemplated?

Professor Baron-Cohen says that we must debate these matters now, before even the possibility of a test becomes a reality. I have no doubt he is right. But I am far from clear which side we should be on.

Every human instinct must surely be against some form of national screening that would offer the opportunity to breed out the wild, the eccentric, the sometimes weird, crazed individualists who break free of routine constraints and offer the diversity on which we thrive. Can we afford to lose a future Einstein?

There is a deeper strain to the debate. Who is to judge where lies the dividing line between madness and norm? As Kamran Nazeer so brilliantly described in Prospect magazine last year, it is possible to convert the apparent drawbacks of autism into an ideal - to learn the art of conversation, for instance, and to become as adept at it as a "normal" member of society.

As the father of a bipolar son, whose understanding of his own condition and whose empathy with his fellow human beings far surpasses my own, I claim no superiority of intelligence when it comes to deciding who is rational and who not. So I shrink instinctively from any notion that we should be given the opportunity of discarding a future human being simply because he or she may be an inconvenience.

If that means holding back science or our knowledge of genetics, even at the expense of suffering families, I think it a price worth paying. To interfere with the natural diversity of the human race runs the risk of impeding natural selection itself. And that, in Darwin's bicentenary, would be a backward step.

The Times 12 January 2009

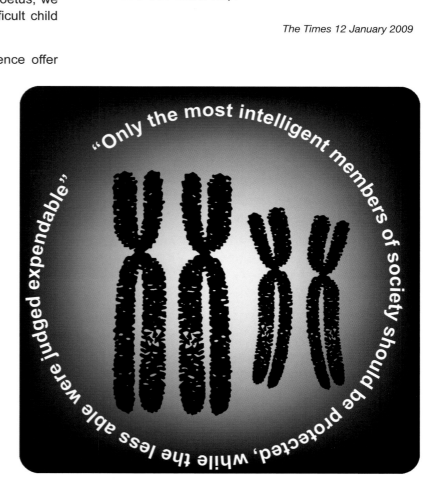

"Only the most intelligent members of society should be protected, while the less able were judged expendable"

Gary O'Donoghue
'My mother once thought of killing us both, life was so hard'

The only blind broadcast journalist in Britain, talks to **Matthew Bell**

On Gary O'Donoghue's first day at the BBC, he was asked to bungee jump off Chelsea Bridge. That was 18 years ago, as a junior reporter on the Today programme.

Now a highly regarded political correspondent, O'Donoghue doubts if a modern-day producer would dare ask the same of a blind person: "Disabled people can be victims of our risk-averse culture. When I joined the BBC, I went to Macedonia during the Kosovo war. Although there was all sorts of training, I'm not sure it would be quite so easy now."

The BBC – where he has spent his entire career, first at Today and then on the World Service – prides itself on its diversity and anti-discrimination policies. But O'Donoghue is the only blind broadcast journalist in the country. Already a familiar voice on radio, he is now presenting more for TV news as well as on the internet. Even for a sighted journalist, working across three platforms can be demanding,

but O'Donoghue is unfazed: "The technology has come on a lot in the past 15 years. I used to have to beg researchers to read cuttings on to tape before going home to listen to them. I would always be half a day behind everyone else."

Now he uses a piece of software on his laptop that interprets emails and text documents and reads them aloud

> "I used to have to beg researchers to read cuttings on to tape before going home to listen to them. I would always be half a day behind everyone else."

> **"There aren't many [disabled people in the media] and there should be more. There is 66% unemployment among blind people of working age. It's an absurd figure."**

in a synthetic voice. Inevitably there are still obstacles – as photographs of text, PDF files cannot be read, for example. But the internet has transformed O'Donoghue's working practices. "When I started, press releases would come in on the fax machine, which is completely useless. I'm quite bullish about it now when bits of paper are handed out. Number 10 did it the

> **"The thing about disability is that in many ways it makes life difficult, but it can also be an asset as it makes you stand out a bit."**

other day and I just said, 'I'm sorry but I can't read it.' They thought about it for a couple of minutes and then emailed it over."

O'Donoghue was born partially sighted but had lost the use of both eyes by the time he was eight. Although mild-mannered and resolutely upbeat, he has had to fight his corner. Last year he was awarded a five-figure payout after complaining he had been unfairly discriminated against when a producer gave one of his stories to another correspondent to present on the Ten O'Clock News. He declines to discuss that episode when we meet, but speaks passionately on the under-representation of disabled workers in the media. "There aren't many and there should be more. There is 66% unemployment among blind people of working age. It's an absurd figure." Should quotas be set? "No, there is no interest in

over-promoting people who aren't up to it – that would be the worst possible thing you can do. But when you come across them then for goodness sake use them."

One barrier to getting more disabled people into the workplace is a lack of confidence, and O'Donoghue recognises that his education played a large part in shaping his "yes we can" spirit.

He comes, he says, from "quite a working-class background", but was sent to a specialist boarding school for blind children in Worcester, and was the first person in his family to go to university, reading philosophy and modern languages at Oxford.

"The school was amazing; we did all sorts of things. It would not countenance the idea that things weren't possible. Football, ballroom dancing – we even went skiing." (O'Donoghue played football for the England blind team –"a very violent game".) He continues: "They also taught us to drive. They would take us to a disused airfield in dual-control cars. It's something you couldn't get away with these days – four blind kids and an instructor in a car charging round an airfield."

O'Donoghue's father was a semi-professional footballer before becoming a taxi-driver, and his mother taught ballroom

dancing before marrying. "She had quite a hard time of it when I was young because in those days there was not a lot of support for parents with disabled or blind children. You were expected to reinvent the wheel yourself the whole time. A couple of years ago she told me that when things got really bad, she seriously thought of killing us both. I think it's a really brave thing to say to your offspring. I think it was quite a dark time."

Now aged 40, O'Donoghue divides his time between a small London flat and Yorkshire, where he lives with his partner, Sarah Lewthwaite, and their seven-year-old daughter, Lucy. During his career he has covered stories in Africa, Asia, Europe and the US, but he seems most at home in Westminster, where he has been stationed since 2004. When we meet, he is about to do a pre-record ahead of presenting the Radio 4 show The World This Weekend for the first time, which he hopes to do more of.

"The thing about disability is that in many ways it makes life difficult, but it can also be an asset as it makes you stand out a bit. There are people who are prepared to take a chance with me. This is the job I wanted for quite a long time, and now I've got it. It's up to me to make the best of it."

*The Independent on Sunday
22 February 2009
© 2009 Independent News
Media Limited*

Photo: BBC

Not childsplay

When Cerrie Burnell got her job as a presenter on CBeebies, the BBC channel for children, she was elated, 'For me, it was the best job in the world,' she recalls. She felt confident that she had beaten the three other shortlisted candidates on merit and that she could do a good job. But just after her first broadcast, hostile comments began to appear on online message boards, with some parents even saying they would forbid their children to watch.

It wasn't anything that she had done or said that caused this reaction – it was how she looked. Because Cerrie, who like many female presenters is pretty blonde and bubbly, was born without a right hand and chooses not to wear an artificial one.

She made the decision to abandon her prosthetic limb when she was only nine years old.

'I simply stopped wearing it. I can't remember what exactly prompted me to stop, but I do remember feeling that this was me, this was how I was born, and if I was happy with it then I couldn't see why others couldn't accept me the way I was, too.'

The BBC received only nine formal complaints, but on the CBeebies website some comments were so nasty that they had to be taken down. Even the more kindly objectors were insulting, with one person suggesting that Cerrie should just pull down her cardigan sleeve a bit so viewers wouldn't have to see her stump.

Others objected that seeing Cerrie would scare their children and give them nightmares and some felt that she had only been given the job because of her disability. Another complaint was that Cerrie's appearance meant that parents were having to discuss difficult issues with their children before they were ready. One parent claimed that a child had "freaked out" on seeing the new presenter, and added: "There's a time and a place for showing kids all the differences that people can have, but nine in the morning in front of two-year-olds is not the place."

But Cerrie's response was typically feisty. She read a few of the comments at first but felt: 'This is the kind of discrimination disabled people face every day of their lives. This attitude still exists precisely because there are so few people with disabilities on television.'

Although she found the criticism upsetting, she didn't take it personally. In fact she

relishes the chance to set a debate going about disability and about false images.

'People need to be represented more honestly in the media,' she says. 'Especially when there is so much emphasis on the body beautiful, plastic surgery and this obsession with trying to look like celebrities.

'When you are not used to seeing normal people, let alone disabled people, then anyone like me is going to create a stir. I think it's really time to start changing perceptions.'

Certainly Cerrie has never let her disability hold her back from jobs – including working in a leprosy clinic in India when she was 19, and later volunteering in Brazil. Some of her Drama tutors did advise her to wear a prosthetic limb for auditions.

'One warned that were I to be cast as Juliet I would have to wear a cardigan,' she said.

'I thought to myself, why would Juliet have to wear a cardigan? Would it be breezy on the balcony? Then the penny dropped – it was to cover my lack of a limb.'

She ignored this advice and still managed to gain theatre jobs as well as small TV roles in Grange Hill, EastEnders, The Bill and Holby City.

She also once worked as a teaching assistant at a special needs school in London, where, she says, neither the children nor the parents were scared of her disability.

'Children are by their nature very inquisitive, and when they see my arm they will ask me questions, and I'm very happy to answer them.

'It may be the first thing they notice about me, but after a while it's the person they see and the disability becomes an irrelevance, which is the way it should be.'

Sources: various

Drugs

Issues to think about and discuss

Just say yes – How would you deal with the issue of drugs? Do you agree with this chief constable that drug laws only protect the users and not the general public?

My father gave me my first hit of heroin – Can you believe that a father gave his son drugs to keep him off the streets and keep an eye on him? Was it really no different from sharing a quiet pint down the local pub? Should this writer still love and miss his drug dealer dad?

Cocaine may not cost much but it certainly isn't cheap – Do cocaine users understand the damage they are doing to others and to the environment – or don't they care?

'When I see a young patient with a heart attack, one of the first things I think of is cocaine' – If the moral issues don't affect cocaine users, might health concerns have more impact?

Drugs

Heroin

Friends

Laws

Heart attacks

Pressure

Legalisation

Drugs

Family

Cocaine

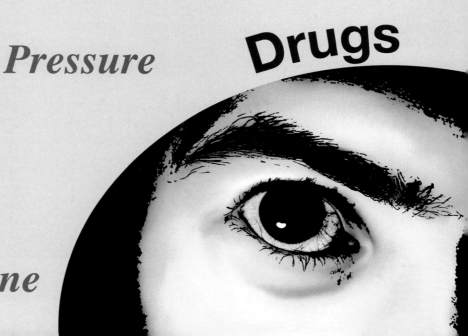

In this article, former Chief Constable, David Pickover, argues th:
all efforts to control the illegal drugs trade have failed and that th
only solution is to make drugs legal.

Just say YES

Despite the best efforts of those who make and enforce the law, the illegal drugs market and connected criminality continue to thrive. **David Pickover** believes it is time for a radical overhaul of how the drugs problem is addressed

THE ARTICLE IN BRIEF:

Governments of all political colours have made repeated efforts to deal with the drug problem. Most of the laws and initiatives brought in over the years have attempted to prevent users from obtaining their drugs. In other words, they have been designed to protect a small group of people from the harmful effects of their own addiction or habit. But in trying to do this, society has been harmed.

The legal steps have not stopped drug use from spreading. The drugs trade has been able to adapt to and counter all attempts to control it. Even large-scale seizures of drugs have no long term effect on the supplies reaching customers.

Because drugs have to be obtained illegally, users who are dependent on drugs are often driven to crime to finance their addiction. A very high number of crimes such as ransom, robbery, theft and fraud, which are committed to obtain money, are related to drug use. It is estimated that 60-70% of all such crime in the UK is related to drug dependency.

The conclusion is that the only way to solve the problem of drug-related crime is to make the possession of most drugs legal and to control the supply through regulated outlets. The poor and those dependent on drugs could obtain free supplies. The only drugs not supplied would be LSD and crack cocaine, two substances which can cause their users to harm other people.

In this article David Pickover is calling for an urgent review of the law.

It is only recently that ACPO (Association of Chief Police Officers) members have spoken publicly of the case for decriminalising drugs, but the notion was first openly aired in police circles in Police Review more than a decade ago.

The time has come to re-visit the topic and for the Government to decriminalise drugs possession and make some substances available through licensed outlets.

Changes in the nature and extent of drug abuse resulted in the Dangerous Drugs Act 1950 being repealed and a new Act with a crusading title, the Drugs (Prevention of Misuse) Act 1964, being introduced.

Perhaps in recognition that preventing misuse was not possible – nor something that should be advertised as a goal, in case it prompted evaluation of its preventative failures – the 1964 Act was repealed and succeeded by the simply named Misuse of Drugs Act 1971.

Nanny state

Designed to protect a minority of people from themselves, I believe that collectively the three Acts exemplify so-called nanny state legislation. It is indisputable that, while purportedly protecting a minority of people from themselves, the legislative measures have proved to be exceedingly harmful to more in our society than the legislation protects.

As well as enacting legislation, successive governments have sought, from time to time, to allay public anxiety and demonstrate their intention to purposefully address the drugs problem.

The last Tory Government offered their strategy in Tackling Drugs Together 1996-98. It failed to have any impact. On taking office, the subsequent Labour Government, perhaps recognizing that curtailing drug abuse presented an insurmountable challenge and they would need someone to carry the can if their drugs strategy was seen by the electorate to have failed, announced the appointment of the 'Drugs Czar' in a fanfare of publicity.

A ten-year strategy aimed at significantly reducing, if not eliminating, drugs misuse was announced. For reasons still not fully explained, the Government dispensed with the Drug Czar's appointment half-way through the ten year term. No fanfares have been heard proclaiming the wonderful overall success of the strategy. Suffice it to say, it too failed to register any measurable impact on preventing drugs abuse.

Minimal impact

In the past, misuse of drugs was principally seen as the prerogative and pastime of those in the upper classes of society and medical professions.

All elements of the illegal drugs trade have responded efficiently and effectively to the challenges designed to eradicate their activities, by way of legislation, a variety of enforcement agencies and education programmes, not to mention all partners in 'inter-agency' co-operation.

The tougher laws that have been called for in the past have been enacted but have proved ineffective in reducing drugs misuse. Implicit in tougher laws is taking tougher action.

Despite substantial increases in the allocation of investigative resources to tackle the problem; despite local, regional, national and international police operations and initiatives, legislation, the police service, HM Customs and Revenue and the Serious Organised Crime Agency have only had minimal impact in disrupting markets, in reducing importation and supplies and in reducing and preventing drugs misuse.

Notwithstanding all the strenuous effort expended, there has been consistent growth in drug availability and an upsurge in the unlawful supply of controlled drugs at levels matching those which business tycoons would boast of at shareholders' annual meetings.

Admittedly, there have been continuous increases in the number and size of

seized. In reality, such seizure rates are unattainable for various reasons, not least on consideration of the simple point that the financial and resource implications of achieving such results are economically prohibitive.

Enormous effort has been expended in preventing drug misuse, ostensibly to protect people from themselves; but today controlled drugs are readily available at inflation-beating prices – cheaper than in the previous decade – a firm indication of the traffickers' success and the minimal impact of legislation.

Paying the price

Drug users can only obtain their preferred substance illegally in the market place of the underground economy and this has resulted in an explosion of drug-related crime. The goal of the legislation has been to protect people from themselves, but by rendering the supply and possession of controlled substances unlawful, the legislation has resulted in far more people being harmed and victimised than it has protected.

The inextricable link between drug dependency and the commission of crime to feed and fund it is well established.

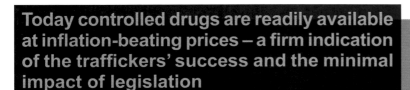

Today controlled drugs are readily available at inflation-beating prices – a firm indication of the traffickers' success and the minimal impact of legislation

Nowadays, however, the £5.3 billion underground economy of the drugs trade is no longer confined to such people, nor to urban and inner-city areas.

Like cancer it has spread – principally through the activities of street traders – and now manifests in all areas and echelons of society, which shows that preventing drug misuse by legislative prohibition is a Utopian ideal starved of practicality.

seizures but the amount of illegal substances seized still represents the tip of the iceberg.

The UK Drug Policy Commission reckons 12% of heroin and 9% of cocaine available on the market is seized. However, the more relevant statistic, often repeated by many studies, estimates the traffickers' market will be seriously damaged only if 60% to 80% of available drugs were

Reducing crime is a more sensible, laudable and attainable objective than blindly seeking to protect people who abuse drugs from themselves using legislative measures.

Although the exact proportion of acquisitional crime to fund drug dependency is uncertain, various studies over the years have estimated it at between 60% and 70% of all acquisitional crime in the UK.

In terms of the gravity of offences, thefts in retail premises to fund drug dependency register at the bottom of the scale. However, proportionately, they are at the top end of the scale. What is the loss to the retail trade? Who cares? We all should, because if shoplifting could be eradicated, the cost of all retail goods could be significantly reduced.

In the overall scheme of things, thefts in retail premises to fund drug dependency are often considered petty crime by the criminal justice system, even though we all pay the price for it; just as much as we all pay the price for drug-related crime in our motor and house insurance tariffs. Cabinet Office figures show the total cost of drug-related crime is approximately £40 billion per year – ultimately in the interest of protecting smack-heads, crack-heads and shit-heads from themselves. It is the costliest protection racket ever known.

Fresh focus

In my opinion, the time has come for a radical approach; instead of drugs legislation being aimed at protecting a minority of the population from themselves, its principal objective should be protecting the majority of people in our society from becoming the victims of crime. I believe this goal is achievable by decriminalising the possession of drugs and making controlled substances, save for LSD and crack – the use of which presents potential dangers to people others than the users because they have a greater propensity to cause users to harm other physically – available through state-controlled, regulated and licensed outlets.

When former prime minister Tony Blair spoke of being 'Tough on crime and tough on the causes of crime', we know it was spin, but there is merit in the concept. Greed is a cause, drink is a greater cause, but the biggest cause is the drugs trade which has flourished because substances are not available through legitimate means. Decriminalising drugs and making them available through regulated outlets – free for the poor and drug dependent – would eliminate all elements of the current trade from traffickers to street traders who, for too many decades, have funded drug dependency by creating new markets and spawning and nurturing substance misusers.

The point is simple: the ineffectiveness of legislation has resulted in the creation of more drugs users, bringing with their dependency, wide-ranging social problems beyond the commission of crime, as can be seen in the increasing number of young people being admitted to hospitals after taking drugs. There has been a 42% increase in under-16s being taken to hospital following drug-use in the past 10 years according to the National Health Service information centre.

There is currently great and justifiable anxiety across society in respect of gun crime and gang warfare. How much of this is drugs related? I believe decriminalising drugs would result in such activities decreasing, just as much as it would reduce turf-wars between gangs. It would also stop women from funding their drug dependency by becoming prostitutes on the streets, which puts them in danger of being assaulted or even murdered by violent punters.

Crime statistics, whether produced by the Home Office or by the British Crime Survey are notoriously unreliable, but in my opinion one thing is sure: if the possession of drugs was decriminalised and substances were to be made available through regulated outlets, crime, as cited above, would be reduced by 60% to 70% (or around at least three million offences per year). As a result, there would be roll-on recurring financial savings of billions per year, some of which could be devoted to drug treatment and rehabilitation programmes and huge cost savings in public services.

Reducing crime is a more sensible, laudable and attainable objective than blindly seeking to protect people who abuse drugs from themselves using legislative measures.

Unpalatable truth

There has been much Home Office and police service drum-beating recently with respect to falls in acquisitional crime. However, it would be foolhardy to suppose this is entirely attributable to increased police efficiency. It may well be that the decrease in crime can be partially attributed to the decrease in the cost of drugs at street level because of plentiful supply and ready availability. Cheaper drugs result in less crime.

Despite valiant efforts and some successes, all previous and current anti-drugs legislation and strategies have failed. With record numbers of users and dependants; the ready availability of substances at street prices which, save for the occasional blip, have consistently decreased over the years; I conclude there is no counter argument.

A Royal Commission on drug abuse and dependency and protecting the public is urgently needed.

It may well be that the Government and society are suffering from a form of dependence and that dependence on prohibition laws is the problem itself. There is no disgrace in accepting that the methods employed to reduce drug misuse have failed.

David Pickover is a former chief constable of West Yorkshire Police and legal editor of Police Review

Police Review 9 January 2009
http://www.policereview.com

My father gave me my first hit of heroin

Caspar Walsh

Crime was part of my life from my earliest memory. Not just the seedy, dark kind, but the day-to-day-to-pay-the-bills crime. This included theft, fraud, robbery and drug-dealing. Mum had left us when I was three. Dad did whatever he could to keep us going. Crime was how we survived, and as I grew older it became a father and son business.

Dad was first released from prison in 1982. We were living in a smart flat in Kensington and he'd gone straight back to dealing drugs to bring in money - getting a job wasn't even on his radar. Part of our income came from a 2kg block of Peruvian cocaine he was holding for a mate. Dad woke me up on my 16th birthday with a massive line of coke neatly presented on an antique mirror. I loved it. It never felt as if he was being irresponsible. It was normal to me.

A few weeks later, I was watching him dealing with two new customers. They were buying heroin. I'd been snorting a lot of coke and had overdone it. The hash was no longer balancing the buzz of the coke. I wanted something stronger. Dad clearly thought smack was something special - he told me it calmed the erratic, euphoric hit of cocaine. I became convinced this was what I needed for my amphetamine-frayed nerves. I'd asked him for heroin plenty of times, but he'd always flatly refused. When it started to look as if I was going to ruin this transaction with the new customers, he took me into the kitchen.

"Look, kid, I don't know what you're up to, but we need their business - I have to pay the rent." He took out a six-inch square of silver foil from the cupboard. "You can have some of this, but only a little, then piss off to your room and let me seal the deal."

My heart beat faster. This was the rite of passage I'd been waiting for, and another step deeper into Dad's world. I knew what to do - I'd seen him do it plenty of times. The narcotic rush that ran through my body was physical and emotional. I instantly understood why Dad loved it so much. It made everything easier, happier and safer. In that moment I felt a deeper connection to my father. It sounds shocking but, for me, it was no different from your average father and son sharing their first quiet pint down the local pub.

> "That day in the kitchen had a dark beauty to it. Taking drugs was part of the way my father and I connected. I'm thankful I was able to get a little closer to him during that time."

This initiation into the world of Class As happened at a time when I was terrified of what the future held. Dad had been locked up for the previous three years, and had missed my transition from boy to teenager. We had a lot of catching up to do.

My smack habit developed quickly, partly from the little Dad gave me to calm me down and partly from the stuff I nicked off him to keep me stoned. I once angrily asked him why he gave it to me and he told me he wanted to keep me off the streets. At least this way he could "keep an eye on me". It was a twisted paternal protectiveness that led to our relationship breaking down completely, and ended with him back in prison and me locked up for the first time in my life.

My father was essentially lazy; crime was a means to getting us to a better place. Long-term, he wanted me to go to college; get some qualifications and a "proper" job. He was well-intentioned, but hopelessly deluded by the painkilling drugs he loved so much.

A while back I heard that the dysfunction our parents hand down to us gives us something to work with, something to motivate us out of the gutter; that's if we're lucky enough to survive our early years. Giving me heroin was a mistake my father grew to regret deeply - I knew this because he told me, many times. It accelerated me to a place to which I was already heading. And, looking back, the quicker I got there the better. My destination was prison, for dealing and taking drugs.

At 21, I was released on bail to go into rehab and I was able to do what my father never managed through all his years in prison, reading books and meditating: I got clean from drugs and alcohol, and I've stayed clean ever since.

That day in the kitchen had a dark beauty to it. Taking drugs was part of the way my father and I connected. I'm thankful I was able to get a little closer to him during that time. Heroin took my father's life, through a deliberate overdose 16 years ago. Bizarrely, it gave me mine. I still love and miss him deeply.

The Guardian 9 August 2008
© Guardian News and Media Ltd 2008

Cocaine may not cost much but it certainly isn't cheap

The cocaine trade turns people into throwaway human containers. That alone should make it unacceptable, writes *Jenny McCartney*

The comedian Robin Williams, a man who knew whereof he spoke, announced in 1990 that "cocaine is God's way of saying that you're making too much money". Not any more. The price of drugs appears to have gone the way of so many consumer goods in credit crunch Britain: it's possible to get some really amazing discounts if you ferret around in the right places.

Cocaine today, at as little as £1 a line, is as cheap as chips, and set to get even cheaper: last week the International Narcotics Control Board warned that prices will continue to fall unless action was taken to block the drug's current supply routes through West Africa and Eastern Europe.

Britain is a booming market for cocaine, which not so long ago was seen as the champagne of drugs, heavily favoured by film stars, models and footballers. That reputation no doubt helped to popularise it in the minds of moneyed, middle-class dabblers, who imagined that cocaine went with cashmere pashminas and "It" bags as one of life's naughty little pleasures.

Now it's more like knocking back a half-pint of Snakebite at the grimy local boozer: ubiquitous, cheap, and quite liable to contain some unexpected rogue ingredients. To Britain's youth, who have so long absorbed slyly-captioned pictures of celebrities such as Kate Moss and Amy Winehouse with little globs of white powder clinging to their inner nostrils, it has now frequently become an unremarkable feature of an evening out.

I have always found cocaine to be one of the less attractive drugs, if any can be said to be attractive. The glassy self-confidence that it engenders in users seems to be in inverse proportion to their ability to say anything interesting. When reminded that the drug works to inhibit shyness, one might reflect that sometimes shyness has its perks.

What is notable, however, is how few users are willing to engage with the ethical dimensions of their hobby, by which I mean not what it is doing to them, but what it does to other people. Many enthusiastic snorters are tremendously keen on lecturing less enlightened folk on the importance of eating organic food, buying Fairtrade products, and avoiding wearing fur because of the unnecessary suffering to animals. But what of the human animals, the drugs "mules" caught up in the increasingly brutal cocaine trade?

According to the International Narcotics Control Board, the most recent trafficking method is simply to flood commercial flights with large numbers of "mules" who have swallowed up to a kilogram of cocaine each. It becomes impossible for customs officials to cope with investigating each and every one, and if a given number get caught, their losses are amply compensated for by the profits of those who make it through. What becomes of the hapless failures is of little further interest to the traffickers.

Of course, quite frequently the mules end up on a hospital trolley: some of the bags that they have swallowed spring a leak, flooding their system with the drug. Their death notices appear regularly and briefly in the newspapers.

Many enthusiastic snorters are keen on lecturing on the importance of avoiding wearing fur because of the unnecessary suffering to animals. But what of the human animals, the drugs "mules" caught up in the increasingly brutal cocaine trade?

A couple of years ago a middle-aged woman was dumped in agony on the steps of St Helier hospital in Sutton, south-west London, shortly after arriving on a flight from Ghana. She managed to tell police that she was Mary Kofi, although they could not confirm that this was her real name, since she had no documents or identification. Some of the 61 inch-long packets of cocaine later found in her stomach had burst, and she died shortly afterwards.

No one ever found out who persuaded "Mary Kofi" to undertake her treacherous journey, or what she was promised, or who planned to receive her cargo. No one discovered how many children or relatives were left bereft by her disappearance. She was a disposable person in the cocaine trade, a throwaway human container, like innumerable others before and since. I don't know about you, but if I were in the regular habit of ingesting what is carted around the world inside endless desperate, nauseous Mary Kofis, I have a feeling that just thinking about it could take the edge off my high.

The Daily Telegraph 21 February 2009
© Telegraph Group Ltd 2008

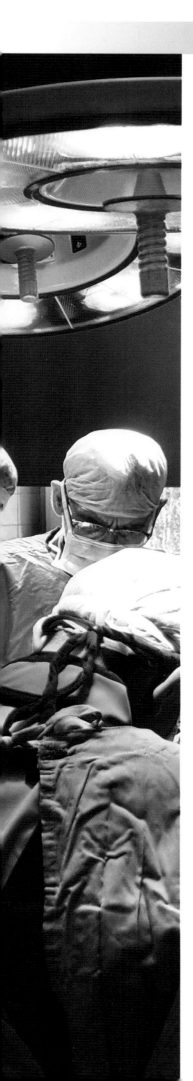

Dr Chris Baker: 'When I see a young patient with a heart attack, one of the first things I think of is cocaine'

Interview: Carl Wilkinson

Different drugs affect your heart in different ways. Coke is probably the one I see most because it causes premature coronary disease, coronary spasm, chest pain and heart attacks.

Cocaine is a powerful stimulant with effects similar to adrenaline. It reduces the re-uptake of noradrenaline and dopamine at nerve endings, increasing blood pressure, making your heart beat faster and more forcefully, and increasing the heart's oxygen demand. It can also cause coronary arteries to spasm, reducing or stopping the heart's blood supply, and makes the blood more sticky and likely to form clots. All of those things can cause chest pain or a heart attack.

Using cocaine a lot seems to give you premature atherosclerosis - that's the furring up of arteries normally associated with smoking and cholesterol. Coke-related heart attacks are more common in people who use cocaine a lot because they get this furring of the arteries, but can it happen to someone who has taken cocaine as a one-off? Yes, it can.

When I see a young patient with a heart attack, one of the first things I think of is cocaine. If you're in your twenties or thirties and you come in with a heart attack, I'll ask you: 'Have you been doing coke?' And I'll probably dipstick your urine to find out. I'll probably even consider it if you're in your forties.

I think people are quite honest. I'm not sure there's so much shame about taking cocaine any more. It is so widespread that certain groups of the population don't feel embarrassed about it.

Oddly, I've treated far more men than women, but that's probably a function of the fact that men get more coronary heart disease than women. In fact, I can't think that I've ever seen a woman with a cocaine-related heart attack.

Cocaine leaves your system within about 48 hours, if you're not a regular user. If you do use it regularly it hangs around that much longer and it's possible that it could still be there for up to three weeks. Of course, if you really want to test for it, it's in the hair.

I now see older people who are taking cocaine. We don't tend to ask people in their fifties and sixties, but I bet there are plenty of people of that age doing a bit of cocaine who have all the other risk factors - cholesterol, high blood pressure, diabetes, smoking and so on.

I think people are aware that if they do too much cocaine they'll lose their nasal septum, but I don't think they're aware that it can affect their heart.

I once came across a couple in their eighties who had been heroin addicts for 35 years. They were very well off and bought very pure heroin, they didn't use much so weren't escalating and they were very meticulous about smoking the drug. If you're very careful you can go on using it for years - although that clearly isn't the case for the majority.

Dr Chris Baker is an interventional cardiologist based at the Imperial College Healthcare NHS Trust in London.

The Observer 16 November 2008
© *Guardian News and Media Ltd 2008*

Education
Issues to think about and discuss

Imagine if we taught maths like PE – a competition, with public humiliation if you got a sum wrong – Is PE to blame for teenage obesity because it is 'emotionally painful and socially humiliating'? What basic life skills are essential for everyone? How can young people be encouraged to take more exercise?

Making students make the grade – Is reporting software an encouragement to learning or an invasion of students' privacy? Do reward systems work in the long term? Why do students need to be rewarded for just doing what they are supposed to do? Who gets rewarded most?

'Now I believe anything is possible' – Is a year at a prominent public school a genuine opportunity for some children from downtown Johannesburg? How do different opportunities affect people's education and chances in life?

It's time to get tough on choosing soft subjects – Reading this article, might make anyone think twice about what subjects to chose at A-level. Isn't it time that universities were more open about what subjects they prefer? Do private schools gain privileges since they 'regularly pick up the telephone to heads of admissions at universities to check exactly what they are looking for, many state schools do not offer even the most basic advice.'

I could never live up to being a child prodigy... – Do child prodigies always live up to expectations? Is it better to develop at a steady rate? Can failure be good for you? In this personal account, the writer explains how her natural gifts meant she didn't learn to work hard.

Education

Education

Expectation

Environment

University

School

Genius

Parental pressure

Opportunities

Imagine if we taught maths like PE - a competition, with public humiliation if you got a sum wrong

Naomi Alderman

At the end of the Olympic games last month, Gordon Brown declared that it was time to "encourage competitive sports" in schools, to end the "medals for all" culture that prevailed in the 70s and 80s. He said that he wanted to see pupils recapture the "all or nothing" attitude in relation to sporting achievement. Barely two weeks later, a study was released demonstrating what any obese child could have told him: competitive sports put pupils off exercise. The study, conducted by Loughborough University, showed that a heavy emphasis on competitive sport in Britain's schools is preventing pupils from developing healthy exercise habits, and doing little or nothing to improve teenage obesity.

As someone who went to school in the 70s and 80s, I can't say that I noticed much of a "medals for all" culture myself. Physical education was taught in much the same way it's always been taught: team games, captains picking their sides, and the inevitable segregation between those who are good at games and are picked first and those rejects left shuffling uncomfortably while the captains try to decide between the fat child, the child in glasses or the child puffing on an inhaler. In other words, physical education was taught in a way guaranteed to give at least some of the children lasting exercise-phobia. Competitive sports may be where exercise becomes "fun" for children who are good at it, but for those who are less talented, it is where exercise becomes not only physically demanding but also emotionally painful and socially humiliating.

To get some sense of the damage this can cause, imagine if we taught maths using the same method. Every lesson would start with two maths captains picking their teams - inevitably leaving those known to be bad at maths to the end. The rest of the lesson would be taken up with public competition in mental arithmetic. Get a sum wrong, and not only would you show yourself up in front of your classmates, but you'd let your team down, too. And as for slow and steady progress, improving your skills and working on your weak spots? Forget it, there's no time for that. There's a reason we don't teach maths like this; it's because we think maths is too important for us to risk leaving some children behind by creating an association in their minds between maths and public embarrassment.

Get a sum wrong, and not only would you show yourself up in front of your classmates, but you'd let your team down, too.

Of course, children who enjoy competitive sports should have the chance to play them, learn new skills and improve their performance. They should be encouraged to take that interest as far as they can. This country has a rich heritage and tradition in sport; both as participants and as whole-hearted supporters. We can all be tremendously proud of our Olympic athletes, of their determination and abilities. But competitive sport is really just one tiny offshoot of PE. Children who enjoy maths should be encouraged to pursue that interest as far as they can, too - to a professional level, if they want. But most of us don't need the skills of professional mathematicians. What we need are basic mathematical life-skills: the ability to plan a journey to get somewhere at the correct time, to make a budget, to work out that paying £20 a month over a year for a £120 TV isn't a good bargain.

In the same way, what many children - particularly those who are less good at sport - need from PE is a grounding in the basics. They need an introduction to the concept of competing against yourself, trying to improve your own performance without reference to anyone else. And they need to be taught how to make exercise a part of their lives. The Loughborough study suggests that schools should offer aerobics or hill-walking as an alternative to competitive sport. It also emphasises that schools should be trying to inculcate the exercise habit in children. You can't encourage exercise to be a lifelong habit by forcing children to do physical activity they don't enjoy.

Unless the government changes its mind about the push toward competitive sport, I'm afraid Brown may get his wish. Children will indeed develop an "all or nothing" attitude towards exercise, with many deciding that, as they can't be winners, they might as well do nothing at all.

$$\sqrt{\chi + \chi \pi}$$

The Guardian 25 September 2008
© Guardian News and Media Ltd 2008

Making students make the grade

Bribery or Big Brother? What's the best way to motivate people to do well at school?

Ever considered dropping your end of year report into a puddle to make it unreadable? Have you skilfully transformed an E grade into a B? Ever persuaded your parents that the teacher must have mixed you up with someone else? Intercepted a Parents' Evening letter? These tried and tested methods will be things of the past if Britain follows the US in using technology to track students. Companies like Edline and Powerschool provide 'student information systems' which allow parents access to grades, attendance and assignments on a daily, even hourly basis, making all the normal reporting and grading activities of a school available online. Homework, missed classwork, revision, worksheets, it's all there online for you and your parents to see.

Parents no longer need to ask "Have you done your homework?" they can see the answer. Teachers don't need to check whether you handed it in - there's a virtual 'drop box' for you to deposit it, so the old excuse of "The dog ate it" is a thing of the past. And this real-time reporting is coming your way! The government wants 'real-time' reporting systems up and running in UK schools – by 2010 in all secondary schools and in all primary schools two years later.

According to the providers, this can only be a good thing - they speak of 'harnessing the power of parental involvement'. One website boasts of "An e-mail response within 24 hours from a teacher; a weekly report on a child's grades; and around-the-clock access to school assignments and schedules." Other sites show videos of parents delighted that they can discuss school progress and events with their children over dinner. The students are apparently thrilled with the way they can manage their work: "I'm in control of my grades" one beams.

Teachers, for whom all this extra reporting would seem to mean extra work, are also quoted as being pleased with the system. They find they get fewer queries from parents - who can find out most answers to "How's my child progressing?" online. Many schools suggest that teachers post student grades once a week and some also show where each student stands in comparison to the rest of the group.

The software also allows parents to intervene when there is a problem: "When my one son turned apathetic toward school three years ago, Edline allowed me to check his homework assignments daily to make sure he was turning them in," says one mother, who feels that access to information prevented further failure. Other parents say that the system means there are no nasty surprises at the end of term and that they can be more actively involved in their children's school lives. Students also find the fact that they get their test results and grades quickly encourages them to work harder.

So everyone is a winner it seems? Not exactly. Facebook is full of groups for whom 'the power of parental involvement' is not seen as wholly beneficial. Some consider their parents to be too involved: "My dad watches it like he watches the stock market" while others have a sense of doomed inevitability: "BEFORE, the screaming and disappointment only had to be endured four times a year. NOW it can happen every night... because of those stupid online grades." As for those cosy chats over dinner: "For anyone that's interested... me and my mom just got in another fight thanks to Edline."

..."MY DAD WATCHES IT LIKE HE WATCHES THE STOCK MARKET ....

....

But even before this technology hits our shores, there are other ways of "harnessing parent power" and motivating pupils – without resorting to full time student stalking. Whether you regard them as bribery or incentives, reward systems are already being used by many schools as a way of encouraging good attendance and behaviour.

Commercial firms such as Vivo are offering systems that allow students to earn points towards tangible rewards. Schools can allocate Vivo "miles" for:

- Attendance and outstanding progress
- Healthy eating and exercise
- Display work or performance
- Taking responsibility in school
- Being a good ambassador out of school

Students accumulate their points and use a "credit card" system to exchange them for goods. As the website tells students: 'It is the 21st century now right? So when you do something at school worthy of a reward you want something a little more interesting than a sticker or a badge from your teacher? Ok, so how about something like your own personal reward card that you can use like you would a bank card? And instead of getting stickers or paper slips you get awarded credits electronically onto your card which you can then use to buy anything from cinema tickets and iPods to mobile phone credits and music tracks?'

And parents can be involved too. As the site says, 'the active involvement of parents in school initiatives is a key way of ensuring children are motivated and supported throughout their learning journey.' This active involvement takes the form of checking on a student's mile count and topping up rewards. Amongst other suggestions, parents are encouraged to use the scheme to 'easily monitor your child's contribution to school life and their own personal development', 'to set targets for your children which can be linked to pocket money' – one suggestion is to 'motivate your child by making a pledge to contribute or match the Vivo total they earn through their good work at school.'

Enthusiastic teachers say that the scheme motivates pupils and teaches them about 'financial capability, the economy and the socio-political system' and that they 'learn to avoid taxes and fines'. One school involved in the scheme, Barnfield South Academy, Luton was said to have spent £28,000 in 2008 on prizes and incentives.

...''THE DOG ATE MY COMPUTER!!!! ....

....

Other schools have their own home-grown system of tangible rewards. At St Mary's C of E High School in Hendon, London, for example, pupils can aim for a range of treats which include trips to Cadbury World, book tokens, postcards home informing parents of good behaviour and privileges such as being fast-tracked through the lunch queue.

...''BEFORE, THE SCREAMING AND DISAPPOINTMENT ONLY HAD TO BE ENDURED FOUR TIMES A YEAR. NOW IT CAN HAPPEN EVERY NIGHT... BECAUSE OF THOSE STUPID ONLINE GRADES''...

Ofsted, which has responsibility for standards in schools, recently praised St Mary's in a report which also said: 'Rewards, such as opportunities to go on trips or to gain awards, were a powerful incentive for students who struggled with school.''

But do reward schemes work? Professor Maurice Galton and John MacBeath, at Cambridge University, published a book *Teachers Under Pressure* in which they said they had found 'little sign' reward systems led to improvements in pupil behaviour, with evidence from the US suggesting that such systems enjoyed 'limited success'. They also noted that teachers were quick to reward 'difficult' pupils' in an effort to change their negative attitudes to school. Such pupils would receive credits for 'simply listening, or being polite to a classmate', while pupils who were generally well-behaved would have to do something 'exceptional' to earn their credit. Other critics say that pupils quickly learn to play the system and that it has little lasting impact on attitudes.

So if children's attitudes are not improved by reward schemes, will constant monitoring by tracking technologies make any difference? If Facebook - a technology students are happy to engage with - is anything to go by, the latest excuse will have to be "the dog ate my computer" - tracking technology and all.

Sources: Various

'Now I believe anything is possible'

In a unique experiment five South African teenagers are studying at Stowe for a year. Tim Ecott meets them

"This half-term holiday is going well because I haven't had to worry about snakes," the 15-year-old girl in her smart school blazer and tie explains. "The last time I spent a weekend away from school I was awake all night, thinking that a snake would come into my bed."

Makgotso Maiko is a South African, currently spending a year at Stowe, one of England's top public schools, in rural Buckinghamshire. Snakes don't seem like an obvious half-term challenge as we sit under the neoclassical columns of the school entrance designed by Vanbrugh and overlooking the rolling grounds landscaped by Capability Brown. However, during her last exeat [weekend break from boarding school], Makgotso found herself staying with the family of a fellow pupil whose pet snake had escaped from its tank.

"I am a bit of a drama queen at the best of times," she giggles. "But in Africa we know that snakes are dangerous, and not to be kept as pets."

Makgotso is one of five teenagers to have been chosen from the Dominican Convent School in downtown Johannesburg to take part in what Stowe's headmaster, Dr Anthony Wallersteiner, says is a unique experiment to give South African children an English public school education for a year.

"Other English public schools have had exchanges, but not to my knowledge on this scale and not where each pupil has been fully funded," says Dr Wallersteiner. Tall and patrician, his pin-stripes and polished black Oxfords are perfectly in keeping with his white panelled study designed by John Soane in 1805 for the dukes of Buckingham. But there is nothing old-fashioned about his ideas for Stowe, or his attitudes towards the pupils. "We're probably less 'talk and chalk' in our approach than the African children are used to, much more about practical based learning."

Those who wanted to apply for a place at Stowe were asked to write an essay explaining why they wanted to come to England. Then every applicant was personally interviewed by Dr Wallersteiner, who flew to South Africa to select the winning candidates.

When [Richard Branson] left school his headmaster predicted he would either make himself a fortune or end up in prison

The five pupils – three girls and two boys – are known as the Branson Scholars, as they are part-sponsored by Sir Richard Branson. The entrepreneur famously left Stowe before completing the sixth-form, and his business empire had its beginnings in a phone booth in the school grounds from where he ran a fledgling music magazine. When he left school his headmaster predicted he would either make himself a fortune or end up in prison. Branson sees no irony in now assisting others to be good students.

"I wasn't particularly interested in school," he admits, "and I suffered with dyslexia, but I believe that this project will open the eyes and the ears of these young South Africans to all kinds of possibilities."

Branson rejects any notion that uprooting five children from humble backgrounds and putting them into the grandeur of the Stowe environment will make them discontented when they return home. "I don't swallow that argument. With every charitable idea, it's a case of doing what you can do. And South Africans are energetic and resourceful. Let's give some of them a chance."

The pupils are thrilled that I have spoken to Branson, whom they have yet to meet. "Please tell him he is our Daddy," says Matshidiso Nhlapo. "And we are grateful."

Sir Richard's partner in the experiment is Mike Parsons, chief executive of Barchester Health Care, whose own son is at Stowe. Parsons, who has family connections to South Africa, provided the original link to the Dominican convent. Although the Africans were flown to England courtesy of Virgin Atlantic, the Stowe fees (£25,500 per child per annum plus extras) are borne by him and the school. Parsons is underwriting the cost of four students, while Stowe is giving one place as a full bursary.

The African pupils arrived at Stowe at the beginning of this term. Sixteen-year-old Vusi Nyhila, the eldest boy, tells me he was the first member of his family to go on an aeroplane. "That was great," he beams. "I never went to sleep."

Vusi reveals that he lives at a church-run children's home in Johannesburg because his mother is unable to look after her six children. At half-term he is staying with a fellow pupil's family in the Home Counties, in the kind of home where owning horses is nothing extraordinary. "They have horses, and they let me try riding," he enthuses.

In contrast in South Africa, Vusi would spend holidays working in a clothes shop for a weekly wage of about £35, most of which he would give to his mother.

It would be easy to imagine that the South African pupils are living some modern-day version of The Prince and the Pauper. However, they seem unaffected by the opulence of Stowe's manicured grounds and the fact that they now play rugby, lacrosse and water polo. All five are confident and articulate.

Fifteen-year-old Matshidiso says her unemployed father is constantly in her mind. Her mother died a few years ago and the family had to sell their house to pay for medical expenses. The family restaurant business went, too.

"I missed several months of school," she says in a low, soft voice as we sit beside Stowe's heated swimming pool where she is learning to dive. "Then, luckily I got a scholarship. My dad tells me that you have to grab hold of every opportunity in life. And I want to make him proud."

Was he concerned that she was going so far away? "He was." She pauses, and there are silent tears. "When he said goodbye at the airport he whispered only one thing: 'Come back home just as sweet as you are'."

The South Africans' own analysis of the Stowe environment is not based on material wealth. I ask if their new English friends are different in any way. Their replies are revealing: "The girls are very concerned with how they look. They don't want to play games so much, they'd rather go shopping. They are all worried about getting fat. And everyone owns an i-Pod."

The boys seem to have no social problems. Khamuka Moloi loves the soccer and rugby, and says the academic work is of the same level as he's used to at his school. Vusi is less interested in the schoolwork, because, by his own admission, he was a late starter. At almost 17 he is three years older than the other fourth formers.

"I didn't start school until I was nine," he tells me unselfconsciously, sitting in a leather armchair in one of Stowe's study areas. "I never dreamed a place like this existed. But now I really believe anything is possible."

Back in Johannesburg, Mike Thiel, headmaster of the Dominican school, keeps in touch with his pupils through email. He accepts that returning next year could be difficult for them.

"These children are tough, and none of them has had it easy," he explains. "But they know that part of the deal is that they come home and inspire other pupils to work hard and strive for a better life. Emotionally, they've got it together."

Dr Wallersteiner agrees. "I hope the children will make friendships with 'Stoics' that will last a lifetime. And maybe, in 10 years' time, someone in Johannesburg will be able to pick up the phone and call one of his mates from Stowe and collaborate on some business venture together."

It's too early to tell what the consequences of this experiment in extending the "old school tie" might be, but Makgotso Maiko is already brimming with confidence.

"I'm thinking of offering my services to Mr Branson," she says seriously, "as a business development adviser."

Sir Richard might just be glad of it.

The Daily Telegraph 23 October 2008
© Telegraph Group Ltd 2008

> **Branson rejects any notion that uprooting five children from humble backgrounds and putting them into the grandeur of the Stowe environment will make them discontented when they return home. "I don't swallow that argument."**

It's time to get tough on choosing soft subjects

Anna Fazackerley

I can hear them now. Parents all over the country are boasting about the A-levels their clever offspring are studying. "Oh yes, Matthew is working ever so hard," they say merrily. "He's taking law, history and business. I don't know where he inherited his brains from!"

But research published this week by Policy Exchange may make them wish they hadn't opened their mouths. Data obtained from 27 leading research universities shows for the first time that the vast majority of them favour traditional A-levels over "soft" subjects, ranging from art and media studies to the more serious-sounding law, business studies and accounting. Yet, crucially, universities are failing to tell students and parents of this.

Currently, only Cambridge University and the London School of Economics publish lists of "non-preferred" subjects. Other universities offer no clear advice on their websites about subjects that may count against students. Based on last year's statistics, if Matthew wants to read law at one of our leading universities, law A-level will be a major disadvantage at many institutions, and the fact that he has unknowingly plumped for two subjects that are non-preferred will almost certainly rule him out of the game altogether.

If tutors think a subject is inadequate preparation for one of their courses they are absolutely right not to accept it. There is no shame in top universities striving for excellence. The real scandal is the lack of transparency

The scandal here is not that top universities are disregarding certain A-levels. If tutors think a subject is inadequate preparation for one of their courses they are absolutely right not to accept it. There is no shame in top universities striving for excellence. The real scandal is the lack of transparency. Vice chancellors have batted this issue off, saying that admissions are complicated and subject preferences vary from department to department. This is certainly true. But nonetheless universities must go the extra mile in spelling out their subject preferences to teachers, pupils and parents.

This is critical if the leading research universities genuinely want a large pool of bright underprivileged pupils to fish in – because the second scandal here is that students at non-selective state schools are the ones who are most likely to trip up by choosing their A-levels badly. Many independent

Cartoon by Ham Khan

and grammar schools don't even offer soft subjects. And, if a gifted state school student is adamant that she wants to take media studies because it is less stuffy than all the more traditional subjects, she is much less likely to be warned that this might reduce her chances of acceptance at certain universities.

Advice about higher education in many state schools is in a parlous state. While sixth form tutors at certain independent schools regularly pick up the telephone to heads of admissions at universities to check exactly what they are looking for, many state schools do not offer even the most basic advice. If we are ever to live up to the much-trumpeted agenda to widen access to higher education in this country this must be addressed as a matter of urgency.

Yet the finger of blame should not be pointed just at universities and schools. The government has failed too. It has been so busy protecting itself by denying that soft subjects even exist, that it has failed to give a clear signal that subject choice matters.

We should be doing everything in our power to make sure that the brightest students can gain access to the very best universities. Right now, for many students, soft subjects are barring the door.

The big research universities have taken such a hammering from the media and politicians on admissions that it is understandable they are hesitant about putting their heads above the parapet on A-level choice. They have been slammed for not letting in enough state school students, and then booted up the backside for being prejudiced against independent schools. They see soft subjects as yet another painful social engineering story in the making and the result is a resounding silence on subject preference.

Yet there is clearly an issue of social justice here. Subject choice has become yet another obstacle that may prevent less privileged children reaching the top of our higher education system. So why aren't ministers shouting about this? The answer is that the mission of widening participation is to push children from less advantaged families into university – any university – to move us closer to that mythical 50 per cent target. This obsession with numbers misses an absolutely vital social point. It is not enough for talented state school students to gain access to a university. We should be doing everything in our power to make sure that the brightest students can gain access to the very best universities. Right now, for many students, soft subjects are barring the door.

Let's stop sniggering about media studies and take action. The hard truth about soft subjects can't be ignored any longer.

Anna Fazackerley is senior adviser on universities at the think-tank the Policy Exchange.

The Independent 4 December 2008
© 2009 Independent News and Media Ltd

I could never live up to being a child prodigy...

Jocelyn Lavin

I don't have many memories of being four, but I do recall my surprise at starting school and finding that my older classmates weren't all fluent readers like me. I think it came as a surprise to my parents, too - since I was their first child, they'd assumed there was nothing unusual in the speed at which I'd learned to read aloud.

Mum and Dad never "pushed" me. They enjoyed my inquisitive nature and answered questions, but I wasn't forced to recite my times tables every morning or switch off the television. I simply enjoyed learning, and when no one else was teaching me, I'd teach myself.

I was a natural mathematician, and later became a gifted oboe player and pianist, too. At 10, I was encouraged to audition for a place at Chetham's School of Music in Manchester. A friend I considered a better musician failed to win a place, so I was surprised and delighted when I got in. I now realise the examiners were judging potential rather than ability, and in those days potential wasn't something I lacked.

During my first year, I was a subject of an educational psychologist doing a study of gifted children. She measured my IQ and found it to be 169 - I've since been told that made me literally one in a million.

Perhaps Chetham's gave me unrealistic expectations. When I finished my maths O-level early, I asked if I could learn astronomy to fill the time. As with everything else, I took the exam and got an A. I thought things would always be that easy. At 17, I'd given my future little

> ## "Having always taken my abilities for granted, it was hard for me to accept they had a limit."

thought. My childhood dream of becoming a librarian on a spaceship remained the closest thing I had to a career plan. Cocooned in academia, it didn't seem to matter. When I left Chetham's with six A-levels, all A grade, even the press took notice.

My decision to pursue maths and astronomy at degree level led to headlines about me "reaching for the stars". I arrived at university with every expectation of proving them right. In fact, I was about to come crashing back to earth. My peers, who had learned to work hard for their A-levels, thought nothing of putting in extra hours at home, but I hadn't developed the self-discipline. Everything had come easily to me at school. I'd dash off homework on the bus and my grades never suffered. Now, for the first time, I found something I couldn't do. My whole sense of self was shaken.

I felt genuine shock. Bewildered, I did everything I could to avoid work. Living away from home for the first time, in London, distractions weren't hard to find, but every evening I came home to coursework that hadn't been done, and every day I found new excuses to avoid lectures and tutorials I couldn't face.

Inevitably, my grades suffered. I received warnings and ignored them. I'd never had to ask for help before, and didn't know how to. Having always taken my abilities for granted, it was hard for me to accept they had a limit. I flunked my second year exams. The sensible response would have been to immerse myself in study. Instead, I spent my third year producing a musical. Inevitably, I failed my finals, too, eventually scraping a third on retakes.

My parents were devastated. I felt terrible guilt, and dwelt on how old schoolfriends would react. Everyone I knew had expected great things of me, and I'd let them all down.

Still, I'm not sure what people expected of me. Rocket scientist or concert pianist? Which star was I meant to be reaching for? The great achievement remained undefined. Having a burden of expectation young makes disappointment almost inevitable. In fact, I went into teaching, which I did happily for 20 years.

The most common interpretation of success seems to involve a long career, good pay, a big family. I've hit my 40s, single, without achieving those things. Someone who is motivated and driven - irrespective of their IQ - will probably find it easier to reach those goals than a "brilliant" individual who lacks direction. On those terms, many people would consider me a failure, but I'm not ready to accept that. I've been thinking about where my real skills lie. Two years ago, I gave up teaching to concentrate on musical arrangement.

It's been a hard slog, but I'm starting to get commissions. I've had some positive responses, and it feels good to receive praise again. At last, I've worked out what I really want to do - and this time I'm willing to work for it.

The Guardian 20 December 2008
© Guardian News and Media Ltd 2008

Environmental issues

Issues to think about and discuss

What China crisis? – "China is building a new coal-fired power station every week and expanding 160 airports" – Is China going to increase global warming or could we learn from its efforts to help the environment?

Poverty or poison – In poor countries recycling of hazardous electronic waste is often done by hand, by children. But it is *our* waste. Is it right even to call this recycling? What should a country like Britain be doing about this? How should we dispose of it? Can we avoid creating this waste?

Fishy on a dishy – Some people avoid meat but still eat fish. Is that a better choice for the environment and for your health? What are the effects of different ways of farming and of catching fish? Does what you choose to eat really matter?

Should you become an ecotarian? – Are animals or the environment the priority? Is eating to save the environment going too far?

No words necessary – What is the illustrator trying to portray with this cartoon? Is it true that there are "No words necessary"? Do you think that art can really tackle issues such as climate change?

An act of extreme, wilful fecundity? – Why was the birth of eight babies greeted as a miracle and then condemned as greed? Should Nadya Suleman have had so many children? Does it matter that she conceived by IVF? Who should decide about the size of a person's family? Do we all have a duty to the environment NOT to increase the population?

Environmental issues

Art

Children

China

Fishing

Recycling

Environmental issues

Climate change

Shopping

Food

Developing nations

Photos: Mike Shearing

WHAT CHINA CRISIS?

China is often criticised for its environmental record, but Mike Shearing feels there is another story to tell

I live in Guizhou, one of China's poorest provinces. It is the size of England with a population to match. There's a saying here that, "no three li [half a kilometre] are flat, no three days are sunny, no three coins are in the same pocket," but despite the poverty and relative lack of sunlight, the flat-topped roofs of the apartment buildings are chock-a-block with water tanks for solar heating. They're almost as common as cars.

The accommodation block stairwells are uniformly grim, but they're all fitted with sound-activated lighting to minimize unnecessary energy consumption. Low-energy bulbs are in all public buildings. One recent innovation has been solar powered traffic lights, mobile devices stationed outside school gates at busy times. And the city's police force has acquired electric-powered vehicles to supplement their petrol patrol cars.

> I've taught in classrooms where it's been down to 7°C, but in those conditions you just put on more clothes and jump around

The Chinese are not profligate in heating either. The emphasis is on heating the person not the space. Northern China has district heating schemes, but south of the Yangzi, households make do with air conditioners or small heaters, wheeling them to whichever room they're using at the time, huddling around them. No one leaves heaters on when they go out.

Most schools have undergone refurbishments – computer labs, all-weather playgrounds, sometimes completely new – but none has heating installed, despite winter temperatures similar to England. I've taught in classrooms where it's been down to 7°C, but in those conditions you just put on more clothes and jump around.

It might not be easy being vegetarian in this part of China, but the Chinese eat every part of the animals they kill. Actually meat consumption isn't high, and it's usually the more resource-efficient pork and chicken, shredded up and intermingled with most vegetable dishes.

Mobile, solar PV traffic lights help school children cross roads safely (below) and roofs laden with solar water heaters (left)

"China is building a new coal-fired power station every week and expanding 160 airports". But some of those new power stations are replacing older, less-efficient plants, and many airports are miniscule

Westerners keen to justify their own high-carbon lifestyles insist that "China is building a new coal-fired power station every week and expanding 160 airports". But some of those new power stations are replacing older, less-efficient plants, and many airports are miniscule. I've seen Scalextric sets bigger than the luggage carousel at Tongren airport.

On a wider scale there are significant initiatives underway. Most National Park buses are LPG-fuelled, and in Xinjiang province there's the largest wind farm I've seen – it takes 10 minutes to travel past on the train. Unlike most countries China hit its 2010 target for wind energy three years early, and a carbon capture project begins next year.

Similarly, while the British Government continues its tortuous shuffle towards packaging legislation, this summer China banned retailers from giving away free plastic bags.

Unlike most countries China hit its 2010 target for wind energy three years early, and a carbon capture project begins next year

The popular assumption is that the Chinese state systematically denies its citizens the quality environment to which they're entitled, but on most environmental issues the authorities are far ahead of the public.

Everything in the Chinese peach garden isn't rosy, but I see more hope for the planet living here than I did when I lived in the UK. Most people live inherently sustainable lives – minimal carbon footprint, minimal food miles. If the West actually makes the necessary changes in lifestyle or technology to deal with the threat of climate change, I'm quite convinced the Chinese will follow. But if they don't, why should China bother?

Mike joined Friends of the Earth in 1984, co-ordinating the Exeter group between 1985 and 1988. He is currently teaching English in China where he has lived for the past four years.

Earthmatters, Autumn 2008
Friends of the Earth
http://www.foe.co.uk

Workers unloading a sea-going container full of imported televisions and monitors at Alaba market in Lagos, Nigeria. Many of these that are not working, will be tossed into the dumps outside of the market.

© 2009 Basel Action Network (BAN)

Poverty or poison
The stark choice facing developing nations

We are all using more electronic products than ever before – and we are throwing more away. This electronic scrap – e-waste – is increasing so rapidly that the developed world cannot deal with it.

Every year, hundreds of thousands of old computers and mobile phones are dumped in landfills or burned in smelters. Thousands more are exported, often illegally, from industrialised countries to Asia and Africa. There, workers at scrap yards, including children, are exposed to a cocktail of toxic chemicals and poisons.

The volume of electronic products

discarded globally has skyrocketed, with 20-50 million tonnes generated every year. Think of it like this - if the estimated amount of e-waste generated every year could be put into containers on a train it would stretch once around the world! E-waste now makes up five percent of all municipal solid waste worldwide. And it is not only developed countries that generate e-waste, Asia discards an estimated 12 million tonnes each year.

E-waste is growing because people are upgrading their mobile phones, computers, televisions, audio equipment and printers more frequently than ever. Mobile phones and computers are replaced

most often. In Europe e-waste is increasing at three to five percent a year, almost three times faster than waste in total. Developing countries are also expected to triple their e-waste production in the near future.

Although recycling can be a good way to reuse raw materials, the hazardous chemicals in e-waste can harm workers in the recycling yards, as well as their neighbouring communities and environment – and under the guise of recycling some countries are actually dumping toxic waste on their poorer global neighbours.

In a 'free market,' toxic waste will always flow towards those areas with the least political or economic power to resist it. The logic of business will be to send hazardous waste to the places where it costs least to get rid of it: where labour costs are cheap, land is inexpensive and there are fewer laws protecting the environment and the workers – in other words, to the developing world. It is vastly cheaper to 'recycle' waste in developing countries; the cost of glass-to-glass recycling of computer monitors in the US is ten times more than in China. In developed countries, electronics recycling takes place in purpose-built plants under controlled conditions. In developing countries however, there are no such controls. Recycling is done by hand in scrap yards, often by children. And governments of debt-ridden countries are willing to take both health and environmental risks in order to obtain hard currency – to swap 'trash for cash'.

E-waste is routinely exported by developed countries to developing ones, often in violation of international law. Inspections of 18 European seaports found as much as 47 percent of waste destined for export, including e-waste, was illegal. Mainland China tried to prevent this trade by banning the import of e-waste in 2000. However, Greenpeace has discovered that the laws are not working; e-waste is still arriving in Guangdong Province, the main centre of e-waste scrapping in China.

Greenpeace also found a growing e-waste trade problem in India. 25,000 workers are employed at scrap yards in Delhi alone, where 10-20,000 tonnes of e-waste is handled each year, 25 percent of this being computers. Other e-waste scrap yards have been found elsewhere in India. This trade in electronic waste began to grow when scrap yards found they could extract valuable substances such as copper, iron, silicon, nickel and gold, during the recycling process. A mobile phone, for example, is 19 percent

© 2009 Basel Action Network (BAN)

A boy hired to haul electronic scrap from Alaba market in Lagos, Nigeria to this nearby informal dump sitting on a swamp. Imported scrap televisions and computers that could not be repaired get deposited and burned.

© 2009 Basel Action Network (BAN)

Electronic waste dumped in a residential area just outside of Alaba market in Lagos. This e-waste is routinely burned here.

copper and eight percent iron. However the conditions under which such metals are extracted would not be tolerated in the countries where the e-waste originates.

Greenpeace is pressing leading electronic companies to face up to their responsibilities and to make clean, durable products that can be upgraded, recycled, or disposed of safely and don't end up as hazardous waste in someone's backyard. Another campaigning group, BAN,

based in Seattle, is committed to fighting e-waste and supporting the Basel Ban, an international agreement to prevent the exporting of toxic waste from the rich to the poor. BAN sees the shifting of e-waste to the poorer nations as "a crime against the environment and human rights".

Sources: Greenpeace, BAN and various

For further information about the issue of e-waste go to:
http://www.greenpeace.org
http://www.ban.org

Market scavenger boy, Alaba market, Lagos, Nigeria

FISHY ON A DISHY

So on we come to sea food, another guilt filled minefield for your average ethical consumer. We sent **Jan Hilmar** down 20,000 leagues to find out if you can combine those essential omega-3 oils with a clear conscience.

OK, so we're used to hearing that eating meat is bad. Bad for the animals that get killed, bad for the environment, and a highly inefficient use of resources.

We know that, yet some of us – including myself – still eat it. Even so, I'm sure we all know a non-meat eater who allows themselves the occasional seafood treat, or even excludes fish from their list of banned food. Is that justified? Is eating fish really any better than meat? If, like myself, you like your fish, what are some things you can look out for when buying it?

My first impulse would be that wild caught is better than farmed fish. To me, "farmed" conjures up images of intense production, massive use of chemicals, and cramming the poor animals into much too small a space. However, over half of the world's wild fish species are in a perilous state. Another quarter are over exploited, and only three percent of all species in our vast oceans are under exploited (a worrying term in itself).

Against this backdrop, farmed fish doesn't sound bad. However, as always the plot thickens. Consider that perennial favourite – prawns. If, like me, you thought prawns had a happy life, frolicking in the open waters, then think again.

Most of the king and tiger prawns we see in the supermarket are farmed in poor countries, which can initially be lucrative to the locals: a company moves in, buys up their land, and offers to hire them at above average wages as shrimp farmers.

Unfortunately, these farms tend to replace mangroves – trees and shrubs that grow in salt-water lakes. These mangroves are important ecosystems, home to a huge number of species, CO_2 sinks and natural flood

defences. The prawn farms can only operate for a few years, until sludge accumulates, making them unusable.

The farm – and workers – are abandoned. Some countries now have stricter laws for the preservation of mangroves, but generally, prawn farming is about one of the least sustainable practices out there. Maybe time to rethink that prawn biryani.

Farming fish like salmon and trout has its problems as well. Here, fish are usually kept in pens in the water and fed special food – including other fish – to make them grow faster. The high density of fish means that diseases spread quickly amongst them, which can also spread to wild fish. They also produce a large

WHERE TO START

The Marine Conservation Society
http://www.mcsuk.org produce a handy leaflet which provides a quick idea of what to buy and what to avoid.

The Marine Stewardship Council http://www.msc.org operates a certification scheme which attempts to identify sustainable sea food. There are now many products in supermarkets bearing their logo. There seems to be mixed feelings about the scheme. Some claim it's a great guide to making quick decisions in the shops, whereas others say it doesn't go far enough. As with anything like this it's good to do your own research, and do what you feel comfortable with.

amount of harmful waste, and it can still take several kilos of wild fish to make every kilo of farmed salmon. Again, organic fish farms avoid some of these problems and some supermarkets are looking for more sustainable feeding stock for the farmed fish that they sell. Another possibility for farmed fish is to consider predominantly vegetarian fish – tilapia, for example, can be grown without using tonnes of other fish to feed them.

It might seem that the best option is to go for line-caught fish, harvested the good old fashioned way. Unfortunately, this is the more expensive option, and although line-caught can mean caught with rod and line, it can also mean long lining involving dozens or hundreds of kilometres of lines with thousands of hooks. Unfortunately this means other fish, turtles and seabirds can be hooked.

So, as usual, life isn't easy for the ethical consumer. The important thing here is to do research, find what you're comfortable with, and never be afraid to ask questions about the provenance of what you're buying.

Friends of the Earth Scotland – What on Earth, Spring/Summer 2008

JARGON BUSTER

LINE-CAUGHT: A lower-intensity method than trawling – but still can indiscriminately catch lots of other species.

BOTTOM TRAWLED: Caught using a huge net, dragging along the ocean floor. Highly destructive to fish populations and the ocean floor.

PAIR TRAWLED: Huge net, pulled by two boats. Catches everything in its path, thus very damaging to endangered species.

Should you become – an ecotarian?

Fair Trade, Free Range, Food Miles, these days there is no end of dietary dilemmas to pull at the moral heartstrings. And yet here's another – say hello to ecotarianism!

Ethical shopping has become a nightmare. While you're keenly trying to work out the food miles of the fair trade organic soya you're about to put into your trolley, along comes another enviro-boffin with a new term to get your head around.

Yet ecotarianism is straightforward in its approach. The basic idea is this: eat foods that have the least impact on the environment. Simple! Or is it? While deciding which tomatoes to put into your trolley, consider this – which have the lowest global-warming potential (GWP) and the least chance of damaging our planet with their acidification and pollution potential. Why is it that these good ideas always fail at the first hurdle?

However, don't give up yet, for there are now bundles of academic papers to help you through this eco-shopping minefield. Use as your bible 'Cooking up a storm' by Tara Garnett from the University of Surrey. In this she has worked out the lightest (in environmental terms) foods to eat, making it easier to decide what groceries make it to the checkout and what gets left to rot in its own planet-destroying shame.

So what does the shopping basket of an ecotarian look like? Well strangely enough, not quite how you'd imagine. The emphasis is entirely on the environment and not on the health and wellbeing of either people or animals, so many parts of this diet are hard to digest.

The key is efficiency of production. Products that have been the most efficiently produced have the lowest GWP. In 2004 a German study compared fruit juice from Brazil with local European versions. It found that even taking into account the distance travelled by the Brazilian juice, the European juice used more energy in its production, and so had a higher GWP. Now that puts a spin on food miles for you.

Another example will really rile the animal welfare campaigners. The problem with focusing on the efficiency of production, is that it overlooks the well-being of live animals. Take poultry and eggs. The ecotarian lifecycle analysis rewards high-efficiency feeds and lower-energy production. This means that non-organic or non-free-range meat and eggs are better for the environment. That doesn't take into account the total barbarity of battery hen production.

On the other hand however, organic non-animal products are best as the organic system uses legumes to fix nitrogen rather than wasting fuel on synthetic fertilisers.

The ecotarian also buys less frozen foods, which should please the chefs among us. Half of supermarket lorries are now temperature controlled in order to transport such products around the country, causing a massive greenhouse-gas burden. The exception however is frozen peas. Following a seminal study, 'Give Peas a Chance', which discovered that the production efficiency of the humble frozen pea is in fact very good, frozen peas are acceptable to the ecotarian.

So all is not quite as straightforward as it seems. Do you prioritise the environment or the animal, the greenhouse-gas issue or the basic instinct to eat what the hell we want? If your moral heartstrings are struck, read 'Cooking Up a Storm' before you next go shopping and avoid carrying yet another environmental burden on your shoulders – or in your shopping bag.

Sources: Various
For more info visit: http://www.sehn.org/

No words necessary: The cartoonists tackle climate change

The Ken Sprague Fund has organised a competition for cartoonists to use humorous images to bring home the reality of global warming. The first prize was awarded to 'Coat Star' by Mikhail Zlatovsky from Russia (see next page). The judges felt that the winner "captured the shabbiness and sleazy way our planet in being devastated."

http://www.kenspraguefund.org

'Coat Star' by Mikhail Zlatovsky

An act of extreme, wilful fecundity?

Why the birth of octuplets in California so speedily turned from a good news story into a finger-wagging morality tale.

Brendan O'Neill

When Nadya Suleman gave birth to six boys and two girls in five minutes on 26 January, it was greeted as a 'midwinter miracle', a story that 'cheered recession-hit America', a 'welcome relief from bailouts and bankruptcies'. Now, it has become a shrill parable about overpopulation, resource depletion, the dangers of fertility treatment and the problem of 'poor mothers'. The story has shapeshifted from a 'ray of sunshine for a nation in the grip of economic meltdown' to a 'tale of seedy self-indulgence'.

To be sure, not many women would make the decisions that Ms Suleman made. Going ahead with a high multiple pregnancy can be dangerous, both for mother and babies, who tend to be born very small and very premature and thus are susceptible to heart, respiratory and brain-development problems. And the news that Ms Suleman, who is reportedly unemployed and not very well off, already had six children – meaning that she now has a brood of 14! – will have made the everyday, always-busy parents of two, three or four kids groan with exhaustive empathy. Yet if we are serious about reproductive choice, then someone like Ms Suleman must be free to opt for a Brady Bunch-style family, just as other women opt to have no children at all.

Midwinter miracle to seedy tale

Behind the understandable 'what was she thinking?' response of ordinary news-watchers, the steady denigration of this story from a 'midwinter miracle' (it is only the second time in American history that a set of octuplets has been born alive) to a 'seedy tale' reflects a broader cultural discomfort with fertility today, with the very re-creation of

Photo: Amy Lang/Landov/Press Association Images

the human species. Many look upon the Suleman babies, not as eight bundles of joy, but as eight carrycots of carbon. The babies are less 'gifts from God' than 'potential polluters'.

In the only statement issued by the mother to date, she described the birth as a 'miraculous experience' – but many see the babies as mere 'users of resources', money-grubbing, nappy-requiring, food-scoffing cling-ons to our already jam-packed planet. The Los Angeles Times reported that Ms Suleman was 'racking up unfathomable medical bills that would, in all likelihood, fall to taxpayers'. Others demand to know 'who is going to foot the bill' for such things as diapers (one website estimates that Ms Suleman will have to spend a total of $23,738 on diapers and $10,000 on baby wipes).

The discussion of the Suleman Eight as a financial and environmental burden, as a strain on both taxpayers and on the planet, as both the users of monetary resources and the flatteners of rainforests, exposes the contemporary cultural view of new human life as being somehow destructive.

A new take on an old-fashioned view

The discussion of the Suleman Eight as a financial and environmental burden, as a strain on both taxpayers and on the planet, as both the users of monetary resources and the flatteners of rainforests, exposes the contemporary cultural view of new human life as being somehow destructive. The old-fashioned view of poor children as a burden on society's economic resources mingles with the new-fangled view of all children as a burden on the planet's resources, giving rise to a handwringing discussion of a remarkable eight-baby birth as something terrible. The more that the planet is seen as a fragile larder of limited resources, the more that phrases like 'human impact' and 'human footprint' become dirty words, and the more that overpopulation comes to be seen as the root of all eco-evil, then the more that new birth becomes a cause for concern rather than for celebration. Society's discomfort with the f-word – fertility – is now projected on to the Sulemans.

Should doctors decide?

For others, the Suleman Eight highlight the dangers of unregulated fertility treatment. It is reported that Ms Suleman conceived her eight babies, and her six other children, with the aid of IVF treatment. And people want to know what kind of doctor willingly implants eight eggs into the womb of 'an unmarried, unemployed California mother who's already raising six children aged two to seven'.

The more that the planet is seen as a fragile larder of limited resources, the more that phrases like 'human impact' and 'human footprint' become dirty words, and the more that overpopulation comes to be seen as the root of all eco-evil.

Commentators slam the 'unregulated fertility industry' for assisting even a family where 'there's no dad, no money, no job, no room and six older siblings'.

Of course it is a doctor's job to advise women who receive IVF treatment of the risks of high multiple pregnancies. And the evidence suggests that they did precisely that in the Suleman case: they suggested to her that she should consider a partial abortion, but she chose to reject their advice. However, the implication behind the widespread denouncement of Suleman's doctors as 'irresponsible', 'negligent' and even 'criminal' is ominous indeed. Are we saying that doctors should decide which women are desirable for IVF treatment and which are not? That they should limit the choices of those women who are 'unmarried, unemployed' and who already have kids at home? And those who have 'no money, no job', too? Since when did it become acceptable again to imply that poor women should not procreate and that doctors should do everything in their power to stop them?

As it happens, it isn't true that the 'fertility industry' (that i-word is always used to create the impression of sinister God-playing laboratories or baby-making factories) is 'unregulated'. As Time magazine reported in response to the Suleman miracle-turned-controversy, 'reproductive medicine is among the most regulated specialities in the US'. All fertility clinics must report to the Centers for Disease Control and Prevention on how many embryos they transfer in every IVF cycle, as well as the number of babies born from every cycle. Some fertility experts are outraged that one unusual multiple birth has been used to problematise the broader, and often truly miraculous, provision of IVF treatment.

Dr James Grifo, professor of obstetrics and gynaecology at the NYU School of Medicine, sensibly said: 'I don't think it's our job to tell [women] how many babies they're allowed to have. I am not a policeman for reproduction in the United States.' That so many commentators post-Suleman are calling on fertility doctors to be precisely that – the cops of baby-making, the selectors of who may be impregnated and who may not – exposes the fragile foundations to the principle of reproductive choice today.

Today, the concern about too much fertility in general sits uncomfortably with a concern about too little fertility in the West as compared with the East. The end result is the rehabilitation of the old discussions of the 'wrong' people having the 'wrong' kind of babies.

It also casts some light on what many observers consider to be the problem with human fertility today, especially of the natural variety: it is unregulated, uncontrolled; pretty much anybody can have a baby, even those with no money and no commitment to reducing their carbon footprint. The fervour with which some want to clamp down on doctor-assisted reproduction exposes their deeper desire, however wishful and forlorn it might be, to limit all forms of fertility – for the sake of the planet, for the sake of the public purse, for the sake of not having too many of the 'wrong' kind of people.

Conspiracy theories

There is even a conspiracy theory doing the rounds about the Suleman Eight. One conservative website says the babies, born to a woman with a clearly Muslim name, might be part of the 'jihad by stealth', where Muslims are procreating in order to outnumber Christians: 'If we want to know what the US will be like in a few years we need only look to the UK. Muslims now have the numbers in Europe to wreak no end of havoc and they are doing it.' The conspiracy theorist even suggests that Ms Suleman might have been 'hired' as a 'brood mare' to help 'populate the planet with more Muslims'. Insane, right? Clearly. Yet this mad conspiracy-mongering can also be seen as simply a more twisted, sinister version of the mainstream Fear of Fertility, only in this story it is American values that are threatened by uncontrollably fecund Muslims rather than the 'health of the planet' being threatened by overly fecund people in general. Today, the concern about too much fertility in general sits uncomfortably with a concern about too little fertility in the West as compared with the East. The end result is the rehabilitation of the old discussions of the 'wrong' people having the 'wrong' kind of babies.

Fertility used to be a nice world. It meant being 'rich in resources or invention', fruitful, prolific, productive. Now it is a dirty word, looked upon as a pastime indulged by eco-thoughtless or the 'wrong' people who must be regulated, controlled or guilt-tripped into changing their ways. A Los Angeles Times columnist described the birth of the Suleman Eight as a 'display of extreme, wilful and not miraculous fecundity'. That can be seen as the elite view of child-bearing more broadly today, which, in a world of allegedly limited resources and too many bad people, is increasingly seen as a potentially 'extreme' and 'wilful' activity.

Spiked 2 February 2009
http://www.spiked-online.com

Family & relationships

Issues to think about and discuss

Are girls better than boys? – Do you need to have a baby boy to 'complete' your family of girls? Is this fair? Where does this idea come from?

Don't lose your bottle – Can a blind father really look after a baby? "Nappies I learnt to change; prejudices... I did not."

Where did childhood in Britain go wrong? – According to various reports, Britain's teenagers are top of the league for all sorts of misconduct and they are miserable. Is life so much worse for young people?

My parents left me home alone – This is what happened to this 17-year-old girl, it sounds great, but how did it really feel?

Zannah's thoughts & **Who's your daddy?** – What does it mean to be a father? Blood relation or carer, who matters most? Was it right for a man to claim back the cost of bringing up the 16-year-old girl he found out was not his?

Caring for the teen parents – Does having a child young ruin your chances? A Russian journalist finds positive aspects to teen parenthood.

Tragic mum's dying wish – A mother is dying of cancer, should the grandmother care for the children once she is gone? But what if she is only just getting her own life back again...?

He blocked the door and pulled a knife & **The lessons that need to be learnt from Baby P** – Two accounts of the life of social workers. Is instinct the most important tool for the job, or is that what led to failure in the case of baby P?

Tiny turns in the right direction – Why would anyone volunteer to spend time with a 'troubled, chaotic teenager'? Can a stranger be a role model?

Adoption

Social care

Violence

Grandparents

Teen parents

Family & relationships

Are girls better than boys?

It's funny, but when I say that I don't care if our next baby is a boy or a girl, no one believes me. Certainly I think adding a baby boy to our family would be wonderful, exciting and a great joy. But I honestly don't think it will be any more wonderful, exciting or joyous than our two girls have been so far, and any future girl would be.

From what I can work out, most people think that the only possible reason you would have a third baby is to "complete" your family by having a full set of sexes. When our second daughter Frances was born I lost count of the people who instantly asked if we were going to "have another crack". Even at the checkout the other day, the lady loading our groceries looked at Maisie and Frances, studied Susie's swollen tummy, then turned to me with a smile and said "Good luck this time!"

And it's not just strangers. My mum has told me on countless occasions how she can't wait to see me with a son. Last week, when she turned her x-ray vision onto Susie's tummy and determined that Susie was having another girl, she asked me if we would have a fourth. Even when I explained that we'd always wanted three kids and we didn't care what sex the next baby was she still wouldn't let it go. Instead she looked at me with that unmistakable 'mum' look, the one that says "yes, but I know what you're really thinking", and simply said "Yes Joe. But a boy would be nice, wouldn't it?"

The fact is I think a boy would be nice. I think it would be nice to have a child whose hair I could brush without needing an advanced diploma in braiding from the Ponds Institute. I think it would be nice to have a child who didn't spend the entire morning trying to co-ordinate different shades of pink for her morning ensemble before heading to creche. And I think it would be nice to have a child who didn't get mortally offended every time I thought she was dressed as a fairy when, in fact, she was a princess.

And while I'm on it, I think it would be nice to have a child who handled his frustrations in logical and socially acceptable ways, such as breaking stuff. I have learnt after long experience with Maisie that when she is frustrated we have to go through this crazy dance of isolating her feelings, discussing those feeling, validating those feelings and then celebrating the closure of those feelings by watching an episode of Dora the Explorer. I think it would be a lot easier on all concerned if the next time she got frustrated she just kicked a ball through a window.

> "Isolating her feelings, discussing those feelings, validating those feelings and then celebrating the closure of those feelings by watching an episode of Dora the Explorer."

I think all of this would be nice. But I know from hard wrung experience that not only are girls nice, but being a dad to girls is pretty nice too. For example, I know it's nice to be invited under Frances's bed to share a picnic with her teddies. I know it's nice that when I do volunteer reading at Maisie's school she gets so excited she stands up every twenty seconds and squeals "That's my dad!" And I know it's nice to always be asked to play the prince whenever the girls play princesses, even though I always end up as the horse or the dragon.

So knowing all of that, I can honestly say I don't care if our next baby is a boy or a girl. My only hope is, if it is a boy, that he's happy to play the horse or the dragon while I play the prince.

Joseph Kelly
Baby Essentials 18 March 2009

Don't lose your bottle

Johny Cassidy was met by tuts and prejudice as his daughter's main carer

Photo posed by models

I think it was Winston Churchill who said that when war begins, throw away the battle plans. That's what it was like for my partner Angela and me when my first daughter, Oonagh, was born in 2001. It was incredible to think how much disruption a seven-pound little human being could bring, but bring it she did.

Three months into the campaign, we agreed Angela would go back to work. It seemed the sensible thing to do.

This meant I would look after Oonagh during the day. How difficult could it be? Poor naïve me.

I soon found that nappies and the inability to see don't mix and at first found it easier just to bath Oonagh when she needed changing. This way I knew she was clean. Just whip the nappy off, a quick dunk in the tub and job done.

Looking back, Oonagh must have been the most bathed baby ever. After the regular mealtime foodfight, where I would put food up her nose and in her ears, she would get dunked again. The mashed carrots, or whatever culinary delight I had created, would vanish down the plughole and I'd have a nice clean baby again. For about two minutes.

I really loved my time with Oonagh and took to it quite well but what I found odd was people's reactions to a blind man looking after his daughter. Everyone had an opinion, from health visitors to friends and neighbours. This was my biggest barrier. Nappies I learnt to change; prejudices and ideas about childcare I did not.

I realise that social services and health visitors have a responsibility to see children are looked after. I think this is why Angela and I had more health checks than our friends. At the time they laughed at the preferential treatment we were getting because of my eyesight but I think it was mainly to monitor how I was doing as the main carer.

"Nappies and the inability to see don't mix and at first found it easier just to bath Oonagh when she needed changing"

Public attitudes were interesting, especially among older people. I remember being in a shop when Oonagh was about six months old. She had been asleep in her buggy but woke up quite grizzly and hungry. I knew she wanted her bottle so she could go back to sleep again but before I was able to locate her mouth with my little finger, I had the bottle snatched from me and put in her mouth by someone else. On another occasion, a friend's daughter's christening, I had to contend not only with tuts and comments but the suggestion that I should join the men at the bar, as if my tending a child made me inadequate as a man and my being blind made me unfit as a father. I was told that I was holding Oonagh wrongly and that she needed winding or changing. When I did change her, I felt incredibly smug that there were no signs of nappy rash but it was hard to keep calm as my nappy-changing skills were publicly scrutinised.

In spite of these upsets the good definitely outweighed the bad. It was a massive learning curve for us all and we all gained. Oonagh is six now and there's no doubt we have a special bond. My white stick has been every sort of toy from a horsey to a magic wand. Maybe some day she can use it to change the world, if she hasn't already.

Disability Now May 2008

Where did childhood in Britain go wrong?

Sue Palmer

Well, it's a start. David Cameron has noticed that health and safety regulations stop schools taking children out on field trips, outdoor activities or just collecting autumn leaves at the park. And the Department for Children, Schools and Families is to issue guidelines about extra-curricular activities, aiming to get pupils back into the real world.

I suppose school-organised, adult-supervised activities are better than nothing. But they're really not good enough. Indeed, excessive health and safety measures at school are just the tip of the risk-aversion iceberg leaving increasing numbers of young people without the emotional resilience, social competence and personal confidence to thrive in our society.

A couple of years ago, the Institute for Public Policy Research found that British youngsters were at or near the top of the European charts for almost every type of teenage misconduct and malaise. Not just knife-crime and antisocial behaviour in inner cities, but underage drinking, sexual activity and drug abuse across the social spectrum.

Something is mightily wrong with childhood in Britain, and after 30 years working with children and teachers (the last eight years of which were spent researching "toxic childhood"), I reckon our risk aversion - not just in schools but in every area of life - is a major part of the problem.

Think back to your childhood. What and where did you play when you were six, seven, eight? Most adults remember building and making (dens, mud pies, forts, go-karts), make-believe and role play.

They remember running, jumping, climbing, and playing outside (the garden, the park, local "wild" places), kickarounds on the playing field or disappearing for hours on their bicycles.

There were no grown-ups to supervise this play - children organised it themselves, and by playing together, often in mixed age groups, they learned to get along, to deal with squabbles, to collaborate, to negotiate.

Now think about children you know today. How often do they go "out to play"?

Over the past 25 years there has been an enormous change in young children's leisure experiences.

When asked recently by the Good Childhood Inquiry what age children should be allowed out alone, many adults suggested 14. And even if they would like to give their children more freedom, parents are prevented by public opinion - any child seen out unaccompanied these days is considered at risk or a possible threat to public safety.

So for most 21st-century children, the word "play" doesn't mean outdoor, physical pursuits or indoor creativity: it means sitting down at a PlayStation, mindlessly gazing at television, or communicating virtually with friends via Bebo or MSN.

Instead of first-hand experiences and real interaction, they have ersatz experiences on screens.

Just as health and safety regulations have stifled the excitement of learning at school, preoccupation with public safety, endless regulation and adults' desire for tidy, orderly communities have helped stifle children's leisure time - and a high-tech, consumer culture has provided an indoor sedentary substitute.

Children in Britain spend an average of five hours, 20 minutes a day on screen-based activities.

Now think what's been lost. All the most essential lessons of life - the personal, social and emotional lessons that make us functioning human beings - are caught rather than taught.

Social competence, self-confidence and resilience, commonsense understanding of the world - not to mention physical health and fitness - all come from being out there in the real world.

If children don't get these vital first-hand experiences, we can't be surprised that many end up as fragile or anti-social teenagers, either risk-averse themselves, or ready to take excessive risks, because they're unable to make sensible judgments.

A combination of parental anxiety, community intolerance and all-pervasive risk aversion threatens the mental and physical health of the next generation. It is becoming a matter of urgency that we reclaim public space for our children and relearn skills that came naturally to our parents.

> So for most 21st-century children, the word "play"... means sitting down at a PlayStation, mindlessly gazing at television, or communicating virtually with friends via Bebo or MSN

Instead of wrapping children in cotton wool, we have to do what parents in the past (and today in other parts of the world) have always done.

First, parents themselves must take personal responsibility for making the local environment as safe as possible for children to play. This means working with other parents, neighbours and shop-keepers, as well as obvious agencies such as the police and housing authorities.

When parents know where their children are playing, they can set safe boundaries and ensure friendly adults are on hand when needed.

Second, adults must train children to deal with any dangers they might meet. This means getting out into the local area with them, teaching road safety skills through example, talking about safety issues and dangers.

If the loving adults in children's lives take control of the situation, they - and the children - can feel confident that today's youngsters are as all right as it's possible to be.

But if we leave it to the heath and safety authorities, they'll strangle us all in red tape.

The Daily Telegraph 15 December 2008
© *Telegraph Group Ltd 2008*

My parents left me home alone

Melissa Blease

Leaving home should be a rite of passage, a time when you say goodbye to your parents to pursue a new life. Supposedly you're the one who ventures out into the world and they're the ones who stay behind. It didn't turn out like that for me. When I was 17, my parents both left home to pursue life-changing experiences and I was the one left behind.

How could this have happened? I'm still not sure. Both my parents were teachers, imaginative and loving towards myself and my sister. I remember growing up as a magical time full of attention, affection and security. My parents were married for 21 years and seemed to be close. There were moments when they argued but as a typically self-centred 16-year-old, I paid little attention to their heated debates.

It came from nowhere, the day it happened. I remember a row and raised voices upstairs. My mother dashed past me on the stairs carrying a suitcase, her face turned away from me. No explanation, nothing. I looked outside and saw a man sitting in a van. My mum got into the passenger seat and they drove off, followed by my dad who dashed after them in his own car.

I don't know what he intended to do if he caught up with them, but he came back shortly afterwards. My sister and I sat in the kitchen too stunned to talk. My dad was distant and uncommunicative.

The next day, he went to visit a friend in Yorkshire where he stayed for the next few days. Strangely I was relieved. He had always relied on me as an ally and confidante but I was finding it hard enough to cope with my own feelings, let alone take care of his. My sister went to stay with her boyfriend's family. My mum, I guessed, was with the man in the van. And that was it: the end of life as my family knew it. I was alone.

The days that followed were bleak, confusing. I tried lamely to relish my new-found freedom, but really I was frantically worried about my parents' wellbeing. My mum phoned, and although she wouldn't tell me where she was in case I told my dad, she reassured me that she loved me, and asked if I was OK. I was keen to assure her I felt fine; I didn't want to worry her.

About a week later, my mum arranged to meet me in a nearby park. She told

> "One by one, the utilities were switched off; the TV was taken away and the furniture mysteriously disappeared. Both parents sent me money (which I spent on extravagant, New Romantic outfits) and guilty letters telling me how much they loved me."

Photo (posed by model) by Bruce Turner

me she was living about three miles away, with a man she'd met at the educational arts project where my parents had once worked. It was the first I knew of his existence. A few weeks later, my dad found a new job in London. He wanted me to go and live with him, but I resented being asked to leave everything and everyone I knew.

I was angry but I couldn't allow myself to admit it to either of my parents. Much easier to pretend I was coping admirably. I threw myself into socialising, inviting friends over for endless all-night parties. The family home I'd lived in for 10 years began to resemble a squat. My parents' bedroom, long since deserted, became a stopover for various friends. I lost the front door key, so we all used to climb in through the front window. The upstairs lavatory fell into the kitchen below.

One by one, the utilities were switched off; the TV was taken away and the furniture mysteriously disappeared. Both parents sent me money (which I spent on extravagant, New Romantic outfits) and guilty letters telling me how much they loved me. Incredibly, social services were never tipped off. I fell through the net; everyone assumed I was being cared for by someone else - even my parents thought the other was looking after me.

Eventually the house was sold, along with many of the family possessions which still filled the shelves and drawers; relics from a time gone by. I moved into a flat with a friend, glad that I could finally leave home myself.

Friends have said my parents were irresponsible to act as they did. I don't see it that way and can't resent them for what happened. I'm close to both of them now and as an adult who has gone through dramas of my own, I find it easier to empathise with their motives. I now know that neither of them intended to end their marriage in such a devastating way. Events and emotions ran away with them and I got caught in the crossfire. I used to feel bad when people asked, "When did you leave home?", not wanting to admit to such a complex, messy truth. Now I don't mind saying, "I didn't leave home - my parents did it for me."

The Guardian 29 November 2008
© Guardian News and Media Ltd 2008

Zannah's thoughts

Susannah (or Zannah as she prefers to be known) daughter of Donor Conception Network founders Olivia Montushi and Walter Merricks was recently interviewed by email for the first book to be written for parents and professionals about donor conception in Germany. Here are her answers to questions from Petra Thorn, a counsellor and family therapist. Zannah, aged 21, is happy for her thoughts to be shared.

I don't remember a specific time when I was told – I have always just known. There was a time when I didn't understand it properly but no young child is likely to understand completely until they are older. It is difficult to say what it was like to be told early because there was never a time when my parents sat me down and 'told' me – the information was just always around and I accepted it as completely normal. It was always an open subject at home – I could ask questions when I wanted to. It has not been a big issue in my life, I don't think about it all the time.

I never felt ashamed about Donor Insemination from day one because of the way my parents told me so it wasn't something I felt I needed to talk about but if we were talking about biology or who looks like who in the family at school I was happy to tell anyone about it. It actually made me feel special and interesting. I liked being different. Although I was rather insecure at school for a long time about many things, this wasn't one of them and never could be.

There has never been a question about who my father is. It seems stupid to me to question this as a father is someone who loves and raises you, not the person who

I have always known from the earliest age that 'Daddy' means love and not sperm.

provided the sperm to make you. I have always known from the earliest age that 'Daddy' means love and not sperm. This did not change during puberty. Actually, as I came to know and understand boys and men I came to realise what a fantastic person my dad is and to love and respect him for being able to face up to his infertility. It takes a real man to do this – my dad taught me what a real man is.

The way to manage DI in a family is to be open and unashamed about your decision. Parents have to let go of their own feelings and focus on the needs of their children – my parents managed to do this and I respect them for it. I can trust my parents totally, feel wanted and loved by them. I have respect for them for 'telling' me, unlike, if I was to find out now, the lack of respect shown to me would affect my relationship with them in the most detrimental of ways. Hiding DI seems to imply that it is something bad, to be ashamed about, that their children are something to be ashamed about.

DI is both very important, because it's about half of my genetic background, and not important at all. It has always been relatively unimportant in my daily life. It may come up in conversation about every two or three months. I am registered with UK DonorLink as I am intrigued about any information that I can find out, but I don't think about this very often. It would be a waste of energy and my life to obsess about it.

Young adults may struggle with DI because of the way it has been handled in their family. I can't really comment any more because their situations are very different to my own. I feel really sorry for anyone who has cowardly parents who cannot face the responsibilities that go with the decision they make to use DI to create a family.

I think donor conception is a completely acceptable way to create a family IF and only IF parents are prepared to be honest with their children AND anonymity is ended everywhere. It is a human right to have the choice to know where you come from.

Susannah Merricks,
http://www.donor-conception-network

It actually made me feel special and interesting. I like being different

Who's your daddy?

Seema Goswami

What happens when a man finds out he's bringing up someone else's kid?

So, what really makes a man a father? Is it the fact that he has bestowed his genes to the fruit of his loins? Or is it that he has spent time and energy – not to mention love and money – in bringing up the sprogs?

I ask this question because of a bizarre case that has all the British tabloid press in a tizzy. A man named Mark Webb sued his former wife to recoup the money he spent on bringing up his daughter, Elspeth, who later he discovered was not his biological child. So, Mark wants his ex-wife and her lover to pay him back for all he spent on raising their daughter.

Mark lost in the English courts, but is not content to let sleeping paternity cases lie. Now, five years after he first found out the truth about Elspeth's parentage (when she was 16) he is appealing to the European Court for Human Rights, asking that the court acknowledge the injustice done to him.

It's not about the money, Mark says to those who ask how he can measure fatherhood in pounds. It is about the larger principle of natural justice – after all, a man deserves to know whether the child he is bringing up is his own or not. And he says he is doing this on behalf of the many men out there who have been hoodwinked by their partners into raising the kids of other men.

Whether the European Court feels Mark's pain or not, this case does raise some interesting points about the nature of fatherhood itself – and indeed, about the shrinking role of men in the reproductive arena.

As far as the nature of fatherhood is concerned, there are broadly two views on the subject. The first lays emphasis on genetic make-up. Your children are yours because they share your DNA. They are your biological link to the future, your claim to immortality, your chance to see your genes survive into the next generation.

If this is your view of fatherhood, then of course you would be gutted to discover that the child you have looked after, loved and cherished was never yours to begin with. That he or she, in fact, shared the genetic code of another man. And if his mother had lied to deceive you on this score, how much deeper would the anger, the pain, the resentment and the bitterness go? It wouldn't just be a blow to your ego but an assault on your sense of self itself.

But there is also a contrary view of fatherhood. According to this, fatherhood has less to do with genes and everything to do with a genuine generosity of spirit. If you have brought up a child, changed his nappies, wiped off his drool, driven him to school, nursed him through illnesses, dreamt dreams for him – then he is yours, no matter who his biological dad may be.

So even if you discover that the child you have loved for so long does not share your DNA, it shouldn't make a blind bit of difference to how you feel about him or her.

But, sadly, the truth is that it does make a difference. Of course it is not the child's fault and you should not make him suffer for it (as Mark Webb did by disowning his daughter and suing her mother). But if you have been lied to and tricked into investing your emotions, your energy and your resources into a child who is not your own you can't help but be devastated by the huge betrayal.

Your feelings towards your partner are going to be riddled with bitterness and anger. Your family dynamic is going to change. So how can your relationship with the child in question remain the same?

No matter how hard you try, you will catch yourself wondering if she thinks of her 'real father'. Is he, in fact, her 'real' father or are you? Does she still love you in the same way now that she has another Daddy? Will you have to compete with him for her affections?

How could things ever be the same in such a complicated scenario?

It is not my case that it is not possible to love a child who is not your own biological offspring. Millions of adoptive parents and step-parents do that every day, pouring their hearts into kids who are not of their own blood. But this is a choice that they exercise out of their own free will. They haven't been tricked into it, manipulated by lying partners into loving kids who are not their own.

That has to hurt. And any man who has been cheated upon in such a manner will carry that hurt with him forever. He may still love the child he brought up. But this love will be always imbued with the pain of betrayal, muddied by the stains of treachery and shot through with all kinds of confused emotions.

At the end of the day, what can you do but pity these men? When it comes to the reproductive arena, women wield all the power these days. They can decide when they want to have babies and with whom. They can trick men into getting them pregnant. And yes, they can lie about who the father of their child really is.

Honestly, when it comes to procreative stuff, it really doesn't pay to be a man. But if you are a man – well, then you must always pay.

Brunch/Hindustan Times February 2009

Caring for the teen parents

Simon Donohue

Britain's shocking record on teenage pregnancy is starkly illustrated by the picture of 13-year-old dad Alfie Patten - a father to baby Maisie having had unprotected sex with girlfriend Chantelle Steadman, 15, only once*.

Perhaps naively, the young pair have vowed to be good parents to the tot, clearly unaware of the huge burden of responsibility now resting on their young shoulders. But they would no doubt be encouraged by the experience of a Svetlana Kolchik, deputy editor of the Russian edition of upmarket women's magazine Marie Claire, who has just spent a week investigating British attitudes to young parenting in Greater Manchester.

She has returned to Moscow with the view that while teenagers here are shockingly relaxed about underage sex, the support network for them is a thing to be celebrated.

In Russia, she says, it would more than likely that a young couple in the same position as Alfie and Chantelle would have sought a termination.

"My message will be that young women choose to keep their babies because society provides them with the opportunities to raise those kids. I think it is positive."

So what brought her here? The journalist was struck by a story in a British newspaper about a generation of 30-something grans whose daughters had also had children.

"It was compelling and I made a resolution that I would come back and investigate further," she says. "I chose Manchester because statistics show that the Manchester area has one of the highest teenage pregnancy rates in the western world."

She certainly found plenty of source material, visiting Moat House, a school in Stockport for young mums, a tough Wythenshawe estate and a mum of the year in Chorley.

"It's ironic to come from a failed communist society and see things here that the communists killed millions in order to achieve, including free health care and childcare.

"We still have free health care but it's very poor. There are free kindergartens but you have to bribe somebody in order to get your children into them."

Teenage pregnancy rates have traditionally been high in Manchester, with the city third behind the London borough of Southwark and Nottingham within England and Wales. Figures for 2007 won't be announced until later this month, but in 2006 for every 1,000 women between 15-18, there were 67 conceptions.

In Russia, there are now moves to tackle a soaring birth rate among younger people. Kolchik says that she witnessed things on her trip to Manchester which would be both amusing and moving back home.

> She was stunned to interview a girl of 14 who has a one-year-old and is at the top of her class.

"I visited one place where teenage mums were playing a game with contraceptives. One of them was 17 and already had two children. It struck me that it was a little late to be talking about contraception," she says.

She was stunned to interview a girl of 14 at the Moat House school in Stockport who has a one-year-old and is at the top of her class.

"She's going to be a lawyer and the father of her child didn't even know that she had a baby," she adds.

A 21-year-old mum of three from Chorley won an award for being a mum of the year. "She had twins at 16. She had planned to have a baby at that age and said it was an overwhelming desire."

She interviewed people from what she describes as Manchester's "underclass" and met the mother of a two-year-old girl who had started going out with boys at the age of nine and had sex for the first time aged 12.

"We in Russia are used to the view of Britain as a post-Victorian society which is almost puritanical and yet kids get distributed condoms at school at the age of 11 and 12 and start having relationships that early. I felt there was a desire to become an adult as early as possible."

In Glossop she was told young people became intimate at an early age because there is nothing else to do.

"In Russia, if a young woman gets pregnant, a man has to marry her," says Kolchik. "But at the same time, it is very easy to get divorced in Russia and so many of those relationships do not last. Abortions are also very common in Russia. It is very easy to have a termination.

"We don't have the resources that are available for youngsters here. I was amazed by the council houses, halfway houses and nurseries.

"I think one can be a good parent at 17 and I admire those young women who want to keep their children. It is such a different experience to that in Russia. Modern women are wanting to have children much later in life. They have so much stress and they want to take control.

"They might take a positive from that. I think women can have it all."

Manchester Evening News
16 February 2009

* DNA tests later established the baby's father was a 15 year old boy, Tyler Barker

'It's not truancy, I'm on paternity leave'

The Daily Telegraph 14 February 2009

Tragic mum's dying wish

Miriam Stoppard

Dear Miriam,

I have two grandchildren aged nine and 13 and their mother is dying of cancer. It breaks my heart to know she won't be with us this time next year.

Her ex-husband never bothers with the kids. He flits in and out of their lives when he feels like it.

My daughter has begged me to raise her children rather than have them go to foster parents. I love them too much to see that happen but I'm frightened of the responsibility.

Already my grandson is acting up, saying I can't tell him what to do. I understand he's scared about losing his mum but it's brought home the impact of having two children living with us permanently.

My husband and I have only been married for two years, it's a second marriage for both of us. He's supportive but didn't sign up to become a step-parent and we won't be able to please ourselves as we have been doing.

There are so many emotional hurdles in front of me, I can't think straight. I don't want to let down my daughter. Can you help me?

Barbara

Dear Barbara,

Few of us plan on raising a second family, especially in such tragic circumstances. You just want to be a grandparent, not a parent. You want to spoil your grandchildren, not discipline them.

It's natural to feel stressed and overwhelmed and it's good you don't have rose-coloured glasses because you will experience ups and downs. Taking on the responsibility of raising your grandchildren will be hard work and a huge challenge but one which your daughter feels you can manage.

Your grandchildren will need your loving support more than ever as they wrestle with their loss and cope with feelings of confusion and vulnerability.

You probably haven't forgotten the basics of raising children but it would do no harm to enroll in parenting classes to update yourself on some helpful new techniques.

Always make taking care of yourself a priority. If you get sick or burned out, what will they do? Accept help from relatives and friends.

Create time to learn something new or join an exercise class. Exercise helps us let off steam, improves our mood and gives us more energy.

Even if support groups aren't normally your cup of tea, it's important to connect with other people who understand what you're experiencing.

Contact the Grandparents Association, 0845 4349 585, http://www.grandparents-association.org.uk, whose services include an advice and information line, welfare benefits advice, publications and support groups. The GrandparentsPlus Network brings together grandparents raising their grandchildren to give them a voice, to share experiences, to find solutions. To join, email info@grandparentsplus.org.uk with your name and address.

Daily Mirror 11 February 2009

'He blocked the door and pulled a knife'

As the Children's Secretary orders an inquiry into the death of Baby P, a social worker reveals the challenges of life on the front line

Sally-Anne Jones

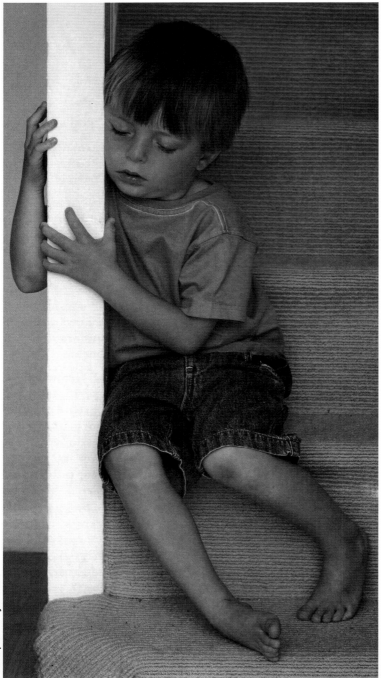

Photo posed by model

Over the past 20 years I've been chased with machetes, threatened with knives and had loads of doors slammed in my face. You don't know what's behind any door, but as soon as you walk into a home you make an assessment of what is going on.

The best tool for doing your job as a social worker is your instincts. Above all, you have to remember that you are there for the child. Most of the time abusers make damned sure they are not found out, so you have to keep an eye out for the little things. Some try to hide their guilt with aggression, others welcome you in for a cup of tea and present little Johnny covered in chocolate – and that's harder. The social worker will think it's good that he's eating and that his mother is allowing him to express himself, but it also covers up the bruises.

> **he admitted the abuse, saying: "Yeah, I hit the little poof," because the boy was close to his mother and wasn't "manly" enough.**

Some years ago, I was involved in a case where a young boy accused his father of hitting him with a metal pipe. He told the school, who reported it to the police and we were called in to see him. The dad opened the door to me. There were pills on the coffee table and a woman sitting subdued in the corner of the kitchen. I told him we had been referred by his son's school - and he admitted the abuse, saying: "Yeah, I hit the little poof, the bastard," because the boy was close to his mother and wasn't "manly" enough. He hadn't done the same to the other sons, he said, because they were more like him.

> **while I was sitting there, surrounded by pills that were clearly [illegal] drugs, he began showing me photographs of his daughter. "Beautiful, isn't she?" They were obviously pornographic**

While I was sitting there, surrounded by pills that were clearly [illegal] drugs, he began showing me photographs of his daughter. "Beautiful, isn't she?" They were obviously pornographic. She was just a little girl, dressed provocatively and sitting on the laps of his friends. I smiled, made appreciative comments and asked if his wife would like to join us. But he said: "No, she won't. She likes sitting in there." Then I gave my usual spiel about why I was there - and the next thing I knew, he had pushed the settee against the door and pulled a knife on me.

I leapt over the settee and legged it all the way to the office. I was pretty fit in those days. The police arrested the guy and found drugs and other knives in the flat. They kept the boy at school and the other children away from him.

> **they moved the mother to the other side of the borough, put her in a safe house and gave the children back to her. Their father was in custody – but the next day, the mother moved back to the old flat to be with him**

The council was able to work quickly then and they moved the mother to the other side of the borough, put her in a safe house and gave the children back to her. Their father was in custody - but the next day, the mother moved back to the old flat to be with him. That's the psychology of the abused. She was a victim, but she had been groomed. It's the Stockholm syndrome.

The older boy didn't want to go back, but the others did. Eventually all the children were removed from their parents because the dad was violent and the mum was unable or unwilling to protect them. So they had to be separated.

For an inner-city London social worker like me, that might be just one of up to 25 cases that you're dealing with. An office may be understaffed, but that won't stop the flow of child protection cases. In every case there is loads of paperwork.

After the referral and assessment, you have to investigate a case immediately to see if the child needs to be protected. You make your initial inquiries and if there is evidence that the child is at risk, or likely to be, you take appropriate action, perhaps removing the child to ensure his or her safety and welfare.

> **for an inner-city London social worker like me, that might be just one of up to 25 cases that you're dealing with**

The investigation is ongoing – which means joint work with the police, medicals to check, and getting in touch with health and education specialists – ahead of a case conference with everyone involved, including any "significant adults" such as childminders and members of the family. In the meantime you will have had numerous strategy meetings to plan the work and timescales, with all the relevant professionals. For example, who will do the interviews with the children and when will they be done?

Of course a register can't protect children, and it's the social worker's assessment and the network that protect the child. But it's a judgment call and sometimes the call is wrong.

Ultimately it boils down to the quality of staff, the management and the training of the social worker involved. That person will be getting s**t from their cases, but they may also be getting the same from their bosses.

If she is being bullied and pressurised at work, she won't be able to do her job. It's like a mother with too many jobs to do: something has to give.

The Times 13 November 2008

The lessons that need to be learnt from Baby P

This correspondent, who recently won an award for her campaign for greater openness in family courts, gives her reaction to the tragedy

Camilla Cavendish

It is important to remember that Baby P was not killed by social workers. He died at the hands of sadists of unimaginable depravity, who were skilled at deception. That is where the greatest fault lies, and there must be real questions about why they face only a maximum of 14 years in prison. Had they treated an adult that way, the verdict would surely have been murder and the sentence would surely have been higher.

Yet evil is abetted by incompetence and aided by secrecy. All three elements were present in this appalling case. There is no doubt that some of the most evil people are the most persuasive, and the most adept at hiding their sadism. Yet it is not easy to understand how so many different care workers and agencies could be involved with a child who was on the at-risk register for nine months, and fail to see what we, from the outside, feel that we would have spotted immediately.

Bureaucracy and lack of communication are often given as reasons for child protection failures. But the tragedy of Baby P is not explained by bureaucracy. There is clearly a problem with social workers being overburdened with form-filling and not having enough time to see families, or to think. But Baby P was visited 60 times by health and social work professionals. They were not failing to talk to each other, according to the Haringey safeguarding report. But they were repeatedly failing to touch or examine him.

When so many people are involved in case conferences... it can lead to bad decisions

To have failed to protect him in the face of so much evidence seems inexcusable. But there is an explanation - given by Beverley Hughes, the Children's Minister. She believes that social workers jumped to the conclusion early on that Baby P's mother was inadequate but not a physical abuser. They then stuck to that in spite of the staggering and mounting evidence to the contrary.

Her explanation strikes a chord with me, because I have seen that pattern over and over in child protection cases with which families have asked me to get involved. Social workers deal almost constantly in uncertainty and

ambiguity, with many families whose cast of characters and income is in constant flux and where children cannot be sure who will be in the house tomorrow. So it is particularly important for them to anchor themselves in a working hypothesis about what kind of risk might be posed to the child. But too often, that hypothesis becomes the official line without sufficient challenge. This is despite the changes brought in after the Laming review into Victoria Climbié*, which encouraged agencies to work more closely together. Or perhaps it is partly because of it. When so many people are involved in case conferences, groupthink can be very powerful. And it can lead to bad decisions.

No amount of child protection legislation can ever substitute for properly trained professionals knowing how to think straight amid chaos

Eileen Munro, reader in social policy at the London School of Economics and the respected author of the *Effective Child Protection* handbook, makes the point that it is human nature to form a view based on first impressions, and stick to it. She says that this "has a devastating impact in child protection work, in that professionals hold on to their beliefs about a family despite new evidence that challenges them. It can be equally harmful whether they are over or underestimating the degree of risk to the child". To counter this, she believes that social workers need to make their first impression explicit, and recognise that it will require a deliberate effort to think of evidence to the contrary.

This kind of psychological approach seems enormously powerful to me. Most people seem to focus on the legislation. But no amount of child protection legislation can ever substitute for properly trained professionals knowing how to think straight amid chaos, with strong leadership from their managers.

The Times 13 November 2008

* Victoria Climbié was killed by her guardians in 2000 aged 8. She had suffered years of abuse despite having had contact with social and medical services and the police.

Photo: ITV News

itv NEWS

Baby P: The Facts

Baby P born: 01/03/06 in his earliest months there was no documented evidence of abuse. Visits to the doctor were for routine matters such as weighing and nappy rash.

Aged 7 months: 13/10/06 taken to GP with bruises to head and chest said to be caused by a fall downstairs.

Aged 9 months: 11/12/06 taken to GP with bruising to his forehead, nose, sternum and right shoulder. Referred by GP to specialists at the Whittington Hospital, north London. **12/12/06** examined again and referred to a child abuse investigation team. **15/12/06** police investigation begins. **19/12/06** Mother arrested and released on bail. Baby P discharged from hospital into the care of a family friend.

Aged 10 months: January 07 Returned to hospital for nappy rash x-rays on his legs.

Aged 11 months: 22.02.07 First home visit by the social worker appointed to the family. 10 visits follow in six months, eight scheduled, two unannounced.

Aged 13 months: April 07 taken to North Middlesex Hospital's A&E unit with bruising to his face and swelling to his head. Notes say Baby P was unsteady on his feet and holding his head to one side. **10/04/07**, referred to a child development centre as 'he likes to bang his head against things'. **11/04/07** discharged from hospital and sent home.

Aged 14 months: mother is interviewed by police relating to her arrest on 19 December. Three days later police visit the family home and take photographs of the child and the furniture and seize one of Baby P's toys.

Aged 15 months: 12/06/07 - 26/06/07 Baby P is looked after by a childminder who claims she warned social services about the child's injuries.

Aged 16 months: July 2007 his mother takes him to the hospital twice to have him checked for an ear infection and an allergic reaction.

Aged 17 months: 01/08/07 a doctor examined Baby P at St Ann's Hospital in Tottenham but failed to notice broken ribs and a broken back. Notes say that he is "quite miserable" and crying and it was not possible to make a full examination. **03/08/07 11.36am** A 999 call was made. Four minutes later, the ambulance arrived. **30 minutes later** Baby P was declared dead at hospital and police were called. **1.45pm** mother arrested.

May 09: The sentences Peter's mother, her lodger Jason Owens and her boyfriend were all found guilty of causing or allowing a child's death. She must serve at least five years and Owens at least three years – but they could serve up to 14 years. The boyfriend was given 12 years for Peter's death and life for raping a two-year-old girl. He must serve a minimum of 10 years.

Sources: Various

Tiny turns in the right direction

His experiences mentoring a troubled, chaotic teenager often led Andrew Graham to wonder: 'Why am I doing this?' Here he explains why, years later, he's still there for him

It's not a question you get asked every day: "How would you have felt if I'd died?" Especially not in the middle of a meat-feast pizza. But it was put to me one Thursday night not long ago as I sat and ate with a 17-year-old boy – let's call him "Luke" – while he was reflecting on events some eight months earlier, when injuries he received in a car accident had left him on a life support machine.

I had just started a new teaching job, and arrived at the intensive care unit exhausted after my first week of work. I found Luke on a respirator, with a less than 50-50 chance of survival. After all we've been through, I thought, as I sat in silent vigil with a nurse in the intensive care unit. The boy I've been meeting every week for the last three years ends up brain-damaged, crippled, or worse. Fine mentor I turned out to be.

Mentor. The word conjures up images of Alec Guinness in his brown robe, instructing young Skywalker in the ways of "The Force". But the reality is more prosaic. Put simply, it's someone who offers to meet a troubled young person and to build a consistent and reliable relationship with them. Basic stuff perhaps, but, sadly, it's something a significant number of teenagers have never had. And it's the reliability a mentor displays that often has the most effect. Exhausted by a week of teaching practice, I would curse Luke's name as I waited in vain at the bus stop where he frequently failed to appear. But the point was I was there, even if he wasn't.

I first met him in the summer of 2003, during an activity day in the countryside. From the start of the trip, he was bullied by each of the other potential mentees in turn. Someone punched him as he got off the minibus. Then his baseball cap was grabbed and chucked in a cowpat. Bullying can often look like a cruel version of pass the parcel, in which physical or verbal abuse is tossed from person to person. Those who can't return the package keep getting thrown it. And without the quick wit or physical dexterity of the other potential mentees, Luke was receiving parcels morning, noon and night. Perhaps it was empathy from my own torments at school, but I really felt for Luke.

Our first meeting was a game of golf, played against the setting sun of an early September evening. Dragging his coat and rucksack behind him like prison irons, he explained how he'd ended up in the back of a stolen car – the reason for his referral from his secondary school (referrals can range from the police to a relative) – and how, once he'd learned to drive, the possession of a Mitsubishi or Toyota would soon be within his grasp. "I really like cars," he noted mildly, an observation that, it transpired, was the understatement of the century.

Like any relationship, there tend to be "good" dates and "bad" dates. Cinema, pizza restaurant, a game of pool... whatever the activity, few of our meetings would go by without him showing me the latest clutch of hastily-snapped car pictures on his mobile. I became a scratch expert on mag

> **Mentoring is not about radical change. It's about nudging someone a few degrees in a different direction. But these degrees can mean the difference between prison and a job, and that really matters.**

> *It's worth asking at this point, as many people did, how he managed to slip through the child protection net. At meetings of teachers, school nurses and social workers I attended, we scratched our collective heads.*

wheel hubs, metallic paint jobs, fuel injection and aerofoils. I could just about tell apart an Impreza from an Isuzu. And I discovered the meaning of NOS – nitrous oxide systems, for the uninitiated. Basically, it makes cars go faster. A lot faster.

But this often fantasy world of flip-top phones and flash motors was in stark contrast to the grim reality of Luke's daily life. At the end of an otherwise picturesque country lane, he lived in almost Dickensian squalor with his vague and disorientated mother. The walls were wet with damp, the cooker baked with an impressionist crusting of filth. I often found him curled up on a hard stone floor in an unwashed sleeping bag.

Lack of boundaries

On top of the dire circumstances of his home, the family was also the subject of regular attack. It's not uncommon for communities to bully a family the way a group attacks an individual, and Luke's house was often stoned or "egged".

Rarely did a week go by during this period when I did not return home to find an answerphone message from the school. He had been in a fight, his phone had been stolen, he was suffering from headaches, possibly hunger-induced. Indeed, school was often the only place where Luke received any sort of nurture.

But, in truth, they were fighting a losing battle against the teenage consequences of appalling childhood neglect. I was never to possess the full picture, but the snapshots were enough. A toddler, witnessed by neighbours, being subjected to half-an-hour of obscene verbal abuse in the garden, for example.

It's worth asking at this point, as many people did, how he managed to slip through the child protection net. At meetings of teachers, school nurses and social workers I attended, we scratched our collective heads. My own private, and largely unprovable conclusion, was that emotional or physical neglect often came lower in the priority points system than active abuse.

Perhaps not surprisingly, given his background, the development of his social skills was a lengthy affair. One Friday evening when we approached the bar of our regular haunt, I asked him what he'd like to drink – non-alcoholic, of course – and he promptly pulled out a half-drunk bottle of cola. "Already got one," he grinned, offering me a swig. Glancing wearily at the landlady, I suggested that she might rather like to sell him a drink of her own.

But mentoring's like that. Always two steps forward, one step back. The mumbled sound of him saying "excuse me" to someone he wanted to step round was a major triumph for

> **But, in truth, as we trudged round town in the rain when Pizza Hut was full, and when he uttered barely a word during two hours of pool, apart from his constant request for more salt & vinegar crisps, I sometimes found it irksome. And during those moments, the question uppermost in my mind was: "Why am I doing this?"**

me. Equally gratifying was his admonishment of me for not taking the empty glasses back to the bar. It showed some sort of milestone had been reached. Mentoring is not about radical change. It's about nudging someone a few degrees in a different direction. But these degrees can mean the difference between prison and a job, and that really matters.

Those incremental gains and setbacks were how our relationship developed over the years to come. Much of it mimicked the uneasy relationship between parent and teenager. There was the teasing that often had a serious intent. "Mind your trainers," I'd say, as he unleashed yet another gobbet of sputum on to the pavement. My refusal to buy him cigarettes, though, when he was, and clearly looked, underage, was a line in the sand. Perhaps inevitably, he managed to get them from somewhere.

More serious were the mini debates we used to have when he had been temporarily excluded from school. My tactic was to gently point out the disparity between his long-term aims – getting a job and, more importantly, a driving licence and car – and the futility of his short-term actions. I also tried to paint a picture outside the consequence-free world in which teenagers are often unwittingly placed. "A fight in a pub is very different to a fight in a classroom," I told him once. Sadly, the incredulous look in his eyes suggested he didn't really believe me.

On such occasions, a question nagged at me that I found difficult to answer: "Why am I doing this?" Certainly, there were enough pats on the back from school and social work representatives to reassure me that I was doing "the right thing". But surely there was more to it than that.

Yes, there was the quiet satisfaction of building a productive relationship with someone so frequently written off. The

moments of humour, the jokes only we could share. His glee as I submitted myself to the electrocution machine on the pier. The look of terrified exhaustion on his face as he got off the back of my motorbike for the first time. I still have on my mantelpiece the model Honda he presented to me shortly after we started meeting.

But, in truth, as we trudged round town in the rain when Pizza Hut was full, and when he uttered barely a word during two hours of pool, apart from his constant request for more salt & vinegar crisps, I sometimes found it irksome. And during those moments, the question uppermost in my mind was: "Why am I doing this?"

Social conscience

My answer was not that I'm possessed of some great social conscience. I'm not. Nor that "if I don't do it, nobody else will". There are plenty of good people around to help him out. The honest and rather uninspiring answer is "because I said I would". I made a commitment to this shambling, often inarticulate youth, with his wisps of brown beard and his fag-burned baseball cap, and I intend to see it through.

It is not that his life now is so much better for me having been his mentor. It is merely that perhaps it might have been that bit worse if I hadn't been around.

As we leave the Italian and slope back to the carers with whom he was placed when he was on the road to recovery from the car accident, Luke says: "You're a bit like a dad, really." I stop for a moment. Pondering my own middle-aged fecklessness, I think of the back-breaking work done by my friends who are real fathers. I feel rather callow. But then, as I remember that he has only spoken to his own father once, and never met him, I think: "Maybe he's right." At which point, he summons up a large gobbet of phlegm, and my heart sinks as I wait for the inevitable expulsion.

The Guardian 6 August 2008
© Guardian News and Media Limited 2008

Financial issues

Issues to think about and discuss

A poor start – What chance does a child have in a place where there is 45% unemployment and where 81% of families are affected by poverty?

In hard times, need is good – Have we been greedy and wasteful? Is a bit of financial hardship a good thing?

Why spending money is like a drug – Have you ever felt a buzz from earning or spending money? Can earning money really become an addiction?

A hold-up at the bank – Are attitudes to money in Egypt very different from those in the UK?

It's time to put a stop to shopping guilt trips – "Can you help a starving child?" – are charities too aggressive in their approach? Should they just let us get on with our shopping?

Financial issues

Shopping trips

Credit crunch

Opportunities

Poverty

Financial issues

Charity

Unemployment

A poor start

The epicentre of UK child poverty is in Birmingham, where children in 81% of families are affected, says a disturbing new report

Chris Arnot

Jim Thompson has just been told that there's no chance of an increase on his £90 loan from the Social Fund. "There's 35 quid left to last us another seven days," he says. By "us" he means himself, his pregnant, unemployed girlfriend Jan Mason, 27, and their 12-month-old baby, Michelle. Thompson slumps wearily over the railings at the side of Ladywood community centre in inner-city Birmingham. Then he straightens up and, for a moment, he looks the part of a 25-year-old former soldier who has served in Northern Ireland, Kosovo and Bosnia.

"I'd rather starve than let them go hungry," he adds with a defiant gesture at his family. "We might be short of money, but we're not short of love." Certainly, Michelle doesn't look short of care and attention. But she will grow up in the constituency pinpointed last week as having a higher proportion of its children living in poverty than any in the UK; 81% of families in the area are struggling, which directly affects some 28,420 of its children, according to figures from the Campaign to End Child Poverty.

Thompson was doing comparatively well until three weeks ago, when he lost his job laying carpets for a hotel chain. "They're not fitting out any more hotels until the economy picks up," he says. Next week, he might - just might - get the redundancy money he has been promised. Meanwhile, the rent is due on the family's two-bedroom flat in a nearby tower block. "Then all I've got to find is the money for food, electricity,

milk and nappies," he adds bitterly. "I've been to umpteen building sites trying to get labouring work, but the construction firms are cutting back as well."

So Thompson and his family become another statistic. The constituency's unwelcome reputation is based on a 45% jobless level, combined with another 36% receiving working tax credit to bolster meagre incomes. This part of Birmingham is no longer packed with factories offering comparatively well-paid work. The local government ward of Ladywood, a largely 1960s-built estate, butts right up against the canal-side apartments and restaurants of the city centre. Not far, indeed, from the International Convention Centre where the Conservative party conference gathered last week. Yet the government that Tory leader David Cameron blames for what he calls "our broken society" has invested hundreds of millions in a parliamentary constituency that includes not only the ward and the city centre itself but also inner-city Aston, Nechells and parts of Handsworth.

However, its neighbourhoods have turned into what Jenny Phillimore, from the Centre for Urban and Regional Studies at Birmingham University, calls "microcosms of super-diversity", with constantly changing populations. "Yes, the government had put a lot of money into regeneration, but, at the same time, Ladywood has become a reception area for immigration," she says. "The poorest people come here because there's a lot of cheap, rented social housing.

> Then all I've got to find is the money for food, electricity, milk and nappies," he adds bitterly. "I've been to umpteen building sites trying to get labouring work, but the construction firms are cutting back as well."

"We've found Kurdish and African families with nine and sometimes 11 people living in two-bedroom flats. Those who are here legally are starting to bring their families in, but they're not entitled to any public funds. Without money for uniforms or bus fares, they're not sending their children to school."

Meanwhile, among the settled population, there's a high level of dropping out from an education system on which children depend for qualifications for any but the most menial jobs.

Kenneth Jeffers, 55, a former education minister in Montserrat, came to Ladywood soon after a volcanic eruption on the Caribbean island in the 1990s. He spends much of his time at the Sky Rainbow Foundation, which tries to raise the horizons of black youths. "In the Caribbean, our children's learning curve starts to improve after the age of 11," he says. "Here, it seems to peak at 11 and then start to decline." Jeffers wants to set up exchange deals between schools in Birmingham and the West Indies.

As it is, plenty of children are too frightened to leave their corner of Ladywood. The gun violence plaguing the area is largely based on postcode territorialism. Former social worker Udel James, 50, holds a photograph of her nephew. A fresh-faced black boy, he was shot dead for being in the wrong place at the wrong time.

James's response is to set up One B Outreach, running a minibus to occasional residential weekends in Bromsgrove, Worcestershire. To these youngsters - white and Asian, as well as black - it's as remote and exotic as the Caribbean. "There's a lot of tension at first," James concedes. "But, by the end of the weekend, they're all asking: 'Why do we have to go home, miss?'" It's an understandable question in the circumstances.

The names of Jim Thompson and his family have been changed at his request

The Guardian 8 October 2008
© Guardian News and Media Ltd 2008

In hard times, need is good
Joanna Blythman

Redundancies, repossessions, retail meltdown... 2009 looks like being a supremely difficult year. Yet there's a bright side to all the gloom of a global recession. Perversely, some things could actually get better.

For starters, all those aspirational property developments of ludicrously expensive yuppie condominiums could run out of buyers, putting an end to the hell-for-leather land grab of recent years that has seen councils permitting prime public waterside and greenfield sites to be sold off to the private sector. Not great for the building trade, but then in our new make-do-and-mend culture, skilled tradesmen will be in more demand than ever. Instead of tearing out original wooden sash windows to replace them with expensive and ugly new ones, we might be more inclined to call in the painter to sand them down and give them a lick of paint.

In our new make-do-and-mend culture, skilled tradesmen will be in more demand than ever.

Cartoon by Robert Thompson. http://www.robertthompsoncartoons.com/

When our fridge breaks down after only two or three years use, rather than buying a new one, that almost forgotten word "repair" might drop into our heads.

Municipal vanity projects, like Edinburgh's 17-storey Haymarket tower, with its last-century emphasis on swanky hotels and office suites for financial whiz kids, already look redundant. Who will afford to stay in pricey hotels apart from debt collectors? What financial institution will be looking to relocate its slimmed-down workforce in brashly prosperous premises when the shareholders are baying for the blood of the CEO? It's only January, but already national vanity projects, like the proposed third Forth Bridge, which spit in the eye of the looming environmental crisis, look like crass misconceptions on a massive scale.

Shopping malls are already reporting a severe downturn in business, so the seemingly endless proliferation of initially glitzy malls that purport to be regenerating the local area but which in reality suck all retail life out of high streets and traditional centres, will look like grotesque white elephants left over from another age.

New supermarkets, which have spread like head lice through a nursery in the last decade, now find that their cherished, high spending "time-poor/cash-rich" customers have overnight metamorphosed into "cash-poor therefore time-richer" bargain hunters.

So the one-stop supermarket and car-based shopping trip that involved a large, once-a-week outlay for food for larders handsomely provisioned in anticipation of a forthcoming

apocalypse might give way to a more traditional "buy what you need just for the next few days" shopping pattern with more emphasis on walking or cycling to shops, and buying less food at a time. Good news for local, independent shops and markets. We'll eat better too. Asda reports that sales of ready meals are down by 40% and predicts that Britain will be cooking more from scratch. The £3 Starbucks coffee and the £4 M&S sandwich can expect to be bumped for last night's leftovers in a packed lunch box.

All that Thatcherite survival of the fittest individualism that deemed anything public as second class looks ripe for junking. Demand for private schools is already down and fewer people are going to be able, however willing, to stump up for the notional privileges of an exclusive education. Private schooling in Scotland has only ever appealed to a tiny minority of families anyway. Expect an exodus of affluent kids from our relatively small number of private schools, a move that will inject more confidence into state schools and produce a genuinely more democratic social mix in them.

In the grips of a recession, unbridled demonstrations of conspicuous "see me, I'm rich" consumption, elitism and wealth will be deemed about as tasteless as a drunken stand-up comic at a funeral.

So, respite at last from all those celebs and magazine columnists who tell women that their ultimate goal in life is to own a £1,500 Chanel handbag. Back to the days when a handbag was there to do a job and £150 was expensive. We still have a battle on our hands to encourage our in-denial PM not to bail out Jaguar Land Rover, but surely the days of all those menacing, super-sized 4x4s with tinted windows bearing down on you at enormous speed are numbered?

As the thrifty middle classes scrutinise their bank statements, items like membership of supposedly-luxurious private health clubs will look increasingly unjustifiable. More people will re-acquaint themselves with the council swimming pool or gym and find that facilities are at least as good, and often better, than their clubby private equivalent. As bookshops lose out to the discounting of supermarkets and online sales, public libraries lending books could undergo a renaissance - and not just as warm places to sit when you can't afford to switch on the heating either. As long as we read books, do we really need to own them? Where do you keep them anyway? Is a broadband connection to a home computer or a mobile phone contract strictly necessary? Couldn't many of us just use the computer in the library or internet café or change to a pay-as-you-go phone? These are questions that we will find ourselves considering.

2009? Scary in prospect, but exciting too.

The Sunday Herald 22 January 2009

WHY $P€NDING MON£Y I$ LIK€ A DRUG

Steve Connor – Science editor

Parts of the brain are stimulated by higher salaries, even when prices rise and purchasing power drops

Money works like a drug on the human brain – and even just the thought of earning a higher salary gives us a physical buzz, a study has found.

Scientists have discovered that thinking about cash stimulates the reward centres involved in pleasure and the higher the salary – even if it is just imagined – the greater the pleasure generated in the brain.

This may be no great surprise, but the most intriguing aspect of the research is that the findings hold true even if what we want to buy costs more, for example in times of high inflation, and our actual spending power drops.

The results of the study suggest that the human brain is innately susceptible to the illusion of wealth that money can bring. This is known

brain that are also involved in irrational or addictive behaviour, even if the purchasing power of higher salaries is reduced by high inflation.

A study by Professor Armin Falk, of the University of Bonn, has found scientific support for the theory of money illusion being embedded in the human mind by examining the brain activity of 18 volunteers who took part in a series of tests involving different salary payments and prices.

The volunteers were asked to earn their "salaries" by performing a series of mental tasks on a computer. The salary rates were at two levels, with the higher level being 50% greater than the lower level.

They could then spend this money on a selection of

"Intuitively, money illusion implies that an increase in income is valued positively, even when prices go up by the same amount"

in economics as "money illusion" – when people get fixated on the nominal value of money, rather than on its actual purchasing power. Some economists have proposed that people behave irrationally when it comes to wages by being happier with higher salary increases in times of high inflation than they are with lower salary rises in times of low inflation.

It has now emerged that more money really does seem to generate the feelings of reward in the

goods listed in two types of catalogue. Each catalogue was identical except that one was 50% cheaper than the other.

In practice, the volunteers had the same purchasing power, irrespective of which salary they earned. But the brain scans show that the reward centres in their brains were far more active when stimulated by the idea of the higher salary.

"Intuitively, money illusion implies that an increase in income is valued positively, even when prices go up by the same amount, leaving

real purchasing power unchanged," Professor Falk said.

"Economists have traditionally been sceptical about the notion of money illusion, but recent behavioural evidence has challenged this view," added Professor Falk, whose study is published in the journal Proceedings of the National Academy of Sciences.

For instance, studies have shown that people report being happier when they receive a 5% increase in their salaries at a time of 4% inflation, compared to a 2% increase in salary at a time of low inflation.

But a limitation on these previous studies is that they rely on questionnaires rather than brain scans, which has led other economists to suggest alternative, more rational explanations. The present study sidesteps this potential flaw in the research

by looking directly at the reward centres of the brain that are directly involved in making decisions, Professor Falk explained.

The scientists measured higher blood flows in regions of the brain known to be involved in the experiencing of rewards, such as the ventromedial prefrontal cortex, which lies directly behind the eyes in the front part of the brain.

"This result means that reward activation generally increases with income, but was significantly higher in situations where nominal incomes and prices were both 50% higher, which supports the hypothesis that activity in the ventromedial prefrontal cortex is subject to money illusion," Professor Falk said.

*The Independent
24 March 2009
© 2009 Independent News
& Media Limited*

A HOLD-UP AT THE BANK

MARIA GOLIA OBSERVES HOW MONEY IS ON EVERYONE'S LIPS, ESPECIALLY WHEN IT COMES BY THE SUITCASE-LOAD.

Until recently, there were two things you never talked about in Egypt: time and money. While it was permissible to discuss things like eternity, you wouldn't dream of announcing the hour you had to wake up or the appointment you had in the afternoon. If people wore wristwatches, they were ornamental. As for money, just as the aristocratically rich find it a vulgar topic of conversation, amongst Egypt's princely poor it was likewise infra dig.

Time isn't as elastic as it once was in Cairo, where the days pass in a Sisyphean loop focused on survival; and money is now so tight it's the very talk of the town. Walking through the city, the snatches of conversation that reach one's ears are no longer phrases or gasps of laughter, but numbers, amounts in Egyptian pounds. People aren't discussing foreign exchange rates or the stock market, but the price of everything they need and can't afford.

Only in the bank is there silence, I noticed this morning, the row of chairs provided for clients occupied by grave-looking men sitting quietly, as if at a funeral. I took a number and joined them. Only two tellers were working, and one of them was busy tallying receipts. To my right, a bearded man with a festering callous on his forehead (caused by fervent friction with the prayer mat) held a mobile phone that rang with the voice of a famous sheikh reciting suras of the Qur'an. To my left, surrounded by several large, bulging suitcases, sat two down-at-heel factotums, come to deposit some bigshot's haul. They were in their thirties, their baggy trousers and shirts so frequently and assiduously ironed that the threadbare creases held together solely by force of habit. The teller called their number and they started transferring their parcels to the window, while everyone in the bank looked on.

Once they'd dragged the cash-stuffed suitcases into position, they opened one, packed solid with neat stacks of various denominations, and began piling them on the counter. As they did so, one could not help observing their faint swagger. It wasn't their money, of this everyone was certain, yet they handled it with pride, as if this transient intimacy conferred a special grace, setting them apart from the men who sat watching, clutching salary cheques of no importance, wondering how they'd make ends meet.

Aware that all eyes were upon them, the trusty factotums slouched casually, one of them leaned his elbows on the counter, and the other probed his ear with a pencil. Both sighed with saintly patience at the task the teller had begun, of running this great hoard, stack by stack, through the automatic money counter. The sound of it, a thrumming flutter followed by a decisive click, created a discomfiting rhythm. The bank customers could see they'd be waiting for quite a while. Some amused themselves counting the number of piles that went through the counter. Others shared pages of someone's newspaper. The man on my right alternately prayed and dozed.

I was probably the only one thinking how easy it would have been to have robbed these gentlemen on the way to the bank, or even now. So far as I could tell, no-one seemed particularly disturbed or bitter at the sight of this mountain of cash, so close yet so far away. Money, for many Egyptians, like time, remains a relative concept; some people have more than others, that is all. People are accustomed to the abyss separating the rich from the poor; it has always been this way and probably always will. But this philosophy is more easily maintained on a full stomach than an empty one, a fact of which Egypt's fat cats are increasingly aware.

Egyptians have never been shorter of cash and options than they are today, largely because there have never been so many of them competing for the same meagre resources. The strain is beginning to show: crime is on the rise, as is drug addiction, those hallmarks of modernity that Cairo had so graciously escaped for so long. The city's clamour seems amplified by the concerns everyone shares regarding their ability to feed themselves and families. It's as if you could hear them all worrying aloud.

By the time my number was called, the factotums had nearly finished their deposit, and we ended up leaving at the same time.

'Let's have breakfast,' one said, trotting down the stairs.

'I don't want beans, let's get macaroni,' said the other.

'Have we got enough?' his friend wondered.

I left them on the street, counting the change they had between them, the empty suitcases lying limply at their feet.

New Internationalist July 2008
© New Internationalist 2008

It's time to put a stop to shopping guilt trips Angela Epstein

The other week, I sat outside a coffee shop in St Ann's Square, Manchester, enjoying a welcome blush of afternoon sunshine. Surrounded by some lovely buildings, including the neo-classical pink sandstone beauty of St Ann's Church, I sipped my skinny latte like a contented tourist on a getaway city break.

Unfortunately as I got up to leave this lunch-time idyll, I had to negotiate one of the less likeable aspects of this pretty place. For crossing St Ann's Square also meant navigating my way past an army of clipboard-wielding stalkers, ready to ambush hapless passers-by.

It didn't get any better on Market Street. This central shopping artery has achieved notoriety by having just been crowned one of the top three obstacle injury hotspots in the country, thanks to the likelihood of pedestrians bashing into numerous bins, lampposts, benches, advertising boards and unseeing mobile phone users.

But even if you survive such perilous obstructions you're likely to get waylaid by what are now being termed charity muggers or 'chuggers' for short: namely fundraising collectors who block the pavement and play on guilt to get shoppers to give to their chosen cause.

Many of these causes are extremely important and provide much-needed aid for the needy at home and abroad. But is this really the best way to get people to donate, or does the brutal hard sell supplant benevolence with resentment?

Some may think even broaching this subject is in itself uncharitable. After all, chuggers are very successful and last year alone, 210,000 people were persuaded to sign up in the street to support charities, according to the Public Fundraising Regulatory Association.

> **Charity muggers or 'chuggers' for short: namely fundraising collectors who block the pavement and play on guilt to get shoppers to give to their chosen cause**

But there has to be a better way to tap into the pockets of Manchester shoppers without literally trapping us as we walk down the street. As well as blocking our pavements, I resent the confrontational and habitually inflammatory approach ('can you help a starving child?') which turns a shopping trip into a guilt-trip.

My humanitarian response is yes, of course. But what I don't want to do is sign up for a direct debit and relay personal details in the middle of Market Street. How does an office worker, caught on the hop after a quick lunch hour dash round the shops, or a weary woman, laden with cheap Primark goodies for her family, be sure she is giving out her bank details to somebody bona fide?

In this age of text messaging, email and even cold calling, there are more appropriate ways to make an approach.

Part of the problem is that we don't know who we are dealing with. New legislation next year will force street fundraisers to apply for a special charity commission permit. But it is also the sheer number of approaches which can hinder the good work of those who are entirely genuine, which is why the new law is to be applauded since it will also give councils the power to reduce the number of fundraisers on the streets.

By adopting less aggressive tactics charities can still rattle their tins and shake our conscience. Outside my local Tesco, for example, there is often a charity desk, where volunteers sit with leaflets and collection tins. There is no pester power, just a polite request to give. It's also a great way to instruct our children in being charitable as they can drop the coins into the box.

There's enough aggression on our streets and as a society we desperately need to become more giving and caring. But making a donation is something the disadvantaged need us to fight for, not to fight about.

Manchester Evening News 6 March 2008

Food & drink

Issues to think about and discuss

Calories and class – Does your social class really determine what you eat – and therefore how fat and how healthy you are? Is the food mentioned in the article really so bad for you? The arguments here and in the next article suggest that it is.

Top stores call them budget food lines. I say they are a disgrace – Sales of supermarket 'value' ranges are soaring, but if a beef pie includes as little as 18% beef can supermarkets really justify their profits? Jay Rayner argues that they are "forcing the very poorest to eat dross". In the next article the Chief Executive of Asda disagrees.

Celebrity chefs risk losing touch – Is it the supermarkets or the customers who are leading the trend towards cheaper food? Are top chefs just being patronising when they tell us to pay more and eat better? If the average family is £4 a week worse off, how should they economise?

All three articles together give an analysis of the issues of food, money and social class.

Kicking the booze and fags was a piece of cake compared to coming off cheese – A lighthearted look at a food 'addiction'. But are there foods that you can become addicted to? What lies behind our food choices?

Let's junk the junk food and save our kids from a frightening future – where burger is king! & **Daddy Cool** – Are parents to blame for relying on takeaways and feeding their children rubbish, as the first writer argues? Or is it better to give in to fussy eaters and avoid a battle? Should children eat what they want, or should they be forced to eat healthily?

Which fast food meals are the healthiest? Anyone's guess! – Before reading this article, which fast food would you have chosen as the healthiest? Should calories be displayed on takeaway foods? When we order our pizza or burger are we even thinking about healthy eating?

Food & drink

Budget food

Addiction

Class

Supermarkets

Fast food

Junk food

Calories and class
Our diet today is as much about class as it always has been.

"The nature of our diets has been entirely shaped by the class system of the 19th century," says Tim Lang, professor of food policy at City University in London. So does this mean that those with less money, have less to eat and so in effect weigh less? You only have to look around to see this isn't the case. As Lang has explained, the class you are from, how much you have to spend, together with what you aspire to eat makes a dramatic difference to your health.

For example, once only the rich could afford white bread rather than the less refined brown or wholemeal. When a cheap version was introduced for the poor – this was seen as progress. In fact the quality was very low. Similarly, in today's diet, exotic foods, once the luxury purchases of the richer and more travelled classes, are packaged in frozen versions, often in two-for-one offers in all the supermarkets. Since it is not possible to produce luxury foods at such low

prices, something has to give – and invariably it is the nutritional value.

Most people try to buy as good food as possible for as little cost as they can. But how does this affect our health? A child born in one deprived Glasgow suburb can expect a life 28 years shorter than another living only 13km away in a more affluent area. According to a three-year investigation for the World Health Organisation one factor in this is obesity, resulting from a poor diet: "Obesity is caused by the excess availability of high-fat, high-sugar foods", the type of foods that appear to give you more for less. In Rotherham, where areas around the town centre have deprivation levels that put them in the worst 6% of the country, one in 10 reception-age schoolchildren is obese. By year 6, 18% of them are obese, while 60% of adults are either overweight or obese.

Which socio-economic class you are born into is still one of the most significant determinants of how healthy you will be. Elizabeth Dowler, Professor of Food and Social Policy at Warwick University,

When you are on a low income you buy the kind of food that will fill you most cheaply

who was recently involved in the government's Low Income Diet and Nutrition survey, says the class differences are stark but complicated. "If you live for more than six months on the minimum wage or on benefits there is growing evidence you cannot afford to buy the food you need for health. It is still to do with class but it's complex to unpick. Food is the flexible area that you cut back on when you are on a low income. Unlike council tax or utility bills, no one fines you if you don't spend on food and no one takes your children away, so that's what you cut, and you have a fag because that takes the hunger away."

When you are on a low income you buy both the kind of food that will fill you most cheaply, but also the kind of food that is most appealing

– the cheapest, most flavoursome foods. Luckily (or not) supermarkets provide high calorie, cheap foods to satisfy this need.

According to Dr Tim Lobstein, Director of the Childhood Research Programme at the International Association for the Study of Obesity, what may seem ignorant choices to others are in fact quite rational. Lobstein has calculated the cost of 100 calories of food energy from different types of food. The cheapest way to get your 100 calories is to buy fats, processed starches and sugars. A hundred calories of broccoli costs 51p, but 100 calories of frozen chips only cost 2p. Good quality sausages that are high in meat but low in fat cost 22p per 100 calories, but "value" fatty ones are only 4p per 100 calories. Poor quality fish fingers are 12p per 100 calories compared with 29p for ones made with fish fillets that are higher in nutrients. Fresh orange juice costs 38p per 100 calories, while the same dose of energy from sugary orange squash costs 5p.

Poor people do not choose to be unhealthy, the way we live, shop and eat all reflect our economic and class system – and those with less are being forced into an unhealthy life in just the same way as their Victorian ancestors.

Sources: IASO 2009 & Various

Top stores call them budget food lines.

I say they are a disgrace

Sales of supermarkets' 'value' products have soared in the recession. But, as **Jay Rayner** has discovered, the quality is dire. Here he asks why highly profitable supermarkets force the poor to buy and eat such low-grade food

Not long ago I sat down with the multi-Michelin-starred chef Heston Blumenthal to taste-test products from the supermarkets' value ranges, the very cheapest of the cheap, the lowest of the low. It was a truly humbling experience. As we studied the prices, all of them measured in pence rather than pounds, we swiftly concluded that whatever aesthetic considerations we might want to bring to bear - did this stuff taste nice? Was it well made? - were irrelevant. Nobody bought these products because they liked them; they bought them because economic circumstance forced them to do so.

Beef & onion pie - 7% beef

Never was that more true than now. Anyone looking for a marker of recession could do worse than go loiter in the value-range aisles of their local supermarket. Hell, you might even be shopping there - and you won't be alone, because supermarket shopping habits are changing. In the past year sales of own-label premium ranges have dropped by more than 6%. Sales of organic products have dropped nearly 15%. Value-range sales, on the other hand, have leapt by 46%.

So what exactly is it they are buying? I happen to know. For the past few months I have been investigating the realities of cheap supermarket food for an edition of Dispatches, to be screened on Channel 4 this week - and it really ain't pretty. What would you say to a beef pie that was only 18% beef, and a few more percentage points "beef connective tissue" - or gristle, collagen and fat, as it's more commonly known? How about a pork sausage that's just 40% pork, with a slab of pig skin chucked in for bulk? Or an apple pie with so little apple - a mere 14% - that you can't help but wonder whether it really deserves the name? I suspect, like me, you would say, "No thanks."

Then again, I have a choice. I don't have to buy cheese slices with half the levels of calcium of the more expensive variety or chicken breasts that have been bulked up with 40% water to give you the impression you are getting more for less. The people who are buying these products generally don't have that choice. They have to take what the supermarkets deign to give them. Which raises the question: is what the supermarkets give them good enough?

Only the most callous could argue that it is. This is not born of some conviction that all supermarkets are Evil as the foodie Taliban like to claim. Sure, they aren't perfect. The economies of scale that help them

to keep prices low mean they can sometimes exert undue pressure on producers. Their impact on small local shops can be devastating. But they provide a level of convenience that serves hard-pressed families - in which time is short because

Apple pie - 14% apple

both parents have to work to make ends meet - very well. They have opened up the range of ingredients available to us and helped to foster a debate on where our food comes from.

In return we have rewarded them with an exceptionally light regulatory regime that has enabled the likes of Tesco, Sainsbury's, Asda and Morrisons and the new breed of discounters - Aldi, Lidl and Netto - to be amazingly successful. Their share of this country's £120bn retail food market has risen from less than 20% in the 1980s to more than 70% now. But with that unfettered access to the market must come responsibilities - and surely that should include improving the quality of the food sold to the very poorest in society.

We can fight long and hard about what the word "quality" means. The supermarkets argue that their value ranges aren't in any way harmful and point out - rightly - that in recent years great efforts have been made to reduce the levels of things such as salt and sugar in very cheap bread. The age of rickets is over. But that still leaves them selling products that contain animal products the vast majority of us would actually throw away rather than cook with. Pig skin is apparently quite high in protein, but would you really choose to have it minced up and put in your sausages simply because it's cheap?

Furthermore, is it outrageous to suggest that the supermarkets should absorb the costs of making these improvements? They make huge profits. Morrisons, for example, made £583m this year. Sainsbury's is behind but has a still sizable £239m. And Tesco, the market leader, has just posted more than £1.8bn worth, despite the tough economic climate. Indeed, their ability to make money has proved remarkably consistent. New research commissioned by Dispatches and carried out by John Thanassoulis, lecturer in economics at Oxford University, has found that the profit margins of the big supermarkets have remained surprisingly steady for decades at around 5%, not just in the good times but during recessions of the sort we're experiencing now as well. Thanassoulis even found evidence that margins actually go up during economic downturns.

Value range sales - up 25%

In short, they can afford to take the hit - because it really wouldn't cost much at all. I asked a food technologist, David Harrison, who has huge experience of the mass-market food business, to re-engineer some standard value-range products. I didn't want him to make a gourmet beef pie. That would be easy. Just throw money and some quality sirloin at the problem. I wanted to make a better pie, keeping within reasonable financial parameters. He started by analysing all the cheapest pies on the market and found that, on average, they had just 18% beef plus a few more percentage points of that connective tissue. (It can go much lower. I came across a minced beef and onion pie that declared a beef content on the label of just 7%.)

Harrison upgraded our generic recipe to produce one that had no connective tissue and 25% beef. The extra cost, to increase the meat content by 38%? A penny a pie. To remove the pig skin from a budget pork sausage and lift the meat content from 40% to 54% cost 0.7p per sausage. To increase the amount of apple in an apple pie by more than 40% cost 0.8p. As the cost of raw ingredients is only a quarter of the finished product's retail price, these really are tiny amounts. All of these improvements, even represented as double-digit percentages, may look marginal but the differences in the finished product are discernible. In a series of blind taste tests that I conducted, the overwhelming majority of people identified our new improved products and preferred them. And if that sounds like banal advertising patter, so be it.

Obviously companies need to make money, or they wouldn't be able to invest in their business, which in

turn means they wouldn't be able to serve their customers. But if absorbing the expense to make these improvements meant Tesco's profits went from that £1.8bn to, say, £1.77bn, if Morrison's made not £583m but £570m, who exactly would weep? Not me.

Unsurprisingly, the supermarket business doesn't quite see it this way. As far as it is concerned, it has never stopped striving to improve the quality and value of its products. "Supermarkets are constantly looking at their ranges, both in terms of the quality and the price that they can offer it at to customers," Andrew Opie of the British Retail Consortium told me. "It's what they do and it's what they do well. So all of the supermarkets will be undergoing reviews of their ranges on a regular basis to examine what's the best-quality products they can get on the shelves at the right price. This is nothing new to the supermarkets."

Budget foods – Disgrace!

Let's be clear. A 25% meat pie is still not a fabulous item. Nor would Blumenthal and I have swooned over a 54% pork sausage. Likewise, we can lecture those in dire straits on the need to eat more fresh fruit and vegetables - where the value ranges happen to score well - though patronising people who are struggling to make ends meet has always left me with a nasty taste in the mouth. The fact is that the items I have looked at are invariably going to be a part of the diet, and that leads to simple questions of respect; of the supermarkets, which do so well out of us in good times, not forcing the very poorest to eat dross when the bad times come.

Not that concepts like this are entirely alien to Britain's big companies. It's called corporate social responsibility and every serious public company, including the supermarkets, has a department entirely dedicated to it. They know their business and environmental practices have to comply with certain standards. They know that their dominance of the market means they are scrutinised in detail. And they also aren't averse to taking a hit on their bottom line. They already sell certain cheap products at below cost as loss leaders. Isn't it time that they extended that principle so that the quality of their very cheapest food, sold to the most vulnerable of their customers, should also become a part of their corporate social responsibility code, too?

The Observer 18 January 2009
© Guardian News and Media Ltd 2009

Celebrity chefs risk losing touch...

While Asda chief executive Andy Bond was guest editor of the Grocer magazine, he took the opportunity to respond to criticism on budget food lines

I can't help feeling the latest series of Channel 4's Great British Food Fight, while entertaining on one level, is slightly past its sell-by date. Hugh may have changed his tune a bit on Freedom Food, but still wants us to pay a pound more for our chicken. Jamie wants to save our costly bacon. And Heston wants Little Chef customers to swap egg and chips for Earl Grey foam on a bed of quail egg couscous.

"It sticks in my throat when celebrity chefs dictate how viewers should spend their hard-earned money."

As retailers and suppliers, we can't afford the luxury of being so out of step with the mood of the nation. Our customers dictate what we sell and how we sell it.

We didn't tell them frozen food was a good idea at the start of the credit crunch. They told us and we all played catch-up. And when I'm in stores talking to customers each week they tell me their priorities have changed. They still want healthy, safe and nutritious food, sourced in an ethical and fair way – ideally from UK producers – but they don't want to pay more for it. And, crucially, they can't afford to.

Asda's income tracker shows the average family is £4 a week worse off compared with a year ago. It probably doesn't sound much to a millionaire, but it's the difference between putting a few extra products in your basket or leaving them out.

And it sticks in my throat a little when celebrity chefs make sweeping assumptions, and preach to TV viewers about how they should spend their hard-earned money. Was I the only one who thought Hugh was patronising to the single mum who he wanted to pay more for higher-welfare chicken?

I'd like to see the reception Hugh got if he joined me on an accompanied shop or customer listening group – not on camera so it turns into a pantomime – so he can get closer to the challenges real people face on a daily basis.

Without a dose of reality, the celebrity chefs risk losing touch, and disappearing into obscurity. Which will hurt them much more than the thought of chickens crammed in a shed.

The Grocer 31 January 2009

I DETEST the diet police. You know, those people, always middle class, who've managed to shrink their political world view down to an obsessive concern over what they, and other people, should eat. Those who believe that feeding kids Big Macs is criminal 'abuse', and that all we need to do to make the world a better place is to make everyone give up red meat and measure our GI intake.

These people who've tried to create a utopia within their inner world (or at least the inner space from mouth to anus), which has, like every other attempt at utopia, become a totalitarian state.

I am not a food fascist. In fact, since their ranks started swelling I've taken a firm stand to eat anything that takes my fancy: 12-packs of doughnuts, spam fritters and an infinite variety of cheap Polish pickles, any time, in any quantity. This is how I fight fascism.

However, at the risk of sounding like a health-Hitler myself, I'm going to have to reveal that my relationship with one beloved foodstuff has recently ended. I believe now that I was a victim of an addiction. This foodstuff would plague my every moment when I was denied it. Sometimes the need woke me at night.

When I tried to give it up, I was overcome with dizziness, cold sweats, weeping, trembling hands, irritability, flashes of anger, lethargy. I've kicked the booze and the fags and, believe me, that was a piece of cake compared with coming off this thing. Mid-withdrawal I even considered going back on the fags as a way of distracting myself from the pangs.

This dangerous substance is called cheese. Camembert, Brie, vintage Canadian Cheddar, Edam. All available without prescription.

Why deprive myself of my favourite fix? It was not the bad breath or the Stilton goo oozing from my armpits. It was snoring.

Ewan Morrison:

'Kicking the booze and fags was a piece of cake compared to coming off cheese'

I read somewhere that there was a link between dairy produce and snoring, and since my nasal noise had become so severe that even the downstairs neighbour had complained, and for that matter, my girlfriend would not have me in the same bed, I decided that something had to go. The snoring or the cheese or maybe even the possibility of a meaningful relationship.

I can now attest that there is a factual and proven link between snoring and cheese consumption. I am a living test tube experiment. After five days without cheese, my nights are now 90% snore-free. My love life has resumed. Of course I miss the aroma of Gorgonzola in my moustache, and there is now an aching chasm in the fridge where my beloved Brie used to be, but when you take out the scales and place a very tasty woman on one side and a human weight of coagulated lactose on the other, it makes the decision a lot easier.

But I'm no food fascist and I absolutely do not recommend that you do the same. So I won't tell you that cheese increases mucous that restricts the breathing airways, or that as the Casein molecules in cheese are digested, they break apart to release opiate molecules. Or that according to campaigners for veganism, many milk products contain measurable quantities of herbicides, pesticides, dioxins and 52 powerful antibiotics.

No, eat as much cheese as you like. Just be aware, next time you reach for that vintage mature Cheddar, that it could consume your life. I was lucky. I got out before it got me.

Ewan Morrison is the author of three novels, Swung, Distance and Menage (all Jonathan Cape) and writes a weekly column for Scotland on Sunday

Scotland on Sunday 15 February 2009

… and I'm telling you that you can't 'hold the cheese' on a cheeseburger!

Let's junk the junk food and save our kids from a frightening future –
where burger is king!

Jayne Dowle

Pizza or chips? It's the half-term holiday in Wakefield town centre, and that was the question I overheard a father asking his son, who looked about eight.

Wakefield boasts a variety of cafés, so "pizza or chips" certainly weren't the only options available.

But when that is the only choice to be offered by a parent, is it any wonder that almost one third of our children are either obese or overweight?

The Government can spend as much money as it likes on healthy eating campaigns, but it won't make much difference to children's health until it tackles the takeaway epidemic. We have turned into a fast-food nation, and nobody – except Jamie Oliver – appears prepared to do anything about it.

This week, the takeaway chain, KFC, announced that it was creating 9,000 jobs in Britain. Subway, the sandwich shop, plans to open 600 new stores and create 7,000 new jobs, and Domino's Pizza, McDonald's and Greggs all report increased trade. This is in a recession when the first thing to go in the family budget should surely be the extras – like food which you pay someone else to prepare for you.

Some business commentators argue that this boom is because

cash-strapped consumers are avoiding expensive restaurants and choosing cheaper outlets. I'm sorry, but I don't buy that one. Every town, city and village has pubs desperately offering "proper" meals at ridiculously low prices to tempt in dwindling custom. I could name you at least half-a-dozen, locally, where you could feed a family for less than £20. But I've heard many a parent lament that they "can't get them to sit down to eat a proper dinner".

So they trough from a polystyrene carton while walking through the streets. And nine times out of 10, they can't even be bothered to find a bin to put it in when they have finished. But the really scary thing is that kids brought up like this will know no different. When they have children of their own, they won't even consider going into a place with knives and forks.

Listening to local radio on the way home from Wakefield, two advertisements came on back-to-back. The first was for the latest government campaign, Change4Life, aimed, earnestly, at getting families to "eat well and move more". It was followed by an exhortation to head to a certain pizza restaurant chain as the ideal way of entertaining children at half-term. I thought of that kid with his dad, and wondered whether he went for pizza or chips, or both.

I recognise that the forces of big business can't be stopped. And in a free country, it would be wrong to single out food retailers for special censure, although Ministers threaten such a sanction if Change4Life does not succeed. In any case, a ban on junk food won't change a culture which has taken such a firm root. I do wonder if the Government realises what it is up against. Its cartoon families seem to me incredibly naïve foot-soldiers in the battle against the takeaway armies.

I wouldn't be human, and neither would my family, if we didn't enjoy pizza or chips, or burgers, now and again. However, there is a massive difference between regarding takeaway food as an occasional treat and relying on it as a staple diet. But I know that many families just cannot be bothered to buy food, prepare and cook it. I even see primary-age kids buying their breakfast from the café near my children's school.

What kind of parent can't put a slice of bread in the toaster, or shovel some cereal and milk into a bowl? I can manage that, even on the busiest of mornings. I would have failed as a parent if I couldn't. It's not shortage of time that is stopping parents from encouraging healthy eating habits, it's sheer laziness.

I know also of teenagers who think it is so "uncool" to take a packed lunch to school that they demand a fiver a day to spend at lunchtime. Sorry, Jamie, school dinners don't even register. That's £100 a month. One A-level student I know goes to the sandwich shop twice a day, at lunch and teatime. I can't even begin to

So they trough from a polystyrene carton while walking through the streets... But the really scary thing is that kids brought up like this will know no different. When they have children of their own, they won't even consider going into a place with knives and forks.

imagine what else he eats when he finally makes it home. Why don't his parents just say no, and withdraw the funds?

If a recession can't stop irresponsible parents from feeding their children rubbish, then I don't know what can. If I ruled the world, I would run an anti-obesity campaign – aimed primarily at ignorant parents – as

If a recession can't stop irresponsible parents from feeding their children rubbish, then I don't know what can.

frightening as the ones which have persuaded millions of people to quit smoking and drink-driving. Instead of waffling on about including lots of fruit and veg in the diet, it would spell out the dangers of kids eating so much saturated fat and processed

junk. Let's get down to basics: heart disease, rotten teeth and thighs so fat that they chafe.

There. Told you it wouldn't be pretty. But neither is your child dying from a heart attack before they are 30.

Yorkshire Post 19 February 2009

Daddy Cool

Andrew Hoyle, Scotland on Sunday's assistant chief sub-editor

I have heard it said that you are what you eat. If that is the case, our three children are 45% mechanically recovered chicken, 25% pork and 30% an artery-narrowing and stomach-churning combination of fat, brine and rind.

Yup, our six-year-old boy, his four-year-old brother and their two-year-old sister are in hot dog heaven. Lured by a recession-busting offer at the local supermarket, I bought a tin – mmm – of frankfurters, eight for 99p if memory serves correctly. The children promptly devoured them with relish – and ketchup. What's not to like?

I bought a tin – mmm – of frankfurters, eight for 99p if memory serves correctly. The children promptly devoured them with relish – and ketchup.

Doubtless smug mockney git Jamie Oliver would choke on his polenta at this culinary calamity, but I couldn't give a flying fig about what the PC food-snob brigade think. I'm much more interested in seeing my children happily devouring every morsel of their meal and then asking for more.

Besides, it's not as if they exist purely on a diet of improbably shaped and processed gristle. Pasta with pesto is currently a favourite with our elder son, his brother's adventurous appetite extends to prawns, mussels, crab and mackerel, while their sister will

happily chow down on pepperoni pizza, plus whatever crunchy nibbles she finds under the sofa or worryingly close to the cat's litter tray.

On occasion, though – and I am sure other parents will recognise this – feeding time does turn into something of a battleground, and an expensive one at that. Each child's likes and dislikes vary day by day but never coincide with their siblings' fluctuating preferences. Take breakfast, for

I couldn't give a flying fig about what the PC food-snob brigade think. I'm much more interested in seeing my children happily devouring every morsel of their meal and then asking for more.

example. Today Number One Son hankers after Frosties, his sister will only countenance Cheerios, while their brother will not permit a spoonful of cereal to pass his lips.

So how is the 21st-century parent to persuade them to eat what is given to them, whether they like it or not? On the face of it, some form of pump and tube connected via the nose to the stomach sounds, in the words of Tony Tiger, grrrreat. It would certainly avoid needless waste and spillage. Or should I threaten the little darlings with a blanket ban on watching Sponge Bob Square Pants for the whole week? Best not – this cruel and unusual punishment would only encourage social services to remove them into care before you could say, "Absorbent and yellow and porous is he."

As it is, I usually end up pandering to their whims – anything for a quiet life, especially first thing in the morning. Now, where did I put that tin opener?

Scotland On Sunday 15 February 2009

Which fast food meals are the healthiest?

When The Food Magazine asked nutrition specialists and members of the public which fast foods were most laden with fats or calories, the results were surprisingly poor.

The lack of clear labelling for fast food meals means that few people really know what they are ordering. We believe it is time to follow the example of cities such as New York and Seattle, and get the fatty facts publicly declared on menu boards.

We are eating out of the home more than ever before, but the food we eat is rarely labelled with nutrition details. In the supermarket, we can look at the labels and make a decision, but in McDonalds, Starbucks, Pizza Hut, KFC or Subway, the display boards show no nutritional information at all. We may find some facts available in leaflets, or on the containers or tray liners, but that information comes after we have made our choice, collected our meal and sat down to eat. All we can do then is say, "I wish I had known before I ordered."

Surveys show that meals eaten outside the home are frequently higher in calories and fats than food prepared and cooked at home. This means that caterers have as much responsibility as supermarkets to ensure we get the facts before we choose.

There are already moves in the USA to force better disclosure. The local health authorities for New York City and Seattle have enacted legislation requiring nutrition information to be available at the point of sale. Exemptions are made for small firms with few outlets, and for companies that have non-standard menus. The fast food outlets are fighting back with legal challenges, but the signs are good that the laws will stick and customers will get the information they surely deserve to have. After all, what are companies trying to hide!

In Europe, no such laws are yet envisaged. The Food Standards Agency is promising to look into the issue in the next year or so, but we believe it is time to press forward now. The logic is clear: customers have a right to know what they are being sold. This is especially true for products that rely for their appeal on salt, fats and sugar to boost the flavours of mass-produced, long-life ingredients. It is not difficult to do in fast food chains as meals are made to standard set recipes.

We believe that fast food is designed to look appealing but can hide a large amount of fat or pack a big calorie punch. To check our beliefs, we went to the experts.

Three chicken thighs and a large fries from KFC will give you about half your day's calories (over 940), half a day's salt (3 grams) and a whole day's fat (a whopping 57 grams). Or you could go for a Tower Burger, with over 600 calories and four grams of salt in the one item.

We visited the European Congress on Obesity, this spring, where some 3,000 nutritionists, obesity researchers and clinicians were gathered in Geneva to discuss the latest science on obesity research, the latest ideas for treatment and the policies needed to prevent people becoming overweight. We spoke to 66 of the experts as they looked at the scientific exhibitions, and we asked them to complete a simple questionnaire containing a set of just five questions about the fat and calorie content of fast food, each with four possible answers. For example we asked:

Which item from McDonalds contains the most total fat?
a: Large French fries (170g portion)
b: Double Cheeseburger (165g portion)
c: Filet-O-Fish sandwich (143g portion)
d: McChicken sandwich (147g portion)

Fewer than half the experts were able to identify the culprit here. Many thought it was the Double Cheeseburger, and several thought the Filet-O-Fish, but in fact the French fries come in at a whopping 30g fat. Then we asked:

Which 15 centimetre (six inch) sub at Subway contains the most calories?

a: Tuna salad (250g portion)

b: Steak and Cheese (278g portion)

c: Italian (Salami, Ham, Pepperoni and Cheese) (243g portion)

d: Cold Cut Combo (249g portion)

Most people said the Italian, and some said the Steak and Cheese, but in fact the Tuna salad packs in the energy at 530 calories. Only seven people got this right.

Out of the 66 specialists, not a single person gave five correct answers. Just five people gave four correct answers. The great majority – three-quarters of the experts – got only two, one or none of the correct answers – little better than pure guess work.

When they were shown the correct answers the experts were surprised, but admitted that if they had a problem making the right choice, then surely the average customer had little chance of guessing which foods were the healthiest.

Testing the public

We did a similar survey with a further 220 people on the street, 172 of whom were regular fast food eaters. Again, we asked questions about the fat and calorie content of fast food. For instance:

Which item from the KFC menu contains the most fat?

a: Large Coleslaw

b: Regular Popcorn Chicken

c: Large Fries

d: Fillet Burger

Only 48 people guessed the correct answer, the coleslaw, which contains 22.4g of fat. Most people guessed Popcorn Chicken, which actually has 17.8g of fat.

How many calories are in a six inch individual pan pizza from Pizza Hut?

a: 508

b: 608

c: 708

d: 808

The rules in Seattle and New York City

In Seattle, chain restaurants with more than ten national outlets and $1m in annual sales must have menus displaying calories, saturated fat, trans fat, sodium and carbohydrate information.

If the restaurant uses a menu board, then this must include calories in each item, and the other nutrient information should be plainly visible at the point of ordering. Only items available on the menu for 60 days or more are required to be labelled.

In New York City chain restaurants with 15 or more national outlets must list the calorie content of standard items on menus, menu boards or display tags. The calorie information should be at least as prominent as the price information.

Most people thought the answer was 708 calories, as opposed to the truth that, at 808 calories, one of these pizzas is just over 40% of the average daily recommended calorie total for a woman.

Out of the 220 people who took part in our street survey, only one person guessed all of the answers correctly. Again, most people only got one or two answers right.

It should not have to be guess work. We have the right to know what is in our food, and to have the information we need to make our choices before we buy.

Food Magazine, July/September 2008
http://www.foodmagazine.org.uk

Written by: Anna Glayzer, with additional research by Tim Lobstein, Nina Sorensen and Hannah Brinsden. Thanks to the Woodcock Foundation for their support of this investigation.

Health

Issues to think about and discuss

Hannah Jones: 'I have been in hospital too much' & **Doctors always listen to the child's views** – Can a child really decide whether to choose life saving treatment or refuse it? At what age is someone competent to make that decision? Who should have the final say? In this agonising story a thirteen year old was threatened with being taken from her parents and forced to receive life saving treatment.

Alcoholism is a choice – I need to believe that it was my genes telling me to drink – Is alcoholism genetic? Are there some people who "don't have a stop button"? Or should they just show some self-control?

Too much too young – Would discovering what alcohol does to a young person's body put you off drinking?

Please stop smoking, Mummy! – Are there things parents should give up for their children?

A curiously French complaint – Do different attitudes to disease reflect national characteristics? Is the French medical system more caring or is it pandering to a country full of hypochondriacs?

Saving lives – Tempted to glamorise her job, a GP recounts the heroics of hospital medicine. But in which role did she save most lives? And why did she choose to dramatise her job?

Health

Health

Diagnosis

Life saving treatment

Addiction

Smoking

Alcoholism

Opinion

Doctors

Hannah Jones: 'I have been in hospital too much'

Photo: South West News Service

Imagine, for a moment, that you are the child protection officer sitting opposite Hannah Jones, aged 13, and she is telling you why she does not want to have a "life-saving" heart transplant. By Elizabeth Grice

She holds you with that steady gaze. She looks through and beyond you because her years of suffering have given her the ability to weigh things up with the imperturbable calm of the realist. Her mind is made up, as yours cannot be, because she is about to persuade you that it is not in her interests to be put through yet another operation. She is suffering from heart disease brought on by treatment for childhood leukaemia and knows her time is limited. She is not asking for the "right to die", as the misapprehension is, but for the right to live as she wants – at home with her parents and her siblings.

You are there to act in her best interests. Doctors say that means removing her exhausted and damaged heart and giving her a new one. But she is a brave and well-informed young girl and she has decided the procedure is too risky. It might kill her. At best, it might give her a slightly extended life of endless medication and more scares.

Grotesque as it sounds to the non-medical world – and maybe even to you – this long-suffering, terminally ill girl has been threatened with being removed by court order from the custody of her parents and forced to have the operation. Her desperate parents have asked you to listen to her, and she begins with heart-breaking equanimity to explain to you the reality of her situation as she sees it. She tells you she has had

enough and wants her illness to take its natural course.

"I put my point straight across," Hannah said yesterday of the momentous hour-long meeting with the officer, held in the bedroom of her five-bedroom Georgian cottage just outside the village of Marden, near Hereford. "I said I have been in hospital too much and I associate it with bad memories. I have had too much trauma. I said: I don't want this thing. I was shocked to hear that they could do such a thing [take her from home].

"I'm not a normal 13-year-old. I'm a deep thinker. I've had to be, with my

It might kill her. At best, it might give her a slightly extended life of endless medication and more scares.

illness. It's hard, at 13, to know I'm going to die, but I also know what's best for me."

Her self-advocacy ended all threats that she might be removed against her will to wait for a new heart to become available. The High Court proceedings were dropped. This may be a girl of only 13 who talks to her friends on MSN, loves reading Enid Blyton and longs to go to Disneyland – if only she could get the insurance – but she has the maturity of a child made wise by illness. According to her father, she made the decision "on her own, a bit like a grown-up really, even though she was only 12 at the time". You wonder, he says, "how she was coping, what her mind was thinking at the time. I have great admiration for her".

Medical intervention for as long as she can remember has given Hannah the right to be heard, even the ability and the competence to make decisions about her limited future. "I know there is a big waiting list for heart transplants," she said yesterday, "and I am happy to save someone else's life. I just decided that there were too many risks and, even if I took them, there might be a bad outcome afterwards. There is a chance that I may be OK and there is a chance that I may not be as well as I could be, but I am taking that chance."

There can't be many more desperate situations in which everyone has acted for the best even though they may be in conflict. Here is the cast: the perfect patient, the loving family, the good doctors, the diligent locum, the righteous health care trust, the listening child protection officer and the right-thinking lawyers – who decided on Monday that the threatened court action should be lifted.

In July, Andrew Jones, an auditor, and his wife Kirsty were told that their eldest daughter had a maximum of six months to live. It is difficult to imagine the turmoil they must have gone through to support Hannah's decision to have no more operations. For their own sake, and that of their three younger children – Oliver, 11, with whom she likes to play ball outside, Lucy, 10, and four-year-old Phoebe – if they had thought there was the remotest chance that those

> ## "If she had the transplant as a child it's more likely she would need another one in four or five years."

six months could be meaningfully extended by a heart transplant, they would have seized it.

But Kirsty Jones was once an intensive care nursing sister and she knows that the heart transplant would probably offer no more than a temporary respite. "Yes, I want her to live and yes, I want a cure," she says. "But this is not a cure. I've worked on a cardiac transplant unit and I've seen good and bad outcomes. If she had the transplant as a child it's more likely she would need another one in four or five years." Moreover, doctors had said the drugs to prevent Hannah's body rejecting the new heart could cause a recurrence of the leukaemia. Against such odds, what parent could put a child through a possibly life-threatening, possibly life-extending but ultimately pointless procedure?

"It was very emotional trying to reach the sort of decision you would never wish on your worst enemy," says Andrew Jones. "We were as low as it's possible to get but I just didn't feel able

offer? What if she had been coerced or was seriously depressed? The GP was damned if he did and damned if he didn't.

As a result of his punctiliousness, out of the blue on a Friday evening, the Joneses received a shocking phone call. Hereford County Hospital was applying for a High Court order to remove Hannah from the family home on the grounds that they were "preventing her treatment". Her disbelieving father said: "We were shell-shocked, really. They were ready to take her that night."

"It was just this one locum doctor who didn't know Hannah," recalls Kirsty. "He was saying, 'Bring her into hospital now or I shall send the police and an ambulance and a nurse to come and fetch her. It was terribly frightening. It was in the evening and you can't get a solicitor and the social workers have disappeared for the weekend, and we have to tell the three young children they have to be good, and be quiet, and Hannah might cry,

> ## Against such odds, what parent could put a child through a possibly life-threatening, possibly life-extending but ultimately pointless procedure?

to influence her. My wife and I agreed that whatever Hannah wanted, we would support her."

What complicated an agonising story is the heavy-handedness of the authorities. A locum doctor at the hospital reported the case to the child protection unit after Hannah had put her arguments against further treatment – successfully – to doctors at Birmingham Children's Hospital (where she had a pacemaker fitted this year) and Great Ormond Street (where the transplant would have been performed).

The doctor acted "appropriately" in voicing his concerns. Who could blame him for raising the alarm that someone so young had decided to reject the best intervention his profession could

she might not want to go. But we have to let her go if they do come, because otherwise we wouldn't be allowed to visit her in hospital."

Their last resort was to let Hannah explain her decision. After the meeting with the child protection officer, whom her mother described as 'fabulous', Hannah's views were conveyed to barristers at the High Court and they decided to throw the order out – leaving Hannah free to have a "normal" family life, for as long as it lasts.

The Daily Telegraph November 2008
© Telegraph Group Ltd 2008

Doctors always listen to the child's views

Can a child, regardless of how eloquent or sensitive they appear, really comprehend the enormity of death? Can they be given the responsibility for making complex decisions about medical treatment?

Doctor Max Pemberton discusses.

For the past few months I have been working in child psychiatry, among children and adolescents with cancer. Many have a terminal diagnosis. I've watched as cancer specialists, nurses, paediatricians and psychiatrists have agonised over how best to manage their care. Meetings go on for hours as they ensure that everyone – most importantly the child and their parents – are in agreement with the plan.

But sometimes the wishes of the patients or parents differ from those of the medical staff, often because of misunderstandings or unfounded fears that are easily dissipated with careful explanations and even second opinions from independent doctors.

Rarely does medical opinion differ wildly from the wishes of parent and child. Here, it becomes a child protection matter, because doctors must satisfy themselves that decisions are made with the full appreciation of their consequences and in the child's best interest.

Research shows that children often have the skill, understanding and maturity to make decisions about their care, leading to changes in the way in which medical management is planned. Their views are now central to any decision a doctor makes. But children develop these qualities at different rates. There can be no clear cut-off point when a child is considered to have capacity (the ability to understand the consequences of a decision) simply because of their years. It is not just intellectual and emotional maturity that impact on their competency; social situations also influence decisions. Are they making a decision simply because they no longer want to be a burden to their parents, for example?

In the 1980s the House of Lords ruled, as a result of the Gillick case, that, providing a child can demonstrate that they understand the issues and consequences of refusing treatment, they were considered legally (or Gillick) competent. But ensuring this is the case can be difficult. (The ruling has since been absorbed by the Children Act 2004 and the term capacity has replaced competency.)

A 14-year-old on our ward said she did not want further treatment for cancer. Her parents said that they would support whatever decision she made and refused to influence her. Staff were distraught that despite a good prognosis with the chemotherapy, she would certainly die if she didn't have it. Although she stated that she understood that by refusing treatment she would die, one reason she gave was that it was interfering with her school work and she wanted to do well at GCSEs so she could become a vet.

On one level, she had demonstrated maturity and understanding and had made an informed decision, but her reasoning was flawed: she would be dead as a result of her decision long before her GCSEs and would never become a vet.

Before the case could be referred to the legal team, the girl changed her mind. The reason? A friend texted her saying she should have the treatment.

The Daily Telegraph November 2008
© Telegraph Group Ltd 2008

The Gillick case

Victoria Gillick, a mother of ten, tried to prevent doctors prescribing contraception or giving advice on birth control to under 16s without parental consent.

In 1985 the House of Lords ruled that if children fully understood the treatment they were being offered they could consent to it without needing parental permission.

"Whether or not a child is capable of giving the necessary consent will depend on the child's maturity and understanding and the nature of the consent required. The child must be capable of making a reasonable assessment of the advantages and disadvantages of the treatment proposed, so the consent, if given, can be properly and fairly described as true consent."

This 'Gillick standard' is applied to all medical interventions, not just to contraception.

Alcoholism is a choice - I need to believe that it was my genes telling me to drink

Tanya Gold

Is alcoholism a chronic disease or a moral defect? I hope it is a disease. I need to believe that it is. Because if it isn't, I am a horrible person. From the age of 19 to 27, whenever I drank - and I couldn't stop drinking - I stole, lied, blacked out and punched police officers. If it isn't a disease, then I chose to do it. I decided to spend my 20s with my face down a drain.

"If your identical twin is an alcoholic you have a 50% to 60% chance of becoming one - even if you were separated at birth"

David Cameron thinks I did. Trevor McDonald thinks I did. Rod Liddle thinks I did; he said so in a Spectator article he wrote about addiction that joked about fat people being burned alive. And many of you want to think I did. In his speech in Glasgow a fortnight ago, the Tory leader listed alcoholism as one of the "social problems [that] are often the consequences of the choices people make".

It was tucked away in his list of evil, but it was there. The doubt. The idea that, should the alcoholic really want to stop drinking, he or she can. Should we - you - pay for the tricky, often impossible, rehabilitation of alcoholics, the morons who keep drinking when all joy is gone? Or should we treat alcoholism as a disgusting hobby, born of moral frailty and a desire to live on incapacity benefit and watch Richard and Judy all day long?

Trevor McDonald, perhaps with the best of intentions, revealed on the News at Ten last week that he subconsciously thinks the same. He said that he hoped Ronnie Wood would "end his alcoholism once and for all". Wood can stop drinking but he can never stop being an alcoholic. He has a chronic disease. Can you "end" diabetes? Or schizophrenia? Or epilepsy?

This so angered me that I decided to research the scientific evidence on the causes of alcoholism. I admit I am biased. But the scientists who conducted these studies aren't. I learned that just 3.6% of the UK population are dependent drinkers (according to Alcoholics Anonymous), but another report has found that if your identical twin is an alcoholic you have a 50% to 60% chance of becoming one - even if you were separated at birth. This shows, surely, that alcoholism is partly determined by genetics.

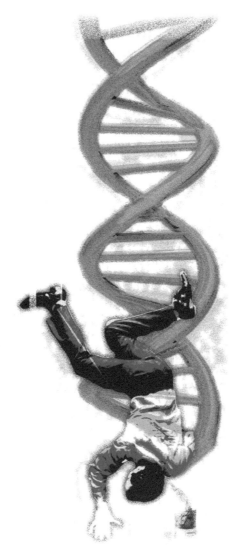

Alcoholics are born with a strong predilection for the disease. We don't have a stop button. We binge-drink from the beginning and we lie to ourselves about it. If you - non-alcoholic reader - were to drink all day, every day, it would be a sign of self-indulgence. You have a genetic profile that makes it possible to stop. We don't have that. Our genetics tell us to drink and drink and never stop.

This is why all recovering alcoholics sound the same, as if they have memorised a pain-ifesto. Alcoholism is essentially a five-act play: they didn't feel safe, they drank, they felt better, they couldn't stop drinking, they lost everything. Curtains. Then they stopped, but they don't know why, and they fear its return every day. Yesterday, at AA, I spoke to a mild-mannered, well-dressed and polite man who described to me how he tried to hang himself from a lamppost in Hampstead Square on his last binge. "That is what booze does to me," he said.

The Cameron-style critics say alcoholics need to take personal responsibility. But they are glib about what they are asking. You can't tell teenagers not to drink on the off chance a disastrous genetic switch in their brains might be activated. Nor can you tell alcoholics to stop drinking or lose their benefits, as the government is considering, because they probably won't do it. Nobody knows why a small number of alcoholics are able to get better and stay better; most alcoholics die of the disease. I am lucky - so far - but I am in a minority. Recovery, for me, seems to be a weird combination of luck, timing and the right help at the right time. It is not due primarily to personal willpower, as these critics seem to suggest. I wish it were.

The Guardian 22 July 2008
© Guardian News and Media Ltd 2008

TOO MUCH TOO YOUNG

THE BRAIN
Alcohol reaches an adult's brain in approximately 5 minutes. In a young person, it starts to affect them in approximately 2-3 minutes.

Alcohol can affect how a young brain works and how it develops. Studies of animals and people suggest that it can cause long-term memory loss and even have an effect on the structure of the brain. Young heavy drinkers have less development in the parts of the brain that control memory. Also possibly affected are the ability to plan, reason and set goals.

A child under 10 has hospital treatment for alcohol-related problems once every three days in England, according to government figures.

We know that under-18s who drink are often involved in other high-risk behaviours, such as unsafe (or unwanted) sex, traffic (and other) accidents, drug use, family breakdown and even suicide.

What is more difficult to assess is the long term health risk to those who start drinking young and may also drink to excess. The research that has been done suggests cause for concern.

BONES
The bone density which is built up in adolescence is important for later life. Alcohol appears to have the effect of stopping cells from forming strong bones. This leads to a risk of fractures and osteoporosis later in life.

THE LIVER
Adolescents who drink heavily have signs which indicate that there is some injury to their livers. Doctors are reporting cases of cirrhosis of the liver among people in their twenties and thirties. This disease normally develops after years of heavy drinking.

HEART AND BLOOD
Among other risk factors is the tendency for young drinkers to be overweight or obese and to have high blood pressure. All of these can lead to heart disease and strokes.

HORMONES AND DEVELOPMENT
A complex balance of hormones is needed for humans to make the transition between child and adult. In rats alcohol has been shown to disrupt this. This could delay the onset of puberty and menstruation in girls. It also appears to suppress the production of testosterone in boys - a key factor in growth, muscle, bone and sexual development.

No one knows yet how much - if any alcohol is safe for adolescents. Nor do we know whether time is a factor: can the body recover from binge drinking? Is moderate consumption a danger? Since the UK has one of the highest alcohol consumption rates in Europe for young people, and since the amount drunk by young people has doubled over the last 15 years, we have a whole generation which is about to find out.

Sources: Various

Please stop smoking, Mummy!

Mum Jo Carter smoked up to 40 cigarettes a day for 30 years until, spurred on by her worried children, she finally managed to beat her habit. Here, the family recalls the toll it took on them.

"It's terrible to see your son gasping"
Mum-of-five Jo Carter, 39, Huddersfield

My son's clothes used to smell so badly of smoke the teachers would accuse him of having a cigarette behind the bike sheds.

They'd pull Mathew aside and he'd have to tell them: "It's my mum!"

Yet instead of dying of shame – and giving up on the spot, I turned it into a joke and said: "So you didn't mention your dad smoking then!"

That's what addiction does to you.

Because your kids are the most precious things in the world, it's too painful to admit you're damaging them, too.

I was 10 when I had my first cigarette. I always knew the risks – I'd seen my grandfather die from smoking-related heart disease. But my philosophy was: "If it's going to happen, it's going to happen."

Over the years, I'd always manage to give up while I was pregnant.

But as soon as my babies were born I would go back.

My eldest, Andrew, is 20 now and back then no one talked about the dangers of passive smoking. Even when it became an issue, I thought I was protecting the children by not smoking directly over them.

When the kids kissed me goodbye before school, I'd turn my head away and blow the smoke out first.

I would get so desperate that I would send my eldest, then 11, to buy cigarette papers.

But even worse was the fact that I smoked around my son Stephen, now 15. He was a very sickly baby. At three he was hospitalised with breathing problems.

As a mother it's terrible to see your son gasp for breath. Not even the bigger warnings on cigarette packets frightened me. But they did scare the kids. They became adamant that I should give up.

A few years ago when I called a meeting to ask them to tidy up, Andrew, turned around and said: "We'd also like to you to stop smoking in the house because it smells and it's bad for you." I was shocked but still I'd turn it back on them.

If they nagged, I'd say: "I'm only smoking in the kitchen now but you still haven't tidied your room, so why should I do what you say?"

My middle son Thomas also has a habit of sucking his fingers. He'd shoot back: "At least what I'm putting in my mouth isn't killing me!"

That's my biggest regret – arguing with my kids when all they wanted was for me to be healthy.

It was only when Stephen's asthma returned with a vengeance when he was about 11 that it finally dawned what it was doing to me, too.

When Stephen went to the doctor's to get his lung capacity checked, I asked if I could try it.

I was stunned to be told mine was lower than his. Straight away I turned to the nurse and said: "Where can I get help to give up?"

That was last year. My partner Russell has given up, too.

But I don't describe myself as an ex-smoker. I describe myself as someone who hasn't had a cigarette for six months.

For 30 years, I smoked up to 40 a day.

But I'd say to other parents, it's never too late to repair some of the damage you've done to yourself – or your kids.

The Daily Mirror 5 February 2009

"I couldn't sleep worrying she'd die"
Stephen Carter-Woodhead, 15

When my teacher asked me to pick a science project, I decided on anti-smoking because my mum smoked so much.

Before that I knew cigarettes give you cancer and they affect your lungs but it didn't mean all that much to me.

Then I went on Google and found horrible pictures of what it does to the insides of your lungs.

But it's when I learned how quickly smokers can die from cancer that I really got scared. That night I couldn't sleep, worrying: "What if Mum dies? It could happen really soon."

Afterwards, when I saw her smoke, I'd drop scary facts into the conversation, although I always tried to keep what I was really feeling to myself.

I don't blame her for smoking. She told me she got addicted very young.

It is frightening having asthma – and not being able to breathe – but I don't blame her.

I'm just glad she's given up – and so proud that she's found the willpower to stick at it.

"Mum doesn't cough anymore"
Bethany Carter-Woodhead, 11

At the dentist's, I would see the poster on the wall saying how bad for you smoking is.

It was a picture of a big, black cancer in someone's mouth. It would give me nightmares because my mum smoked a lot and I knew she could get it, too.

As soon as I was old enough I would read the warnings on her cigarettes. The one that said Smoking Kills was the easiest but it also scared me the most.

Even though I was frightened, I didn't think I could ask Mum to stop, because she's a grown-up. But when the TV ads came on, me and my brothers learned the words by heart.

We said them out loud, too, especially the one about: "I'm afraid of my mum smoking."

I liked it because it gave children a chance to say something.

Now I am glad all the smoke's gone. The house smells nicer. And my mum is different. Her voice has changed and she doesn't cough any more.

Her teeth are whiter, which makes her prettier, too!

A curiously French complaint

Emma Jane Kirby
BBC News, Paris

When I was a student, living in Avignon in the south of France, I remember waking up one morning shortly before Christmas, feeling shivery and as if someone had spent the night sandpapering my throat.

After a couple of days of wheezing and coughing, I took myself to the doctor and explained that I was feeling a bit ropey. One hour later I had been diagnosed with a severe lung infection, mild asthma and had in my hand a prescription for six different types of medicine, an appointment at the local hospital's radiology department and an emergency referral to a specialist in pulmonary disease.

The next day I flew home to the UK for the Christmas holidays where my worried parents persuaded me to visit their local GP for a second opinion. After five minutes in his consulting room, I emerged empty-handed but with a new diagnosis. I had a cold.

Hardening attitudes

I am not suggesting that the French are a nation of hypochondriacs but they do take their health very seriously. France is the biggest consumer of antibiotics in Europe. The government has recently tried to wean the country off its dependency with a series of TV advertisements which reassure the ailing that they do not always need drugs.

A Parisian GP I know, Dr Auber, believes that France enjoys a reputation for having such a great health service simply because its doctors routinely prescribe more medicines. Now he says they are "Anglicising" the system, turning away from the indulgent "There, there" approach and moving towards a much more "Get along with you now" stiff upper lip attitude. It is not going down too well.

Dr Auber claims that many of his patients are deeply disappointed if they do not get a prescription after a visit to his practice and he is quite sure that many go off mumbling that he has not bothered to treat them.

Dr Auber told me that a French colleague of his, who recently moved to join a surgery in London, was staggered to see her British colleagues telling patients complaining of blocked ears, to just go home and pour olive oil into them. In France she said, her patients would have demanded a medical prescription to shift the unwanted wax and she would have felt obliged to write one out.

French malady

But while stuffed-up orifices may be a common symptom on both sides of the Channel, there is one disease that only the Gallic appear susceptible to, and in fact, according to Dr Auber, it is one of the illnesses French people complain about most. Correct me if I am wrong, but have you ever heard a British person complain they are suffering from "heavy legs"?

Fascinated by a malady to which British people appear immune, I went to my local pharmacy and asked the smiling young chemist if she could advise me on remedies

I explained that I was feeling a bit ropey. One hour later I had in my hand a prescription for six different types of medicine, an appointment at the local hospital's radiology department and an emergency referral to a specialist in pulmonary disease.

Worried well

With the current cold snap here, everyone is feeling pretty grotty and congested. Even the sky looks bunged up and it is continually snivelling and spluttering sleet onto the Parisians who in turn are sneezing and rasping into handkerchiefs.

On the Metro, disease hangs thickly in the warm air, and people eye one another warily, sizing up which passenger is likely to be carrying the plague, before choosing their seat and tightening the protective scarves around their throats. At least they have their medicines to console them.

for heavy legs. "Oh, bad luck," she said indicating two entire shelves of pills and potions. "Do you get heavy legs in the winter too? I only suffer from them in the summer," and she handed me a cream with "real grape seeds", assuring me it was very effective when rubbed vigorously twice daily from the ankle to the knee.

I have often wondered if one can get signed off work with heavy legs. I am almost tempted to call my editor to try out the scenario. "Oh yeah hi, it's Emma Jane. Look I'm really sorry but I'm not going to make it in today - I'm afraid I've got heavy legs again." Unfortunately, my boss is a

In the UK my worried parents persuaded me to visit their local GP for a second opinion. After five minutes in his consulting room, I emerged empty-handed but with a new diagnosis. I had a cold.

regular listener to this programme, so by now he will be aware of my British immunity to the illness and would presumably tell me to hop it.

Dr Auber confirms that British people simply do not suffer from this mysterious weightiness of the lower limbs, and adds that the French consume more than a third of the entire world's supply of heavy legs medicines. Curiously though, he has noticed that since the French health insurance companies stopped paying for heavy legs remedies a couple of years ago, consumption of these products is now one-tenth what it used to be.

Emergency treatment

A couple of years back, while skiing in the Alps after a tiring stint in Afghanistan, I noticed my legs were covered in small red spots and I was feeling lethargic. Could I finally have contracted the elusive heavy legs syndrome?

"No!" said the alarmed French doctor, "you have a tropical illness and you need to go straight to hospital."

Laughing to myself at the typical Gallic solicitousness, I popped a Paracetamol and headed straight back to the slopes.

Two days later, delirious with fever and covered in enormous black lumps, I was lying in the isolation unit of a London hospital, howling in pain and terrified what my test results would reveal.

Alerted by my cries, a masked nurse popped her head around the door.

"Oh for goodness sake," she said brusquely. "Anyone would think you were dying. You've only got suspected leprosy."

From Our Own Correspondent
BBC Radio 4
13 December 2008

SAVING LIVES

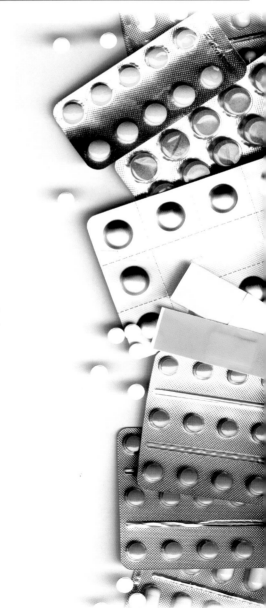

The other day I gave a careers talk at a local school. A boy came up to me afterwards and said, "Miss, have you ever saved anyone's life?"

"Of course," I replied. "I'm a doctor. Saving lives is my core business."

"Tell me about some," he pleaded.

I picked some stories to entertain and inspire the lad. I told him of shocking someone out of ventricular fibrillation when carrying the cardiac arrest bleep; the hypovolaemic teenage victim of a road crash I managed pregnant woman with advanced pre-eclampsia: two lives saved. And I told him about administering adrenaline and hydrocortisone to a patient with anaphylactic shock.

Afterwards I wondered why I had chosen all these heroic examples. What is it, to "save a life"? Why did I not tell him of the hundreds of middle aged people attending with sore throats or sore knees to whom I've said, "Let's just check your blood pressure while you're here"? Or the countless smokers who have left my consulting room

> I WONDERED WHY I HAD CHOSEN ALL THESE HEROIC EXAMPLES. WHAT IS IT, TO "SAVE A LIFE"? WHY DID I NOT TELL HIM OF THE HUNDREDS OF MIDDLE AGED PEOPLE ATTENDING WITH SORE THROATS OR SORE KNEES

to get a drip into; and the woman gasping with pulmonary oedema who responded within seconds to my syringe of frusemide.

"I'd like to do that," he said, with shining eyes. "How many would you save in a week?"

I explained that those stories were from a previous life as a hospital doctor and that I didn't save many lives now as a general practitioner. He was disappointed, so I recounted how I had once spotted the rapidly spreading rash of meningococcal septicaemia and given the urgent shot of penicillin and another time called a "no delay ambulance" for a with a dose of what is known in the literature as "brief advice"? Or those interminable diabetes clinics where I've worked with patient after patient in an effort to align the medical ideal of "tight control" with the lived reality of work and family life?

It's 25 years since I qualified as a doctor. Depending on how you define "saving a life," my personal tally amounts to fewer than a dozen in my entire career – or several thousand.

Trisha Greenhalgh is a professor of primary health care, University College London

BMJ 25 October 2008, Volume 337; a2202

Internet & media
Issues to think about and discuss

Television, teenagers and pornography – Teenagers can easily access 'unsuitable' material online. Should a parent be worried? An amusing comparison of then (1977) and now.

We could turn our back on Jade – if we chose to – The headlines tell the story of a life and death in the media spotlight. Did Jade Goody deserve her treatment - good and bad - in the press? Did the media use her just to make money or did she use them? Is our attitude to 'celebrities' hypocritical?

What does censoring Wikipedia tell us about the way the internet is policed? – Should anything be censored on the internet? Is blocking a Wikipedia page sensible protection or heavy-handed cyber policing?

Wiki-d sense of humour of the online encyclopedia hoaxers – Can you trust everything you find on the internet? Anyone using Wikipedia to help with an assignment had better watch out for Wiki-hoaxers.

Wasting time for fun – Facebook allows a comedian to annoy his wife and lose friends.

Online POKER marketing could spell the NAKED end of VIAGRA journalism as we LOHAN know it – Is it right for journalists to get your attention in this way?

A wireless wonderland – Wireless technology could enhance our safety and medical care by alerting doctors instantly if you have a car crash or a heart attack. But will we really want a microchip telling us what we can and can't eat?

Filling in a digital black hole – Useful online material can disappear instantly. How can we make sure that important information is not lost to future generations?

Reading for the world: Locking up freedom – The power of books to free the mind. And why some states and people want to restrict access to them.

Internet & media

Wireless

Celebrity

Internet

Pornograph

Television

NEWS

Censorshi

Digital

Television, teenagers and pornography

I cannot equate a 1977 Playboy centrefold with what is now online – Brian Viner

My 15-year-old daughter Eleanor has just finished her mock GCSEs, and has done pretty well despite my conviction, aired at regular intervals, that she was spending too much time at the computer on social networking sites when she could have been revising. It is eerie to find history repeating itself, to say nothing of chemistry and physics. When I was 15, my mother took the draconian decision to have the television set removed. She asked Mr Williams from No 54 to store it in his garage while I kicked the habit.

Similarly, my wife and I have resolved to stop Eleanor's access to MSN messenger if we feel that her schoolwork is suffering, an exercise much easier than that undertaken by Mr Williams, who reportedly tripped over the front door step in his haste to get the telly out before I got home from school, exuding teenage malevolence.

Nonetheless, these two examples of parental angst, a generation apart, are instructive. As parents in the danger-strewn 21st-century it is important to maintain a sensible perspective, even in the light of a report just published by market research agency ChildWise, which after surveying 1,800 children at 92 schools claims "a major boost to the intensity and the independence with which children approach online activities".

Teenagers have always found ways to worry and alienate their parents, and always will. It is part of their birthright, just as parents are entitled to fret that their children are exposed to more pernicious influences than they were at the same tender age.

The relentless march of technology makes this unequivocally true, of course. My children can access pornographic images without leaving the front room, whereas I had to rely on reliable contacts in the shoplifting business. Just to bring my mother back into this story, incidentally, I vividly recall my horror one day at finding that my secret stash of pornography had disappeared from its impregnable hiding place under my bed, and how horror turned to mortal embarrassment when my mum casually said: "If you're wondering where your girlie magazines are, I've put them with your Look & Learns. That seems to be the category they belong to."

Now, it would be disingenuous of me to equate a 1977 Playboy centrefold with the images that my kids can download, but the point is that I trust them not to, and since trust is one of the most valuable commodities there is in the relationship between parent and child, I'm not going to let go of it without a struggle. Admittedly, it is a struggle intensified by the myriad of online attractions, especially once you add games consoles to the equation. Indeed, this report reckons that children between the ages of five and 16 are spending almost six hours a day peering at screens of some sort, and if that seems decidedly alarmist, I yield

to nobody in my dislike of the spectral glow that bathes Eleanor's face late into the evening as she messages the school friends she has spent all day with.

But then 30 years ago precisely the same objection was levelled at teenage girls for spending ages on the phone. As for boys, in 1977 the eminent psychologist William Belson published Television Violence and the Adolescent Boy, a report which suggested that teenagers who watched The Sweeney were 49 per cent more likely to duff someone up. That seems as quaint now as the ChildWise report will be to Eleanor, when she's dealing with my 15-year-old grandchildren.

We could turn our back on Jade – if we chose to

Paul Taylor

Photo: Steve Parsons/PA Wire/Press Association Images

PUBLIC LIFE Jade Goody is a 'flawed heroine' to a generation that dumps their partner by altering their Facebook profile

I have always baulked at the idea of describing Jade Goody as a 'reality' TV star. There was nothing, in the parade of attention-seekers and their hissy fits on Big Brother, which bore any resemblance to my reality.

In fact, I baulked at mentioning Jade at all in print. I did not want to add to the sneering, vindictive din of pundits relishing Jade's ignorance. "East Angular... that's abroad!" she had said. She was, the cruellest pundits snidely observed, a 'Miss Piggy look-alike'. Thick and ugly, then. Let's all have a laugh at her expense. It was like shooting fish in a barrel.

But sometimes mentioning Jade has been unavoidable. She has been

the most successful graduate of a 'famous for being famous' school, there for all these past six years in the peripheral vision even of those who tried hard to ignore her.

There was some proper 'reality' to be had from Jade's return to the Big Brother house in 2007 as a 'celebrity' – another word whose meaning has been so warped as to become utterly meaningless. Mean-spirited bullying and racial slurs against the Bollywood actress Shilpa Shetty showed us a reality we knew and despised.

And then suddenly, in among the silly chat-mag spreads, the fatuous interviews, the autobiography, the low-rent scent, Jade Goody gave us

the harshest reality of all. Here was a 27-year-old mother of two young sons, informed (and on camera, no less, during the Indian version of Big Brother) that she had cervical cancer. Now she is coping – also in a blaze of publicity – with a diagnosis that her cancer is terminal.

Still to come will be the poignancy of Jade's wedding to her boyfriend Jack Tweed, more heart-rending tabloid spreads on how she is coping with her treatment, getting her affairs in order and explaining as best she can the fragility of life to her two boys.

"I've lived in front of the cameras. And maybe I'll die in front of them," says Jade. Her spokesman and friend Max Clifford says Jade will remain in the public eye, firstly to make as much money as possible for her children, secondly to give her something to think about besides her illness and thirdly to encourage other young women to be aware of cervical cancer.

What mixed feelings this throws up. The woman willing to show herself to the world in her greatest distress, hoping for a better future for the children she will never see grow up – she is surely to be admired. The woman who is so addicted to publicity that she chooses even to make her last journey with the TV cameras rolling – that's a strange tale of our times.

She will be far from the first woman to choose to face death under an unrelenting media gaze. Jane Tomlinson ran, cycled and squeezed every ounce of life out of her final years, raising £1.5m for charity. In 1990, a 21-year-old woman, Mandy Turner died having spent her last year raising £1m for a scanner at Tameside General Hospital, demonstrating a quite inspirational bravery in the process.

Jade has no such big purpose to fulfil, no charity goal to reach. Instead she is continuing to do what she has done these past few years, standing as a now-tragic, flawed heroine of a generation which forgot about the notion of privacy. This generation would tell the world when they became single again by altering their Facebook profile – sometimes even before informing their other half. They would give Twitter updates before and after, perhaps even during a sexual encounter. They would, as Jade did, go into a house where their every word and movement would be broadcast to a TV audience which would judge them worthy or unworthy with a stab of the phone keypad.

When I wrote on this page about the first series of Big Brother in 2000, I recalled a caustic quote from Warren Beatty, captured in the fly-on-the-wall documentary In Bed With Madonna. He and Madonna went into a doctor's surgery and the doctor asked whether she preferred to speak off-camera.

"She doesn't want to live off-camera, much less talk," said Beatty. "Why would you say something if it's off camera? What point is there in existing."

Having parlayed her slender appeal into a lucrative career, Jade goes on being Jade. The human soap opera continues even as the plot turns dark.

It would be somewhat hypocritical of us to wish she would retreat from the public glare now she finally has something important to say. But the decision of when to turn away, when to stop treating Jade Goody as public property is ours to make. It's no good pondering the ghastliness of Jade choosing to die in the public eye if we the public seem incapable of looking the other way.

17 February 2009
Manchester Evening News

Big Bro Bimbo's Crime Shame

Jade Baddie

BB Jade sobs off to India

How will Jade cope when she finds out she's the most hated woman in Britain?

Jade has cancer

This article was written before Jade Goody's death on 22nd March 2009. It nevertheless sums up the controversial nature of her fame and the difficulty of assessing her life and influence.

Our tears for Jade

The Big Question:

What does censoring Wikipedia tell us about the way the internet is policed?

Archie Bland

Why are we asking this now?

The internet is commonly thought of as a pervert's playground, a lawless domain beyond the normal strictures of national legal systems, with plenty of dark corners where the usual limits of decency are suspended. But a recent decision by the UK's internet watchdog is not merely a fringe matter: it has made a page from the online encyclopedia Wikipedia inaccessible to most internet users in this country. The decision and its aftermath raise the question of exactly how far online censorship should go.

So what was the web page in question?

The entry that is now banned is not obviously explicitly sexual in its content: at first glance it seems like any other page in Wikipedia's vast repository. This one deals with an album by 1970s German metal band Scorpions called Virgin Killer. The element of the page that makes it problematic is the picture of the original album cover that accompanies the text: the image shows a girl aged about 13 posing naked with only a crack in the camera lens covering her genitalia.

Who decided it was illegal?

The British body that regulates what content reaches internet users is called the Internet Watch Foundation, or IWF, which is a charitable body mostly funded by the British internet service providers. It also receives some funding from the EU. The IWF is entrusted by the Government and police with judging which online content is illegal and should therefore be removed.

How does the IWF work?

The IWF only makes assessments of websites where the content in question is brought to its attention by a submitted complaint. Once it is informed of a particular case, it makes a judgement about whether the content is "potentially illegal" or not, and assesses the severity of the offence on a five-point scale. (Most of the examples it looks at, including the latest Wikipedia case, are potential child abuse images – but the organisation also bears responsibility for other categories of criminal content, including racist abuse and extreme or violent pornography.) If the organisation's assessors decide that the law is being broken, it places a

block on the web address in question that is picked up within 24 hours by the internet service providers that subscribe to the service – which cover about 95 per cent of British internet users. The web page in question still exists, but almost anyone attempting to access it from within the UK will be met with a message saying that the page cannot be found.

How active is the body?

Last year, the IWF reviewed more than 34,000 submitted URLs, compared to just a few hundred in the year it was founded, 1996 – a heavy workload for its four members of staff that are trained to assess the material. Of that number, around 3,000 contained images or text that the organisation deemed to be potentially illegal.

And is the approach successful?

It is hard to say, precisely: much of its effect will make itself felt in areas where statistics are hard to come by, such as the number of attempts to access illegal material that are denied. But the IWF points to one powerful piece of evidence for its success: it says that when it was founded, 18 per cent of the reports it received referred to British web pages, a proportion that has now dropped to less than one per cent. It has also been successful by another measure, too. The body was founded as an attempt by the Internet Service Providers and authorities to avoid regulation, which the ISPs feared would be expensive and difficult to comply with. So far, the approach has proved broadly acceptable to both parties.

What general criticisms are there of the body?

Most in the industry think that it does a good job. "The Internet Watch Foundation has a tough job and an important role in protecting our

This replacement cover was released in some countries

children," says a spokesman for one of the ISPs. "We just have to support them – we can't pick and choose." But advocates of internet freedom may feel some unease over the fact that the IWF can effectively make unilateral decisions about whether online content is illegal or not. While the material that is banned is officially deemed "potentially illegal", no one has ever successfully brought a court case that has disputed the IWF's designation. On the one hand, this could be seen as evidence that the organisation makes excellent decisions; on the other, it could be seen as proof that the body has an unhealthy level of control over the material that is allowed by British ISPs, and that there is bound to be a chilling effect that dissuades those who would dispute the IWF's conclusions from pursuing their case.

How has the Wikipedia community responded to this instance?

Mostly unfavourably. Many users of the website feel that this is an example of unjustified censorship: they argue that few potential

paedophiles will be using Wikipedia as their source for illegal material, and that a widely viewed album cover that has been in public circulation for decades should not be so easily removed from public access. Some of the anger is the result of the fact that this is the first time the IWF has censored a web page with such a mainstream audience. There is also an argument that the internet comes in for unfair special treatment on this kind of matter, partly because of public concern about the use of the internet as a way for paedophiles to access child pornography. David Gerard, a Wikipedia volunteer and spokesperson in the UK, points out that it is available offline as well: "I personally find it distasteful. But is it illegal? Are the police going to go into libraries and rip out the offending page?"

Why is Wikipedia the only site to have been censored?

The IWF is in a difficult position because its charter limits it to making decisions about websites that are brought to its attention by third parties. It cannot unilaterally decide that a website should be banned. That means that the image from the Scorpions' album cover actually remains easily available on a wide range of other sites accessible in the UK, including Amazon's American operation. Since the initial decision was reached, another complaint has been brought to the body's attention, about the Amazon version of the image. That instance may be acted on shortly; but it is unlikely that every web page on which the image can currently be found will be removed from the list of available content.

Are there any alternatives?

In the UK, the IWF is the main gatekeeper. Worldwide, there are 33 other organisations that do similar work under the umbrella of an international association called the International Association of Internet Hotlines, or INHOPE. But that means that there are many other countries with very little regulation of the content produced within their borders. As long as that situation applies – and it looks likely to for a long time – the IWF looks bound to stay.

The Independent 9 December 2008
© 2008 Independent News
& Media Limited

Is the IWF the right way of keeping illegal material off the internet?

- The system has worked well, with few complaints about its operation, for more than 10 years

- Any system that can avoid imposing additional legislation has to be a good thing

- The IWF is able to respond much more quickly to potentially illegal material than alternatives could

- An organisation that polices illegal material by banning 1970s album covers has its priorities wrong

- It is not right for such a small organisation to make such significant decisions on a daily basis

- The fact that the IWF is funded by internet service providers may lead to claims of a conflict of interest

---

WIKI-D SENSE OF HUMOUR OF THE ONLINE ENCYCLOPEDIA HOAXERS

Titian's Diana and Actaeon was at the centre of a Wikipedia row

The death of Titian is the latest proof that there's lies, damn lies and Wikipedia. Sarah Freeman reports

In the current dour world of British politics, Wikigate has provided some much needed light relief.

It all began in the World Economic Forum in Davos when Gordon Brown decided to liken himself to the artist Titian who, he said, completed the last

of his great paintings aged 90. Not so, said David Cameron. At this week's PMQs the Tory leader told the house Titian had died at 86 and Brown's artistic faux pas was further evidence of his inability to get the facts right.

It was just another day in the tit-for-tat battle of political one-upmanship. That was until some bright spark in Conservative Central Office decided

to help things along with a dabble on Wikipedia. Shortly after PMQs, an as yet unidentified staffer, no doubt trying to please his boss, logged on to the online encyclopaedia and finding Titian's entry gave credence to the PM's theory, decided that wouldn't do and promptly changed his date of death from 1576 to 1572.

When word got out, it all looked a

little childish, but it was not the first time Wikipedia, which can be edited by anyone, anywhere at anytime has been open to abuse.

Since it was founded in 2001, Wikipedia has more than 12 million articles in 200 languages and its influence is growing. Four years ago, the First International Wikimedia Conference was held in Frankfurt and, despite on-going doubt as to its accuracy, the site has become the first port of call for many, including journalists.

Its flaws were roundly exposed following the death of veteran BBC television composer Ronnie Hazlehurst in 2007. He wrote some of TV's most memorable theme tunes, including The Two Ronnies, Last of the Summer Wine, and Blankety Blank, but when the obituaries appeared, there was a curious entry on his CV.

Numerous newspapers reported that Hazlehurst had emerged from retirement a few years before to co-write the S Club 7 hit Reach. It might have been a surprising departure for the composer, but not surprising enough for anyone to bother to double-check the entry. When it emerged the obituary writers were hapless victims of a Wiki-hoaxer, corrections and clarifications were quickly made, but much of the press was left with egg on its face.

What's perhaps most surprising about the Hazlehurst incident is that it doesn't happen more often. Wikipedia relies on an army of volunteers, many of whom are experts in a particular field, to edit and check the entries, but the sheer scale of the operation provides a happy hunting ground for online mischief makers.

For the most part, the additions and errors are trivial stuff, but every so often a dark side emerges. Three years ago, the profiles of various US Senators were found to have been altered, removing unpalatable facts about voting records and their past political allegiances. One contributor decided to add "most annoying Senator ever" to a list of one politician's achievements.

FOR THE MOST PART, THE ADDITIONS AND ERRORS ARE TRIVIAL STUFF, BUT EVERY SO OFTEN A DARK SIDE EMERGES

As those involved sought to restore their reputations, one man knew exactly how it felt to be the subject of Wiki-abuse. The founding editor of USA Today, John Seigenthaler, took action when he discovered his own entry incorrectly linked him to the assassinations of President John F Kennedy and his brother Robert.

Seigenthaler had been a confidant of the Kennedy dynasty and it emerged the unfortunate turn of events was the fault of a man called Brian Chase, who said he was simply trying to trick a colleague.

Wikipedia's success is down to its simplicity, but this is also its downfall. It takes just a few idle key strokes to mislead a global audience. When Senator Ted Kennedy collapsed following the inauguration of Barack Obama, some eager contributor

decided he hadn't made it and posted news of his death.

Kennedy was, in fact, very much alive and while the entry was swiftly amended, Wikipedia's founder decided enough was enough, arguing some entries may have to be vetted before any amendments go live.

He might as well have suggested he was in favour of child chimney sweeps, such was the outcry from those who feared it was against the principles of the original site. They have a point.

Wikipedia may not be 100 per cent accurate and anyone who blindly puts their trust in the entries deserves to be undone, but if it has the power to make politicians squirm it must be doing something right.

The Yorkshire Post 13 February 2009

Wasting time for fun

Comedian Steve Day has a good return from thousands of hours on Facebook: one gig booking and one lost friend

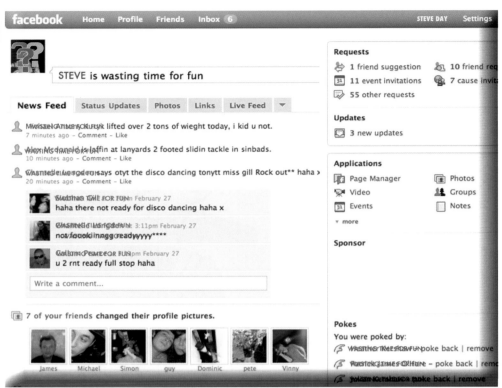

Internet? Nah, never use it. Except all the time. I log on to Facebook for five minutes at half past eleven and the next thing I know it's 2am. As I look back over the time I have spent there, I can at least take comfort in what I've achieved in the last 14-and-a-half-hours. Nothing.

I did once get a gig booking from Facebook, so the 11,000 man-hours haven't all been wasted. I was on MySpace a lot, too, but it feels like the club that no-one goes to any more. In fact, Facebook caused me to fall out with my best friend, Chris McCauseland, who like me is a comic. He's blind, though, so we've got to be friends for that one reason because we're always put on the same bill together. People think, ooh, we've got the blind bloke, let's get the deaf bloke, see

the synergy we could make there! What they really want is the Special Olympics of comedy, "The Aren't They Marvellous Show".

"Aw! Look at the way they're coming up, trying to make us laugh!"

"They're just like people when they do that, aren't they?"

This has gone on for the last five years and in all that time I've never heard him and he's never seen me.

I've fallen out with Chris because of the top friends thing on Facebook. You can have 52 top friends, but what is the point of being somebody's 51st best friend? So I've cut mine down to eight. The problem, though, is that when you get a new friend and want to put them in your top eight, somebody close to you has got to go.

You don't get that problem on Bebo, though, because

someone there is quite likely to have committed suicide and you've always got a vacancy, but on Facebook it's a problem. I had a new friend, far better looking than my ugly mugs. What was I going to do? Then I thought: I know what I'll do, I'll get rid of Chris. He's blind, he'll never know.

I'll get rid of Chris. He's blind, he'll never know.

Two hours later he sends me an email demanding to know what he's done wrong.

Turns out he's got some paranoid blind person's software thing, reporting it all back to him in a voice.

Anyway, the internet. I'm a big one for the online papers. The Guardian and the Telegraph are best for lily-livered liberalism and pedantically-detailed reports of neighbourly disputes over shared

driveways gone tragic respectively.

sportinglife.com keeps me up to date with sports I'm most often watching on TV at the same time. I use Digitalspy to find out what happens in the soaps so I don't have to actually watch them but can spoil them for my wife.

"He dies, doesn't he?" being one of my favourite lines.

YouTube passes me by, due to lack of subtitles. Maybe one day. Same too for the BBC iPlayer. I long for a repeat of Ann Widdecombe on the news saying, "Let me give you an analogy," which came up on the subtitles as, "Let me give you anal joy."

Sorry, I have to go, an event of great importance has occurred. Someone has requested on Facebook that I complete a questionnaire about my favourite ways to be romantic whilst skiing. Byeee.

Disability Now August 2008

Online POKER marketing could spell the NAKED end of VIAGRA journalism as we LOHAN know it

Charlie Brooker

Miley Cyrus, Angelina, Israel vs Palestine, iPhone, 9/11 conspiracy, Facebook, MySpace, and Britney Spears nude. And not forgetting Second Life, Paris Hilton, YouTube, Lindsay Lohan, World of Warcraft, The Dark Knight, Radiohead and Barack Obama. Oh, and great big naked tits. In 3D.

Let me explain. Last week, I wrote a piece on 9/11 conspiracy theories which virtually broke the Guardian website as thousands of "truthers" (painfully earnest online types who sincerely believe 9/11 was an inside job) poured through the walls to unfurl their two pence worth. Some outlined alternative "theories". Some mistakenly equated dismissing the conspiracy theories with endorsing the Bush administration. Some simply wailed, occasionally in CAPITALS. Others, correctly, identified me as a paid-off establishment shill acting under instructions from the CIA.

NEXT TIME A BOMB GOES OFF, ARE WE GOING TO READ "TERROR OUTRAGE: BRITNEY, ANGELINA AND OBAMA ALL UNAFFECTED AS HUNDREDS DIE IN SEXY AGONY"?

Now to sit here and painstakingly rebut everything the truthers said would take three months and several hundred pages, and would be a massive waste of the world's time, because ultimately I'm right and they're wrong - well-meaning, but wrong. What's more, I've woken up with an alarming fever and am sweating like a miner as I type these words. On the cusp of hallucinating. Consequently my brain isn't working properly; it feels like it's been marinaded in petrol, then wrapped in a warm towel. So I'm hardly at my sharpest. Actually, sod it: you win, truthers. I give up. You're 100% correct. Inside job, clearly.

Whatever. Now pass the paracetamol.

Anyway, because it contained the words "9/11 conspiracy", the article generated loads of traffic for the Guardian site, which in turn means loads of advertising revenue. And in this day and age, what with the credit crunch and the death of print journalism and everything, the use of attention-grabbing keywords is becoming standard practice. "Search engine optimisation", it's known as, and it's the journalistic equivalent of a classified ad that starts with the word "SEX!" in large lettering, and "Now that we've got your attention . . ." printed below it in smaller type.

For instance, according to the latest Private Eye, journalists writing articles for the Telegraph website are being actively encouraged to include oft-searched-for phrases in their copy. So an article about shoe sales among young women would open: "Young women - such as Britney Spears - are buying more shoes than ever."

On the one hand, you could argue this is nothing new; after all, for years newspapers have routinely jazzed up dull print articles with photographs of attractive female stars (you know the sort of thing: a giant snap of Keira Knightley doing her Atonement wet T-shirt routine to illustrate a report about the state of Britain's fountain manufacturers). But at least in those instances the actual text of the article itself survived unscathed. There's something uniquely demented about slotting specific words and phrases into a piece simply to con people into reading it. Why bother writing a news article at all? Why not just scan in a few naked photos and have done with it?

And if you do persevere with search-engine-optimised news reports, where do you draw the line? Next time a bomb goes off, are we going to read "Terror outrage: BRITNEY, ANGELINA and OBAMA all unaffected as hundreds die in SEXY agony"?

And wait, it gets worse. These phrases don't just get lobbed in willy-nilly. No. A lot of care and attention goes into their placement. Apparently the average reader quickly scans each page in an "F-pattern": reading along the top first, then glancing halfway along the line below, before skimming their eye downward along the left-hand side. If there's nothing of interest within that golden "F" zone, he or she will quickly clear off elsewhere.

Which means your modern journalist is expected not only to shoehorn all manner of hot phraseology into their copy, but to try and position it all in precisely the right place. That's an alarming quantity of unnecessary shit to hold in your head while trying to write a piece about the unions. Sorry, SEXUAL unions. Mainly, though, it's just plain undignified: turning the journalist into the equivalent of a reality TV wannabe who turns up to the auditions in a gaudy fluorescent thong in a desperate bid to be noticed.

And for the consumer, it's just one more layer of distracting crud - the bane of the 21st century. Distracting crud comes in countless forms - from the onscreen clutter of 24-hour news stations to the winking, blinking ads on every other web page. These days, each separate square inch of everything is simultaneously vying for your attention, and the overall effect is to leave you feeling bewildered, distanced, feverish and slightly insane. Or maybe that's just me, today.

Actually, it's definitely just me. Like I say, I'm ill, my brain's not working. Which is why opening this piece with a slew of hot search terms probably wasn't a brilliant wheeze.

Perhaps if I close with a selection of the LEAST searched-for terms ever, I can redress the balance. Worth a shot. Um . . .

JOHN SELWYN GUMMER . . . PATRICK KIELTY NUDE . . . UNDERWHELMING KNITTING PATTERNS . . . FULLY CLOTHED BABES.

Yup. That should do it.

The Guardian 27 July 2008
© Guardian News and Media Ltd 2008

SEXY OBAMA BRITNEY ANGELINA TERROR

A wireless wonderland

Within two decades, our lives could be ruled by radio waves, says
Claudine Beaumont

This week, a government report provided a tantalising glimpse into the future of technology. Sadly for those who grew up reading Fifties' science-fiction comics, there wasn't a flying car, tinfoil jumpsuit or stun gun in sight.

Instead, what we can look forward to is a wireless world in which doctors can be instantly alerted when you have a heart attack or crash your car, and intelligent sat-navs can advise you whether driving to your destination is the quickest route or whether you should let the train take the strain on this occasion.

The report, from Ofcom, the communications watchdog, outlined several major areas in which new technology could enhance our healthcare system and transport network, potentially revolutionising the way we live.

And far from being a distant projection of a wireless world 50 years down the line, Ofcom predicts that many of the advances it identified could be a reality within the next decade or two - in fact, some of the technologies mentioned are already at an advanced prototype stage.

While Ofcom's role in this future-gazing might not be immediately clear, it makes complete sense. It will be wireless technology that underpins all of these future technologies, and Ofcom - as the guardian of Britain's radiowave spectrum - needs to ensure this finite resource is used wisely.

Predicting the possible ways in which wireless technology might be used enables the regulator to plan ahead and manage the spectrum to meet anticipated new demands.

However, before we all get carried away, a word of warning: Ofcom made it clear in its report that while developing some of these new technologies could prove relatively easy, actually implementing them could be a harder task - "especially where there are a number of inter-related parties or where government plays a key role".

The regulator also acknowledged that there will need to be a debate about the impact of some of the new technologies. For instance, Ofcom envisages a time in which "in-body networks" - devices inserted into patients following an operation to monitor their health and recovery, and manage their care plan - could be considered as intrusive as they are useful, and there will need to be discussion and debate about how far people are prepared to accept modern technology having an impact on their personal privacy.

So what kind of technology will be an integral part of our daily lives in the next 20 years? And how far away are we from turning comic-book fantasy into a 21st-century reality?

INTELLIGENT SHOPPING

The vision: All foods sold in the supermarket will be embedded with a chip, known as an RFID tag, which operates across a short radio frequency. These tags could be read by a scanning device, and tallied with the personal medical records of individuals. The RFID tags could contain important nutritional information and communicate with the scanning device to alert people with food allergies if they pick up an item that could cause a reaction. It also means that diet and health advice could be delivered as you shop.

The reality: Radio Frequency Identification technology (RFID) is well-established. Linking this technology with embedded data would be a fairly simple procedure, but does raise privacy issues: could warning you about your shopping habits be a "nanny state" step too far? One of the most likely future uses of RFID technology will be in our kitchens - intelligent fridges will scan the tags embedded in all food stuffs and be able to alert you when you're out of milk.

SMART DRUGS AND SOCIAL NETWORKS

The vision: People with medical conditions will receive automated reminders when it is time for them to take their tablets. And some medicines, such as asthma inhalers, will be able to wirelessly connect to a handheld device to get updates about pollution levels and atmospheric conditions that may exacerbate a condition. The inhaler will then be able to adjust the dosage. Smart medicines will even be able to help people form social networks, putting them in touch with fellow asthma sufferers and pointing them to virtual clinics.

The reality: This technology is at a very early stage, but it has the potential to save the NHS millions. The problem is, a lot of organisations need to be involved to make this technology work - everyone from the drug manufacturers to the doctors surgeries - and that's going to take time. We're unlikely to see it in action for at least a decade.

BEAT THE JAMS, AVOID PRANGS

The vision: Cars will communicate wirelessly with other vehicles to warn them when they are about to break sharply, reducing accidents. Cars will also boast intelligent sat-nav systems, wirelessly connected to a transport hub relaying real-time road and rail info,

capable of planning the fastest route by road and of informing you when it would be faster to take another mode of transport. Tickets will be automatically booked at the touch of a button, and paid for using a pre-pay card.

The reality: This kind of in-car technology is already well advanced: parking sensors alert drivers to hazards, while auto-braking on some vehicles will bring the car to an emergency stop. Combining this technology with that which powers self-driving cars is the next logical step. Sat-nav systems are already able to access real-time traffic updates; improving this to make it link into a central database would be easy enough - the difficulty comes in developing a software platform used across the whole transport network that will allow operators to share information in a consistent, usable format.

MAYDAY ALERTS AND ENHANCED MEDICAL CARE

The vision: Cars of the future will contain a "black box" style communications hub that will be able to alert the emergency services if you have a crash or pass out at the wheel. If the person involved in the crash has their medical details embedded on their person, paramedics will be able to access them and decide on the most effective course of treatment.

The reality: Crash-response technology already exists and is an extra on many high-end vehicles. Enhancing this technology to alert the emergency services in the event of any accident will be relatively straightforward. And software already allows people to store their medical records on their mobile phones. However, finding a way to securely and confidentially embed them in wearable technology will be the main challenge.

The Daily Telegraph 8 May 2008
© Telegraph Group Ltd 2008

FILLING IN A DIGITAL BLACK HOLE

Dame Lynne Brindley, Chief Executive of the British Library

Research shows that nationally we all suffer from what I call personal 'digital disorder'. Few people have their thousands of digital photographs stored so that their grandchildren will be able to look at them. It's my job to ensure that this does not extend to our national memory.

At the exact moment that President Barack Obama was inaugurated, all traces of President Bush vanished from the White House website, to be replaced by images of and speeches by his successor. Attached to the website had been a booklet entitled 100 things Americans may not know about the Bush Administration – they may never know them now. When the website changed the link was broken and the booklet became unavailable.

The 2000 Sydney Olympics was the first truly online Games with over 150 websites – but these sites disappeared overnight at the end of the Games and the only record is held by the National Library of Australia. These are just two high profile examples of a huge challenge that faces digital Britain.

There are approximately eight million .uk domain websites currently, and that number grows at a rate of 15-20% annually. The scale is enormous, and the value of these websites for future research and innovation vast. But online content is notoriously ephemeral. And if websites continue to disappear in the same way as those on President Bush and the Sydney Olympics – perhaps exacerbated by the current economic climate – the memory of the nation disappears too. Future researchers and citizens will find a black hole in the knowledge base of the 21st Century.

People often assume that commercial organisations such as Google are collecting and archiving this kind of material – in fact they are not. The task of capturing our online intellectual heritage and preserving it for the long term falls, quite rightly, to the same libraries and archives that have

> **IN THE BRITISH LIBRARY THE UK HAS AN INSTITUTION CAPABLE OF LEADERSHIP AND A TRACK RECORD OF DELIVERY TO ENSURE THAT OUR DIGITAL FUTURE CAN BE A RICH GOLDMINE AND NOT A BLACK HOLE.**

over centuries systematically collected books, periodicals, newspapers and recordings – and which remain available in perpetuity, thanks to these institutions.

Olympics fans will be pleased to know that the British Library is undertaking a collecting and archiving project for the London 2012 Games. With appropriate regulation, we aim to create a comprehensive archive of material from the UK web domain. We are also working hard with publishers, government and the other UK legal deposit libraries to make a reality of the national archive of electronic publications envisaged by the 2003 Legal Deposit Libraries Act. This extends our statutory responsibilities to collect UK printed publications to include UK digital outputs such as websites, e-journals and e-documents. We are working with international partners to tackle the difficulties of preserving this content and providing long term storage and access for researchers in 10, 50 and 100 years.

This is truly a public service, ensuring an independent and trusted bedrock for education, research and commercial innovation within a public institution with long term perspective and mission. I am fortunate to spend my

> **AT THE EXACT MOMENT THAT PRESIDENT BARACK OBAMA WAS INAUGURATED, ALL TRACES OF PRESIDENT BUSH VANISHED FROM THE WHITE HOUSE WEBSITE**

working day in one of the world's greatest libraries, a unique storehouse of 150 million items from ancient oracle bones to this morning's newspaper. Our treasures range from Magna Carta to the lyrics of the Beatles.

Digital Britain must include digitising this goldmine of content. Access to a digitised British Library ought to be the right of every citizen, every household, every child, every school and public library, universities and business. That's a vision worth delivering on. We've made a start. One of the jewels of our collection are our 17th and 18th century newspapers. This magnificent archive provides

a vivid and direct insight into two centuries of British history – including the reporting of the French Revolution, the great financial scandal of the 1720s, the South Sea Bubble, and the inauguration of George Washington.

Because of their great fragility, access to such newspapers is severely restricted, but earlier this month, a digitised and fully searchable version of the collection became available, for free, to UK Higher and Further Education institutions.

I welcome the Government's strong vision of a Digital Britain and keenly anticipate tomorrow's interim report from Lord Carter. It adds up to an agenda of fundamental importance for the UK's cultural, creative and economic future in the global digital environment of the 21st Century. But the vision of a 'Digital Britain' must include the critical public service of preserving Digital Britain's collective memory and digitising the unrivalled content within the British Library.

Anyone who watches television, films or reads novels can see how the UK is now reaping the benefit of systematic public investment in its rich heritage over centuries. David Starkey couldn't have made his forthcoming TV series on Henry VIII without the British Library's collections. Anthony Horowitz used the Library for research when writing the popular television series Foyle's War and the actor Alun Armstrong researched for the part of Albert Einstein by listening to the only sound recording of him at the British Library. Creativity does not simply emerge from nowhere.

In the British Library the UK has an institution capable of leadership and a track record of delivery to ensure that our digital future can be a rich goldmine and not a black hole. For my part I commit to championing this effort on your behalf to the very best of my ability.

Dame Lynne Brindley, Chief Executive of the British Library
With kind permission of the British Library 2009

Reading for the world: Locking up freedom – Beverley Naidoo

Literacy is at the heart of the campaign to ensure all the world's children go to school. A specially written story by Beverley Naidoo offers a remarkable picture of the power of education

Believe it or not, the library at my school was kept locked! I have no memory of going inside and choosing a book for myself. What's more, when I asked our vice-principal to sign a form so that I could join the Johannesburg city library, she refused. I can still hear her voice with her Irish lilt… "And what would you be wanting to read more books for, Beverley? Have you not got enough with your textbooks already?"

I was puzzled at the time, but later I realised that the nuns who taught me felt that it was their duty to control the books we read. In class, when we read a story, a poem, a novel or a play by Shakespeare, we were told what the author meant. Our teachers told us to write down what they said and learn it. To them, teaching included teaching us what to think. At least I was lucky to have some books at home that I would read for pleasure. I would lose myself in them and my imagination would roam.

This was all a long time ago - more than 50 years - but the idea of keeping young people away from books and controlling their ideas still angers me. You see, I was brought up in apartheid South Africa. I was a white child in a whites-only school and none of my teachers encouraged me to ask questions, let alone question the racism all around us. It's a bit like we children were little donkeys with blinkers, who had to follow instructions from teachers and adults who also wore blinkers.

I was a white child in a whites-only school and none of my teachers encouraged me to ask questions, let alone question the racism all around us

After I left school, I was very fortunate to make friends at university with people who helped me to tear away the blinkers. For the first time, I began to read books that invited me to see the world around me in new ways. I began to realise that for black South Africans the country was like a vast prison, and I began to ask the questions that I'd never asked before. What I saw, with my own eyes, was shocking, but at least I was now beginning to choose my own journey.

That led to me being locked up in jail for eight weeks in solitary confinement, with no charges. I was still a "small fish" in the resistance to apartheid, but my brother and his friends, who challenged the system, were locked up for years. Reading and discussing books was important to them, because books allowed their minds to travel outside the prison walls. Books helped them keep their minds free.

I began to realise that for black South Africans the country was like a vast prison

I started writing when I was living in exile in England and had two children. Their father and I weren't allowed to return to South Africa, where we had both been born. That made us refugees from our home country and I wanted to find a way for our children, and others, to imagine what apartheid was like. If I could tell them a gripping story, they might want to know more…

That was the beginning of Journey to Jo'burg, my first book for young people. Once it was published, it quickly travelled around the world in many different languages. I began to receive hundreds of letters from readers telling me their thoughts and asking me questions. But there were no letters from South Africa, because the apartheid rulers banned the book until the year after Nelson Mandela was released from jail. Someone could be put in prison or made to pay a fine if they were found with it.

Not having books is not always about lack of money, but about what we value. Books are "mind food". One of our most important freedoms is surely to read, imagine, think and ask our own questions about the world.

*With kind permission of Beverley Naidoo
The Guardian 27 January 2009
Originally appeared in 'Stories in support of education –
The Big Read 2009'*

For more information about 'The Big Read' go to:
http://www.campaignforeducation.org

Language

Issues to think about and discuss

There's all the difference between a silly lad and a murderous racist & The naming of hate – In a challenging article, Howard Jacobson argues that intention is more important than the words we actually use. The same word, he says can be used as an endearment or a missile. But, in Disability Now a writer feels that these words are always 'manifestations of hate' and 'an assertion of inferiority'. Using them in any context makes these attitudes seem legitimate. Who is right? How hurtful can words alone be?

Mind your language – Is it a good thing that the language takes on new words, and changes existing ones? Why do some of us want to resist some changes?

At the end of the day, English is fairly unique! – How many of the most annoying phrases do you use? Why do people find these annoying?

For the latest way to say 'I love you' simply try 459 – Is texting changing the language?

Language

Racism

Offence

Intention

hange

Language

Cliché

Texts

There's all the difference between a silly lad and a murderous racist

Howard Jacobson

Yid, Nigger, Paki, Coon, Chink, Paddy, Raghead, Kike, Sambo, Honky Faggot, Jewboy, Taffy, Bulldyke, Zionist – the list is endless. So? Put 'em together and what have you got? Bippety boppity boo.

We were not appalled when Prince Harry went to a fancy dress party as a Nazi (a good place for a Nazi uniform – on a dickhead at a piss-up), and we are not appalled by what he called his pal Ahmed Raza Khan. And had he called him "Sheeny" or "Hymie"? We would not have been appalled by that either. Not in the context. And please don't tell me contexts are no excuse. Without a context we understand nothing. A context explains an intent. And without an intent we understand nothing either. A word on its own tells you absolutely zilch. Words are innocent. Words await what the user means to do with them, and then await interpretation at the other end. They are no more malicious in themselves than alcohol is inebriated in the bottle. Only where people go about in primitive terror of gods and goblins do words have the magic properties of evil. And we are not such people, are we? We are liberated from superstition. We don't think a word is imbued with malevolence no matter who employs it, how he employs it, where he employs it, to whom he employs it, and regardless of what he hopes will be the consequence of his using it.

Phrases such as "Kill Jews", which you can find sprayed on walls in north London right now, or the latest catchy Dutch refrain "Hamas, Hamas joden aan het gas" – that's "Hamas, Hamas, Jews to the gas", if your Dutch isn't up to scratch – are toxic not by virtue of the words they contain but by virtue of the actions they propose. Haroon Siddique, writing in The Guardian believes we must call a racist a racist. "I was shocked when I heard that [Harry] had used the word 'Paki'. But what surprised me even more were the attempts to play down the nastiness of the term or to pass it off as a term of endearment."

This is a circular argument. If the term is in itself without exception "nasty", if nastiness inheres in it as surely as bacteria inhere in shit, then of course we should not allow it to be passed off as an endearment. But the position Mr Siddique is offering to counter holds that there is nothing intrinsically and unequivocally vile in the word "Paki", that it all depends on the whys and wheres, a position he himself adopts later in the same piece when he concedes, "I admit I have some very close friends who would jokingly call me 'Paki' in a certain context and I would not take umbrage, but they would say it to my face – not behind my back (as far as I know) or while I was asleep."

There it is then. Once context and personality are "admitted", as they must be, that's an end to the intrinsicality argument. If the word is vile and only vile and vile wherever and whenever it is used, then Haroon Siddique must take umbrage no matter how jokingly it is employed, and regardless of whether he wakes or sleeps. But he cites an exception identical to the

> Words are innocent. Words await what the user means to do with them, and then await interpretation at the other end

exception which those who defend Harry cite. The Harry defence is that he used the word "Paki" in the context of friendly joshing. So what's the difference? That Harry is white? That "Paki" is for internal use only? That no white – particularly no privileged white – can be a friend of someone who comes from Pakistan?

I know and understand that line of thought. Jews think the same. We are licensed, exceptionally, to call each other what we like. And without doubt there are things I have been called by Jewish friends I would not take from non-Jewish enemies. But isn't that only because I know them to be my enemies and because the words they use they use as missiles?

It happened to me once in Melbourne that a drunken non-Jewish Australian acquaintance (if that's not a tautology) climbed into my bedroom hoping to steal the woman with whom I was then living. Why he didn't just ask, I don't know. Alcohol, I suppose. In fact he found me alone in my bed. "You bloody Yid," he said. I won't pretend I wasn't frightened.

The palace is still no place to acquaint a boy with the ironic locutions of the street

Such things don't happen every night, even in Australia. "Go home, Lee," I said. He wouldn't. He sat on my bed and started stroking my nose. "You Yid," he said again, and then suddenly he bit me. On the nose. Not a savage bite, though his teeth marks remained for several weeks. But still, not an action you welcome. And yet there was something about the way he did it that reminded me of a caress. A bite is not unlike a word. It is innocent in itself. We bite in lovemaking. And this was a kind of lovemaking. "You Yid," he said again, before offering me a handkerchief to dry my nose and descending the way he'd come.

Was that a racist attack? No. Should he have done it? No. Was I offended? No. Would it have been reasonable for a third party to be offended on my behalf – a vigilante of the political decencies, say, a protector of the Jewish people, a personal-space-violation agent? No. It was between Lee and me. We brewed the dramatic context up between us. As Harry did with his friend Ahmed Raza Khan.

I would be surprised if part of that context wasn't royal ineptitude. Harry had some of the Charlie knocked out of him by his mother, but the palace is still no place to acquaint a boy with the ironic locutions of the street. And now transplant those palace anachronisms to a barracks where everyone is playing the game of being men. No man really knows how to play the man game. The conventions bemuse even the most laddish of lads, which is why they're always fighting. So Harry's attempts were bound to end in tears. But a clown is not necessarily a racist.

A girl was thrown off Big Brother a couple of years ago for using the "N" word. But it was perfectly clear her only crime was gaucherie; she was a middle-class white girl who wanted to show she had mastered street talk, an ambition (whose poet is Ali G) for which the word is sycophancy, not racism. There is a terrifying amount of truly murderous racist hatred out there. It is a matter of life and death that we learn to tell the difference.

The Independent 17 January 2009
© 2009 Independent News & Media Limited

The naming of hate

Prince Harry's open use of an overtly racist word has put the "political correctness gone mad" lobby into attack mode. One ex-soldier speaking on the radio contended that the attitudes of those of us who object to such things "ruins people's lives". What? Why? How?

Surely it's the use of racist, sexist, homophobic and disablist terms which ruins lives. They are manifestations of hate; an assertion, from one group to another of inferiority. They encapsulate the views that what people are makes them worthless. So their use in other contexts where, it's argued, they don't necessarily carry the same amount of vitriol, remains inappropriate because it legitimises and institutionalises them.

In the case of the word used by Prince Harry, the evidence is incontrovertible. "Paki bashing" was the targeting for violence by gangs of white skinheads of Asians in Britain.

Surely it's the use of racist, sexist, homophobic and disablist terms which ruins lives.

In the same way, disabled people who experience hate crime often report the use of derogatory disablist words before and during attacks – assuming they live to tell the tale, not all of them do. People who are tipped from their wheelchairs may have the action reinforced by being called "fucking cripple". Action and speech equal attitude.

"Spastic" attained more universal status as an insult because it passed into more generic usage in the playground, the workplace and the pub.

There's also the question of power and where it lies. Not just in the obvious example of a prince referring to someone of less elevated status. The use of many racist words goes back to the time of empire when words were coined in the dominant culture and used with reference to those over whom power was exercised.

Similarly, we as disabled people subject to abuse cannot simply accept it as part of life. To do so is to relinquish what little power we have.

Disability Now February 2009

Mind your language

The Guardian style guide editor on... the linguistic barbarians at the gates *David Marsh*

The excitement of the Olympics may be over for another four years but the controversy continues. I refer, of course, to the outrage provoked by the use of the verb "to medal". A sure sign, according to some, that the linguistic barbarians are not only at the gates: they have battered their way through, pulled up a chair, helped themselves to a beer and are now undermining our very way of life by rewriting our grammar books to suit their evil purpose.

I don't recall such a fuss at Athens in 2004. But Great Britain didn't win so many medals then. Perhaps the question of whether our sportsmen and women can be said to be "medalling" has only really arisen at this Olympics because of our unprecedented success.

In fact, the term has been common among athletes for years. Here is a typical quote from the official Team GB website, long before we got to Beijing: "The team includes athletes who have medalled at Olympic, World and European level, so this is an exciting proposition for the Games."

But while as a headline writer I would have loved to see "Tweddle medals" in the Guardian (sadly, Britain's top female gymnast came fourth), there's no doubt that the expression sends a shudder through many people when used by commentators speculating over when yet another of our cyclists or rowers will "medal".

As editor of the Guardian style guide I've learned that, for some readers, our worst offence is to submit to what they regard as the creeping "Americanisation" of English, which they blame on television, pop music, the computer and similar new-fangled inventions.

Language changes, however, and the diehards generally lose the battle (which is not to say it is never worth fighting). I came across a copy of the 1950 edition of the Manchester Guardian stylebook recently and among "Americanisms" that it insists should be avoided are: balding, boost, call on the telephone, teen-ager (sic), and top secret.

So is "medalling" just another example of the way our beautiful language is being dragged to hell in a transatlantic handcart?

Well, not quite. As a letter writer to this page has pointed out, the OED lists examples of using "medal" as a verb as long ago as Byron, in 1822: "He was medalled." And this is Thackeray, writing in the mid-19th century: "He went home medalled by the King." The OED gives these two quotations in support of its first definition of "medal" as a verb: "to

I've won gold for medalling with the language

decorate or honour with a medal; to confer a medal upon as a mark of distinction". Admittedly this is a transitive rather than intransitive usage, but not so far in spirit from the second definition, the one we heard so often in Beijing - but dated by the OED from 1966: "to win a medal (ie to come first, second, or third in a sporting event or competition)".

There's nothing illegal, or immoral, about using a noun as a verb, despite what one American columnist calls "anti-verbing prejudice" from some people. He goes on: "Do these dogmatic whiners really eschew verbs derived from nouns? Not a chance. You can bet that they mouth off, mentor pupils, and head committees on proper usage. They probably even phone home, fax contracts, and Google people."

Gary Glitter has more chance of a Christmas No 1 than I do of persuading Guardian readers that "to medal" is OK, but I have to say I have no problem with it. It's quite useful to have an alternative to "win a medal". One of my Guardian colleagues has gone so far as to coin the excellent "outmedal" (as in "Bank on Britain's best squad for a generation to outmedal Italians").

If you are troubled by "medalled", I have to warn you: there is worse to come. As far back as 1992, an Australian newspaper quoted an athlete who hadn't won an event all season, "but has podiumed a couple of times". This seems to be going too far and bloggers have detected an "odium against podium". However, don't bet against Team GB "podiuming" a record number of times in 2012.

The Guardian 25 August 2008
© Guardian News and Media Ltd 2008

At the end of the day, English is fairly unique!

Do you find it's a nightmare mastering the English language? Find yourself saying things 24/7 that you shouldn't of? With all due respect, it's not rocket science (neither apparently is rocket science). I personally couldn't care less, at this moment in time. Do you agree? Absolutely!

And so there, within a not very unusual headline and a couple of sentences go the top 10 most annoying phrases in the English Language. Freelance lexicographer, Jeremy Butterfield, compiled the list as part of his new book *Damp Squid (the English language laid bare)*, and yes for those highly irritated ones among you, the term is actually Damp Squib.

Nowadays squibs (small explosive device) are insulated from moisture, older uninsulated squibs needed to be kept dry in order to ignite, so a "damp squib" was literally one that failed to perform because it got wet. The phrase has since come into general use to mean anything that fails to meet expectations. But why is English such a Damp Squib? Whose expectations is it failing to meet? Well probably most of you who are reading this it seems.

[He looked at] the jargon, poor grammar and meaningless expressions which litter modern speech, and how stupidly irritating we all find it.

Butterfield sourced the book from the Oxford Corpus, a vast electronic collection of modern written and spoken English, which is used to compile the Oxford English Dictionary. It looks at the jargon, poor grammar and meaningless expressions which litter modern speech, and how stupidly irritating we all find it.

As well as clichés, tautology is another bugbear – using different words together that effectively say the same thing twice. For example, "I personally" – which I am personally very guilty of and "new innovation" – how can an innovation be anything but new? The use of "shouldn't of" instead of "shouldn't have" is another common gripe among the linguistic perfectionists.

For those short on time, phrases such as "fairly unique" are just meaningless, long-winded over-complications – something is either unique or it isn't. And while you're wasting energy uttering "at this moment in time" instead of simply "now", they have already written their letter of complaint to the language department in your brain!

While you're wasting energy uttering "at this moment in time" instead of simply "now", they have already written their letter of complaint to the language department in your brain!

But since part of the uniqueness (no half measures here) of the English language derives from its history of constant flux, how can people get so irritated by variations and changes arising in the language norms today? "It's a mix of reasons," explains Butterfield,

TOP TEN MOST ANNOYING LANGUAGE HABITS

★ 1 **At the end of the day**

★ 2 **Fairly unique**

★ 3 **I personally**

★ 4 **At this moment in time**

★ 5 **With all due respect**

★ 6 **Absolutely**

★ 7 **It's a nightmare**

★ 8 **Shouldn't of**

★ 9 **24/7**

★ 10 **It's not rocket science**

"people don't like long-windedness – 'at this moment in time'. They dislike a phrase being flogged to death, like 'at the end of the day'. But for a lot of people, the issue is change itself. Modifications to language upset them. This is odd, since we actively seek change in other areas – look at Barack Obama's victory."

But change goes on. Tautology, time wasting and over-emphasis are what we do best with the language aren't they? Absolutely – another pet hate, I only needed to say yes, and yet many of us exaggerate things with 'totally' or 'absolutely' when we needn't be having such fun. It is also not unusual to hear the word "literally" used wrongly, such as "I literally bit his head off", which you might do to the next person you hear uttering one of the top 10 most annoying phrases.

Sources: Various

For the latest way to say 'I love you' simply try 459

Stephen Adams

Text messaging and other types of technology are producing an array of new slang terms that are seeping their way into everyday language, say experts.

Numbers including 404, 35 and 11 now have meanings beyond the mathematical.

And words like book can mean something completely different.

All are being driven by our increasing reliance on technologies like mobile phones, computers and Oyster travel cards.

Lexicographer Jonathon Green, editor of the recently published Chambers Slang Dictionary, said: "What we're seeing is the influence of technology coupled with current events and, inevitably of the young, who in many cases drive language.

How to talk 'textese'

Numerous expressions related to new technology are now making their way into everyday language. They include:

RAB = A tactless and/or career-limiting move. Named after a 'Ross And Brand,' the BBC Radio 2 presenters whose careers were damaged when they made lewd on-air prank calls to the actor Andrew Sachs.

P999 = Parents alert. Literally 'Parent 999'

Code 18 = Technological dinosaur. From an IT expression used to refer to a problem that does not originate from faulty software or hardware, but from those whose brain-dead faces hover 18 inches from the screen.

GOOD job = Bad job. Generation X term for a 'Get-Out-Of-Debt' job taken solely for its monetary reward, with few career prospects. Now adopted by bankers. And everyone else.

"It's focused on this world of mobile phones - these abbreviations are perfectly suited to those little screens."

While teenagers who spearheaded the use of l8 (late) and lol (laugh out loud) and brb (be right back) are now well into their 20s, a new generation are using so-called 'textese' to communicate in the real world.

So if someone says you are 'book' do not take it as an insult. It does not mean you are a nerd - quite the opposite in fact.

It means you are 'cool' - derived from the fact that when using predictive texting on a mobile phone, this is the first suggestion that will appear on screen when one taps in the corresponding numbers, 1-6-6-5.

But if someone calls you a 404 that is definitely not a compliment - they are saying you are clueless. It comes from the '404 error' message displayed on an otherwise blank page when an internet browser cannot find a website.

More pleasantly, the numbers 143 and 459 can now be the most thrilling in the world. They might not have attracted the interest of numerologists before, but now they can both mean 'I love you'. Both are abbreviations - 143 after the number of letters in each word, and 459 because these numbers denote the first letter in each word on a mobile phone key pad.

Nowadays 35 and 11 can mean 'broke' and 'out-of-date' respectively, thanks to Oyster cards used on London's transport network.

A Code 35 is the message an Oyster user receives when their card is out of cash, while a Code 11 is displayed on a card reader at tube stations when the card is out-of-date.

So if someone says your dress is "a bit Code 11" at the Christmas party, make sure to tell them they know 404 about fashion.

Mr Green, who spends his life charting the influence of slang on language, defended people's use of the new expressions. He said: "It's just another form of the Queen's English - not better, not worse."

He added that such abbreviation was nothing new: " SWALK, for Sealed With A Loving Kiss and NORWICH, Knickers Off Ready When I Come Home, were used in the First World War.

"It has long been dictated by technology. The difference is that the technology in 1918 was a small grubby postcard, while today it's that little screen."

However, while most assume people use such short-cuts because they make communicating faster, an Australian study contradicts such thinking.

It found that while writing 'textese' is quicker, reading it back is not.

Dr Nenagh Kemp of Tasmania University found it took twice as long to read such messages back compared to standard English versions.

That suggests an important reason for using such expressions is not speed, but to be seen to be book.

The Daily Telegraph 11 December 2008
© Telegraph Group Ltd 2008

Law & order
Issues to think about and discuss

Insult after injury – Should compensation depend on how sober the victim was? Do rape victims contribute to crime if they drink too much? An article and two letters offer opposing views.

Victim of a class-war crime – In a horrific case of gang rape, boys who were "not really like that" acted like an invading army. Why did being together change them so much? What does this tell us about gang culture? Can the circumstances someone is raised in turn them into a criminal?

To whom it may concern – Blame the victim for not backing down, blame your mum, blame your dad, blame all white people .... one by one, Lennie James analyses the circumstances - or excuses - that lead people to carry knives. Is this heartfelt and powerful plea to those who carry knives likely to have any effect?

Crime: the writing's on the wall – Can litter & graffiti encourage much bigger crimes? Would a zero tolerance approach to these be the answer?

Ian Tomlinson: The man who was trying to get home – Who was to blame for Ian Tomlinson's death during protests in London? Could it have been avoided? Imagining the point of view of both the victim and the police, the writer hopes that the incident will provoke a debate about the way the police force operates.

A pensioner who uses the wrong recycling bin is fined more than a violent thug. Call that justice? – What does this say about justice in our country today?

How dare these men get sympathy – Some men kill their children and yet are still seen as loving fathers. One mother who has suffered argues for a change of attitude.

Knife crime

Gangs

Rape

Police

Law & order

Protest

Murder

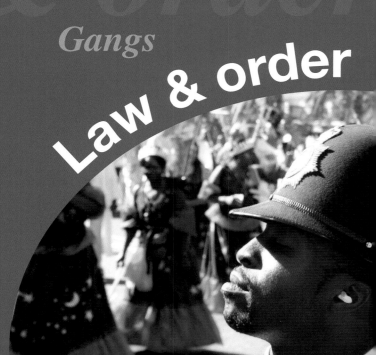

THE ISSUE THE ISSUE THE ISSUE: RAPE & ALCOHOL

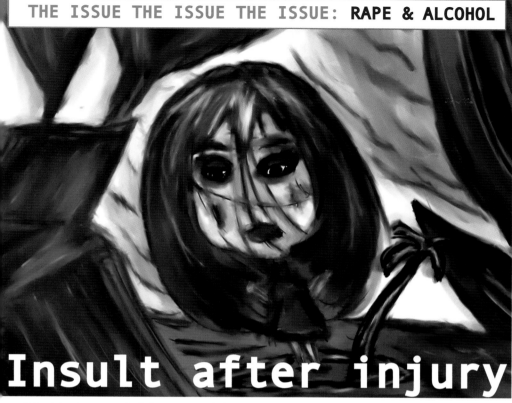

Insult after injury

"I just had no words." One rape victim tells today's Guardian of her stunned reaction to an official letter telling her that she had contributed to her own plight by drinking. The slight was eventually reversed, but it was especially painful as it came from the Criminal Injuries Compensation Authority (CICA), a body charged with supporting victims financially. But in this rape case - as in a total of 14 over the last year - a point was made of cutting the funds because the victim had been drinking.

The battle to put responsibility for rape where it belongs - squarely with the perpetrator - has been hard fought over the decades. There have been successes. For instance, there are now safeguards against trials descending into a farcical inquiry about why a victim wore a short skirt. And in connection with alcohol, the law was changed to respect the reality that if a woman was in no condition to give consent then she did not give it. But reduced payouts for intoxicated victims could be seen as turning back the clock to the days when misogynistic moralising clouded views about where responsibility for rape belongs.

The argument here is not about whether excessive alcohol consumption is a major social problem, which it indisputably is. Nor is there any need to dismiss the fact that drinking raises the risk of suffering rape, just as it increases the dangers of suffering from other violent crimes. No, the argument is that

with rape there can be no divvying up of the blame. When a fight ends in injury or death, the question of who threw the first punch can be relevant - and alcohol can make that question harder to settle. With rape, however, there is no equivalent of the first punch: notions of provocation have no place when it comes to sexual violence.

When the CICA cuts awards on grounds of drink - as in 1% of rape payouts last year - it clumsily applies broadbrush rules covering a range of crimes. Cuts may be justified when a victim's drinking precipitates certain violent attacks - but rape is not one of them. Reassuringly, the CICA says its general policy is not to cut rape payouts due to alcohol. But even if cuts are only made exceptionally, they still imply that some victims are coauthors of their misfortune.

The low conviction rate makes compensation for rape especially important. For the 17 in 18 victims who never see their attacker brought to justice, compensation offers the prospect of formal recognition through another means. That recognition should give the money more than financial value. But the rules on alcohol can leave it providing the opposite of recognition. These rules must change - or at least be applied more sensitively - so that compensation never again compounds injury with insult.

The Guardian 12 August 2008
© Guardian News and Media Ltd 2008

AGREE:

The act of rape is a disgusting one and my sympathy goes to the many victims who suffer it; victims who through no fault of their own have been violently attacked and violated. However, if a woman chooses to go out and have too many drinks then she is not necessarily the only victim if things turn ugly.

I can imagine it must be hard for people under the influence to distinguish a genuine come-on from simple flirtation. How can a person under the influence know that they have clearly given the signals that they do not want to have sex? If a woman chooses to go and have too many drinks, she too has to take the responsibility when things go wrong.

Anonymous, Middlesbrough

DISAGREE:

Under no circumstances is a woman who has been raped, ever responsible for the awful act that has been committed upon her. By altering compensation payouts according to the victim's soberness the compensation board is indicating that some rape victims are more worthy of compensation than others, which is just not so.

No matter how tipsy, or dare I say it, drunk a woman is, she never deserves rape and is never responsible if it happens. She can only ever be the victim. No matter whether the victim was drunk, wore revealing clothing, flirted and enjoyed herself, she is always entitled to say no to sex and her attacker is never entitled to rape. Ever.

Anonymous, Glasgow

Gang rape is used
by soldiers as a
bonding exercise.
And that's why
rootless teenagers
nearer home do it –
Joan Smith

Victim of a class-war crime

In April last year, while a 14-year-old girl was being subjected to a series of unbelievably brutal rapes in a stairwell on an estate in east London, she recognised one of her assailants. The boy had been to a party at her house and she appealed to him for help. "I can't, because I am with my boys now," Cleon Brown told her. "I can't help you." Then he joined in the attack.

It was one of the more harrowing moments described by the girl in a lengthy interview on Friday's Today programme. Another was her recollection that a woman with two children saw her being dragged to another location, where more teenage boys were waiting to assault her. The woman asked the girl if she was all right, yet did nothing to help her.

The interview was breathtaking. So was the fact that the rapes were planned for the most trivial of reasons: the gang's 15-year-old leader O'Neil Denton, who used the name Hitman, wanted revenge because the girl had slighted him.

These events happened not in war-torn Sudan, but on a housing estate in Hackney; and last week seven teenage boys were convicted

of rape and false imprisonment. The eldest of her attackers, Weiled Ibrahim, is only 17. Two other boys did not take part in the rapes, which took place over three locations, but were found guilty of preventing her escape.

> Her attackers were "not really like that"; they behaved differently, she said, once they got together in a gang

In one of the most poignant sections of the interview, the girl still seemed to be in a state of disbelief, suggesting that her attackers were "not really like that"; they behaved differently, she said, once they got together in a gang.

The problem of young males egging each other on to commit grotesque acts of violence is well

known, although it doesn't in any way reduce the horror of what these particular boys have done. The vicious and sustained assault on the girl – she was also orally raped – has striking similarities with those committed by soldiers in wartime.

One of the most notorious examples has only recently come to light. At the end of the Second World War, the victorious Red Army rampaged across Prussia, gang-raping German women. Many of the victims were too traumatised to speak about what happened, and the extent of the sexual violence only emerged years later in Antony Beevor's book Berlin: The Downfall, 1945.

In the book, Beevor revealed how Russian soldiers dehumanised German women and girls, ignored social norms, took pleasure in humiliating their victims and used rape as a bonding mechanism. So did the Hackney rapists; thus it was more important for Cleon Brown (now 15) to keep the "respect" of his mates than to behave with courage and humanity.

Knife crime has attracted intense coverage in the past year, but there

is anecdotal evidence that the true extent of gang rape is hidden because victims are too frightened to report it. The Metropolitan Police say that around one in 15 of all rapes in London involves three or more assailants, but the Hackney attackers boasted that they had assaulted other girls and got away with it. Indeed, it seems that for boys who live on run-down inner-city estates, it's a matter of luck whether they come to our attention as victims or perpetrators, which offers a clue as to why they are attracted to gangs in the first place.

In the Hackney case, the girl's attackers were certainly no strangers to violence: Cleon Brown's father was shot dead resisting a robbery in Jamaica five years ago, and a boy aged 15, who can't be named for legal reasons, saw his brother fall to his death from a flat as they tried to escape a masked gang armed with knives. The rival gang was pursuing the 15-year-old and Jayden Ryan, 16, another of the youths convicted of the Hackney gang rape.

Arguments rage over the causes of rape, but it is clear that some cultures have much higher rates of sexual violence than others. The Red Army soldiers who took part in horrific gang rapes returned home and reverted to "normal" behaviour once they were removed from a theatre where social taboos had

broken down. The families of some of the Hackney rapists, by contrast, are still making excuses for their sons and blaming the victim. "Cleon tried to help her and this is how she repays him," Cleon Brown's mother angrily told a newspaper.

> The Red Army soldiers who took part in horrific gang rapes returned home and reverted to "normal" behaviour once they were removed from a theatre where social taboos had broken down

No matter how great the revulsion caused by this case – and it is hard to imagine a more sickening ordeal than the one they put their victim through – it is important to understand that there are

circumstances in which teenage boys become habituated to violence. Absent fathers, low expectations and an acceptance of violent crime all play a part; these boys expect to be on the receiving end of it and they expect to inflict it on others, usually someone who is weaker than them. Girls, for obvious reasons, are often the victims of choice. In that sense, there is a danger that focusing on knife crime in deprived areas misses an important point, which is the role of gang rape in boosting insecure male identities.

In her Today interview, the Hackney rape victim came across as articulate and courageous, despite her youth and her dreadful ordeal. And that is why she is struggling, as are the rest of us, to understand just how a single harmless remark could unleash such a storm of sexual violence against her.

The Independent on Sunday
14 December 2008
© 2008 Independent News
& Media Limited

From left to right: O'Neill Denton, Weiled Ibrahim, Yusuf Raymond, Jack Bartle, Jayden Ryan, Alexander Vanderpuije, Cleon Brown

To whom it may concern...

...I want to talk to you about the knife you're carrying

My name is Lennie James. I am a 42-year-old father of three. I grew up in south-west London. I was brought up by a single mother. I was orphaned at 10, lived in a kids' home until I was 15 and was then fostered. I tell you this not to claim any special knowledge of how you've grown, but to explain how I have, and from where I draw my understanding.

I want to talk to you about the knife you're carrying in your belt or pocket or shoe. The one you got from your mum's kitchen or ordered online or robbed out of the camping shop. The knife you tell yourself you carry for protection, because you never know who else has got one.

I want to talk to you about what that knife will do for you. If you carry it, the chances are you will be called on to use it. It is a deadly weapon, so if you use it the chances are you will kill with it. So after you've killed with it, after you've seen how little force it takes for sharpened steel to puncture flesh. After your mates

have run away from the boy you've left bleeding. When you're looking for somewhere to dash the blade, and lighter fluid to burn your clothes. When your blood is burning in your veins and your heart is beating out of your chest to where you want to puke or cry, but can't coz you're toughing it out for your boyz. When you are bang smack in the middle of 'Did you see that!' and 'Oh, Jesus Christ!'

Here's who to blame...

Blame the boy you just left for dead.
Blame him for not believing you when you told him you were a bigger man than him. Blame him for not backing down when you made your chest broad, bounced into him and told him about your knife and how you would use it. Blame him for calling you on and making you prove yourself. Tell yourself if he had just freed up his phone or not cut his eyes at you like he did, he wouldn't be choking on his blood and crying for his mum.

Then blame your mum.
When the police are banging down her door looking for you, or she hears the whispers behind the 'wall of silence', tell her it's all her fault for being worthless. Cuss her out for having kids when she was nothing but a kid herself, or for picking some drug or some man over you again and again. Even if she only had you and devoted herself to you, even if she is a great mum, blame her anyway. Blame her for not being around more to make sure you took the chances she was out working her fingers to the bone to give you.

Christian Adams, Daily Telegraph, 14 July 2008 © Telegraph Group Ltd 2008

When you're done with her, blame the man she picked to make you with.

Blame him for being less than half the man he should have been. When he comes to bail you out and starts running you down for the terrible thing you've done, tell him straight: 'I did what I did coz you didn't do what you should have done.' Even if he did right; respected your mother, worked to provide for his family financially and spiritually, taught you right from wrong and drummed it home everyday... Even if he nurtured you as best he could, blame him for the generation of men he comes from.

The one that allowed an adolescent definition of manhood to become so dominant. The one that measures a man by how many babymothers he has wrangling his offspring, or by how 'bad' his reputation is on the streets of whatever couple of square miles he chooses to call his 'ends'.

Damn them for letting you believe that respect is to be found with gun in hand or knife in pocket. Damn them and everyone who feeds the myth of these gangsters, villains, thieves and hustlers. Anyone who makes them heroes while damning hard-working, educated, honest men as weak, sell-outs or pussies.

If you are black, blame white people

for the history of indignities they heaped on you and yours. For the humiliation of having to go cap-in-hand or get down on bended knee or having to burn shit down before you are afforded something so basically fundamental as equality. If you are white, blame black folk and Muslims for taking all your excuses. Failing that, blame a class system that keeps you poor and ignorant so the 'uppers' and 'middles' can feel better about themselves.

You have good reason to blame them all.

I wouldn't be you growing up now for love nor money. Your generation has so little room to manoeuvre. We had more space to step around the bullshit. We weren't excluded at the rate you lot are. Teachers hadn't given up or lost their authority over us. They still tried to protect and guide us even through our most disruptive years.

The police stopped and searched us, but we fought that right out of their hands - we hoped into extinction. But they want to bring back that abusive practice. They are still hooked on punishment rather than prevention. They seem ignorant to the fact that they are feeding you acceptance of an already prevalent gang mentality. As far as you can see, the police are not protecting and serving you, they are coming at you like just another street gang trying to boss your postcode.

When I was where you are now, generations of state agencies, social services, policy-makers and politicians had not abdicated all responsibility for me. We weren't left to our own devices like you have been. Is it any wonder that you end up expressing yourself in such a violently pathetic way?

We should be ashamed. I am. You have shamed us into a desperate need to do something about ourselves. We have collectively failed you and we should take all the blame that is ours for that... but so should you.

I blame you. I blame you because as a generation you are selfish, self-centred and have little or no empathy for anyone but yourselves. You are politically stunted and socially irresponsible and... you scare us. What scares us most is that you would rather die than learn. Your only salvation may be that still most of you aren't playing it out dirty. The vast majority of young men, even with all that is stacked against them, are finding their way around the crap. The boy you will kill, should you continue to carry that knife, almost certainly had the same collective failures testing him. He probably felt no less abandoned and no less scared. He also, almost certainly, wasn't carrying a knife.

Whatever it seems like, whatever you've read, whatever you tell yourself about protection being your reason, statistics show the life you take will be that of an unarmed person. That is what that knife will do for you. It will make you escalate a situation to where it is needed. It will give you a misguided sense of confidence. It will make you the aggressor. That knife will make you use it. It will bring you nothing worth having. There is no respect there. The street may give you some passing recognition, but any name you think you might make will soon be forgotten.

Your victim will be remembered long after you. Name me one of the boys who killed Stephen Lawrence. Once you've bloodied that knife you may as well be dead because you'll be buried for 10 to 20 years. Banged up for that long, only a fool would look back and think it was worth it. You'll be nothing more than a sad, unwanted, unnecessary statistic.

If you were mine, this is what I would tell you. I would make myself a big enough man to beg. I'd get down on bended knees if I had to. I would beg you to take that knife out of your pocket and leave it at home. I would tell you that I know you are scared and lost and that I know the risks involved in what I'm asking you to do. I know that what we could step around, you have to walk through, and that there is always some fool who isn't going to make it any other way but the wrong way. I'm just begging you not to be that fool.

Be a better man than that. Let the story they tell of you be that you exceeded expectations... that you didn't drown. Don't spend your days looking to be a 'bad-man' - try to be a good one. Our biggest failure is that our actions have left you not knowing how precious you are. We have left you unaware of your worth to us. You are precious to us. Give yourself the chance to grow enough to understand why.

Be safe.
Lennie James

The Observer 8 June 2008
© Guardian News and Media Ltd 2008

What scares us most is that you would rather die than learn.

Crime: the Writing's on the Wall

THE PRESENCE OF GRAFFITI, LITTER OR OTHER SIGNS OF INAPPROPRIATE BEHAVIOUR IS A BREEDING GROUND FOR MORE SERIOUS TYPES OF CRIME, ACCORDING TO A REPORT FROM A TEAM OF DUTCH ACADEMICS

The report, The Spreading of Disorder, argued that signs of disorder and petty criminal behaviour cause criminality to spread under what they explain to be an extension of the 'broken windows' theory.

OBSERVING THAT OTHERS HAVE ACTED INAPPROPRIATELY WEAKENS AN INDIVIDUAL'S DESIRE TO ACT APPROPRIATELY

The original theory argued that petty criminality is copied, but the new report claims that petty criminality leads to more serious criminal acts being committed.

During six experiments conducted in the Netherlands in December 2009, the report found that when people saw 'that others violated a certain social norm, they are more likely to violate other norms or rules, which causes disorder to spread.'

The report stated: The probability that a participant litters in a littered setting is enhanced when a lot of litter is present or when the participant watches someone littering.

It added anti-graffiti signs in areas already blighted by graffiti were much less effective than a sign in a non-graffitied area, a phenomenon known as the Cialdini effect whereby people reason: If a lot of people are going to do this it is probably a wise thing to do.

Observing that others have acted inappropriately weakens an individual's desire to act appropriately, strengthening their hedonistic desires and making them more likely to commit crime, the report added.

In one experiment carried out by researchers, the presence of graffiti more than doubled the amount of people that littered (69% of 77 observed members of the public).

Another experiment found that the number of people willing to trespass on private property more than trebled when other crimes had been committed (82% of 49 people).

There is a clear message for policymakers and police officers: Early disorder diagnosis and intervention are of vital importance when fighting the spread of disorder. Signs of inappropriate behaviour like graffiti or broken windows lead to other inappropriate behaviour.

The study said criminal damage can trigger more crime

To read the full report, go to **http://www.rug.nl/staff/ k.e.keizer/research**

Police Review 16 January 2009
http://www.policereview.com

Ian Tomlinson: The man who was trying to get home

Trust in the police was plunging before the death of Ian Tomlinson and the resignation of Met Assistant Commissioner Bob Quick. **David Randall** asks why

You are a police officer on riot duty in the City of London for the G20 protests. It's nearly 7.30 in the evening, and you've been on the go, tense, and with adrenaline pumping, since the briefing at 4.30am. Boy, that was something – they really wound you up – made it sound as if Armageddon could kick off in Threadneedle Street at any moment. And this bloody uniform and helmet are hot, and even though the overtime's good, you just want to go home.

But you can't. Not until the last of these bloody protesters leave. Oh God, here comes one now. Strolling along in his Millwall top, hands in his pockets. Why won't he just get behind the lines? He's taking the piss. Go on, you go, get out of it! And you give him a shove. Silly bugger goes over like he's made of paper. Stays there, gets up, then goes over again. Stretcher, ambulance, gone. And then you hear he's died. Heart attack. Jesus! How were you to know he wasn't protesting, but just an old boozer on his way home. Of all the luck ...

Or maybe on that day you were a father of four with a bit of a drink problem. Which is why you don't live at home but in a hostel up Lindsey Road. It's warm, it's OK, and it's cheap. And it's where you go after you've had a long day on your feet selling Evening Standards outside Monument Tube station. And the hostel's where you want to go now, but you can't, because every route you try to take there are bloody coppers poncing about in their riot gear, acting like hoodies with night sticks, and telling you to get over there or piss off.

And everywhere protesters. You don't know, and don't really care, what they're protesting about, but it's all getting right up your nose because it's your city and you don't see why you can't walk the Queen's streets like you normally do. Then wallop! Over you go. Christ, you feel awful. Some copper's clattered you. Someone helps you up. You go on a bit, then, suddenly, nothing. And the next thing everyone knows, you're a headline. A case. A cause. A dear old dad who's been battered by the coppers and dies.

Somewhere, between these two extremes, the truth about the death of Ian Tomlinson lies. But finding its precise whereabouts won't be easy. Sure, there is film; there are witnesses; and there is a police force which, with its swift suspension of the officer who gave that shove, shows that some lessons have been learnt from the cases of Blair Peach, felled by a police radio at an Anti-Nazi League demonstration in 1979, and Jean Charles de Menezes, shot by a police squad which thought he was a terrorist.

But there is also instant myth-making and finger-wagging punditry that has formed its views at the pace of a rolling news channel rather than that of a coroner's court. And, most of all, there is the widespread idea that we have self-serving police forces whose word cannot be relied upon, whose competence is often questionable, and whose senior officers are rewarded out of all scale with their performance.

It is a view no one does more to promote than the police themselves, last week's example being Assistant Commissioner Bob Quick. Not only did he think "Top Secret" meant "display document on top so people could see how important you are", but he then departed with a pension worth, at the age of 49, £110,000 a year. No doubt directorships await.

So what, before the straight facts are completely hijacked, do we know of Ian Tomlinson and the events of Wednesday 1 April? Mr Tomlinson was 47, a Derbyshire native who moved to London in his teens, became a roofer, and who once lived on the Isle of Dogs with his wife, Julia, their four children, plus five of hers. More than 13 years ago, his drink problem caused him to leave home and live rough for a while, before starting work as a news vendor in the City and moving into a hostel near Smithfield. His friends called him "Tommo". His addiction to drink remained unconquered.

Mr Tomlinson spent most of the day of protests selling newspapers by Monument Tube, and the first evidence of his encounters with police are photographs taken a few hundred yards away in Lombard Street just after 6pm. He is seen standing in the middle of the street, apparently obstructing a police van, being moved away by officers, and, possibly, being pushed. Witness Ross Hardy said Mr Tomlinson had been drinking.

This evidence refutes earlier reports that Mr Tomlinson had not left his newspaper pitch until 7pm. Fully 80 minutes

Photo: Jeff Moore/Jeff Moore/Empics Entertainment

after his Lombard Street brush with the law, he is just a few hundred yards away, off Cornhill. Here, according to several witnesses, he is assaulted by police, allegedly hit with a baton. Then, less than 10 minutes later, as he walks down Royal Exchange Passage just in front of a line of riot police, he is shown, in pictures and video shot by an American, being roughly shoved from behind by one officer. Other footage broadcast by Channel 4 shows Mr Tomlinson being aggressively hit on the legs by an officer with a baton.

He fell awkwardly, cried out at police, "What the fuck are you doing?", was helped up by a protester, got to his feet, but went only a little further before collapsing again. With his face a deathly pale colour, and it being obvious he is in urgent need of attention, a protester rings for an ambulance. Reports vary about the degree of

assistance from police, but Mr Tomlinson was stretchered from the immediate vicinity. He died shortly afterwards.

The officer who gave the push, a member of the Met's Territorial Support Group, reportedly passed out from shock at home when he learned of Mr Tomlinson's death. The rest of the aftermath is now mainly a matter of public record, especially the police statements that showed, once again, the Met's capacity for self-harm.

There was the crude deceit that a hail of missiles from protesters prevented police leaping to Mr Tomlinson's immediate assistance; and the ones that followed, which reminded one of a recidivist being interviewed under caution who deadpans all questions "until my brief's here". Just as some approximation to the full story had to be dragged from the Met with the shooting of Jean

Charles de Menezes, and still remains to be discovered with the shooting of barrister Mark Saunders in Chelsea.

And then there is much that we do not know. How long had the officer concerned been on duty? What was his level of riot training? What was Mr Tomlinson's medical history? Were any words exchanged between the officers and Mr Tomlinson prior to the shove? How many incidents of unduly aggressive policing took place that day but remain unknown because their recipients did not suffer a coronary? Was Mr Tomlinson really drunk, or was his shuffling gait a symptom of a man in the early stages of a heart attack? Was this the once-in-a-blue-moon, accidental consequence of the bolshie behaviour shown by either side when police and demonstrators clash?

Seeking the answers to these questions will now be the Independent Police

Complaints Commission (IPCC), the Crown Prosecution Service and the coroner. The context in which they will do so raises an issue more intractable than even the precise causes of Ian Tomlinson's death. It is that, over the past decade or so, the relationship between public and police has been badly, and unprecedentedly, corroded.

Some of this is the fault of those with warrant cards, especially the Met. Here, seen at its worst in the de Menezes saga, a sort of old lags' culture obtains: you admit nothing until your dabs are proved in court to have been all over the offence in question (and then fail to act on the findings). Here, too, is a management that seems to spend much of its time suing each other, or threatening to do so, and then collecting large sums; where senior officers have pension arrangements that would not disgrace a banker; and where there is a look-after-your own attitude that is positively Masonic at times.

Nor are we free of blame, with our ever more publicly aggressive citizenry proclaiming their rights, and our expectation that a force, by definition, of conservative, tradition-respecting officers should constantly adapt to an ever-changing multicultural, multi-faith, multi-sexualised society.

And some of the greatest fault is that of the political class: forces obliged to use speed cameras as revenue-raisers rather than for road safety; and police stations battered by a permanent hailstorm of targets and new laws, both set centrally to placate the latest orthodoxy or catch a headline.

All that, plus continuously shifting priorities that never seem to include sending officers to deal with the crimes that most damage the quality

of life in Middle England, such as household burglary, vandalism and noise. The result? A police force less trusted, more resented than at any time since the 19th century. You could see it in the near glee with which Assistant Commissioner Quick was attacked for displaying secret documents to a press camera, and you could feel it in the relish applied to the reporting of the G20 death.

There seems something very rotten in the dislocation between British society and its police. If the death of Ian Tomlinson serves to prompt a debate about that, then he will have performed a far greater service than some of the officers tasked with wielding not only batons, but also speed cameras, targets and asinine laws on our alleged behalf.

12 April 2009
© 2009 Independent News and Media Limited

G20 stands for the group of 20 Finance Ministers and Central Bank Governors from important industrialised and developing economies. They meet regularly to discuss global economic stability. On April 1st 2009 they met in London.

Thousands of protesters gathered to demonstrate against a range of issues such as the financial system and climate change. They were also angry about the banking crisis and that those responsible seemed not to have had to face any penalties. The majority of protesters were peaceful, but some smashed bank windows and threw items at police.

The police used the tactic of 'kettling' – confining the protestors in small areas and not allowing anyone to leave, often for many hours. At 7pm senior police officers gave the order to use "reasonable force" to clear the streets.

For excellent photojournalism on the protest go to:
http://www.boston.com/bigpicture/2009/04/protests_at_the_g20_summit.html

Timeline

1 April 7.20pm Ian Tomlinson is struck and pushed by a police officer. He collapses and dies later. The case is referred to the Independent Police Complaints Commission (IPCC).

3 April A postmortem finds Mr Tomlinson died of a heart attack. City of London Police investigate.

5 April The IPCC criticises The Guardian for upsetting Mr Tomlinson's family by printing photographs and witness statements suggesting he was assaulted by police. Other journalists are told there is "nothing in the story."

6 April The IPCC confirms Mr Tomlinson "had contact" with the police.

7 April Video footage passed to The Guardian shows Mr Tomlinson being hit with a baton and being shoved in the back by a riot policeman.

8 April The IPCC reverses its decision to allow City police to investigate. It will launch a full criminal inquiry.

9 April The Met suspends the officer shown in the video, but 48 hours later he is still to be interviewed by the IPCC.

11 April The first post mortem on Ian Tomlinson said he died from a heart attack. A second one gave the cause of death as internal bleeding. Results of a third post mortem are awaited.

Background information:

In April 1979, Blair Peach, a special needs teacher, died from serious head injuries sustained during a demonstration against the National Front. According to witnesses he had been hit by police with truncheons. Although six officers were named in an internal report no one was charged.

In July 2005, Jean Charles de Menezes was shot dead by armed police who mistook him for a terrorist. No officer faced disciplinary charges over the shooting and even one who had tampered with evidence was found to have done nothing wrong.

In May 2008, Mark Saunders fired shots from his home. After a five hour stand-off he was shot nine times by police. His family questioned the use of such extreme force and his sister is suing the Metropolitan Police.

In April 2009, Assistant Commissioner Bob Quick was forced to resign after press photos showed him with secret documents carelessly displayed on the top of papers he was carrying to a meeting.

A pensioner who uses the wrong recycling bin is fined more than a violent thug. Call that justice?

Marcel Berlins

It all started when I idly noticed that a sign on the back of a London bus warned motorists that the fine for driving in a bus lane was £120.

Coincidentally, contrary to my usual dismissive practice, I'd been reading a few of those ubiquitous newspaper stories about householders who'd been fined by their enthusiastic local councils for leaving their dustbins 2cm too near the kerb, or putting a piece of paper into the wrong recycling aperture. For some reason, most of the penalties imposed for those grievous offences were around £100 or £110. In a further coincidence, I needed to know more about the on-the-spot fines that the police are increasingly handing out to perpetrators of what are described as "low-level" crimes. But these allegedly petty offences, it's become clear, can include acts of violence against the person, albeit not the gravest kind. The usual fines for such assaults is £80. Driving while talking on a mobile phone comes even more cheaply, at £60, even though such conduct is a proven cause of accidents, sometimes fatal. I know. A student of mine was killed when she lost control of her car because she was on the phone. Is there anyone who believes that interfering in a small way with the free flow of public transport (though you get fined even if there are no buses in sight) is more heinous than beating someone up? Or that failing to be a perfect recycler of household rubbish is worthy of greater punishment than irresponsible driving which puts lives at risk?

My point is this. People may be understandably shocked by the amount of the fine for driving in a London bus lane. I certainly am. But that shock turns to anger when they start making comparisons, when they read of a drunken thug getting away with an irrelevant fine while a forgetful pensioner who put out her bin on the wrong day is stung for her week's pension. That's what I call offensive disproportion.

In my utopian world of fairness and justice, there would be a Minister for the Abolition of Offensive Disproportion, whose sole job it would be to look at the kind of cases I've been describing (there are many more) and to pronounce upon them: "This cannot be right. Assault is worse than incorrect dustbinning. That's the moral truth. Either raise the penalty for one or lower it for the other. But don't leave it as it is; that's not what our society's about." Of course there can never be such a guardian of sense and moral proportion. But is there nothing that can be done in real life, to take one example, to stem rampant local authorities from treating absent-minded householders who make binning mistakes as ever more profitable milch-cows?

The examples of offensive disproportion I've given above have come from the lower end of the financial scale, though none the less infuriating for that. And they don't have to involve penalties for wrongdoing. The same sense of unfairness can be felt when we're talking huge sums at the other extreme. It has generally been estimated that the Iraq war has so far cost Britain around £6-£7bn. But last year the government was willing to gamble with - which often means losing - more than £50bn of taxpayers' money. For what? To ensure that an irresponsible bank called Northern Rock did not go bust. That disparity shocked me. I'm not saying we should be spending more on Iraq. But I found it astonishing and disturbing that the government thought it perfectly in order to stake seven or eight times the amount spent on a five-year long foreign war just to keep one incompetent financial institution (not even one of the country's largest) alive. Was there no one sensible or courageous enough to tell Alistair Darling or whoever: "This is wildly disproportionate and wrong. It will not do"?

The Guardian 3 September 2008
© Guardian News & Media Ltd 2008

In June 2008, there was widespread shock as yet another father murdered his children in an apparent act of revenge against his estranged wife. In what appears to be a chilling and growing trend, Brian Philcox, 53, gassed himself, Amy, seven, and Owen, three, to death, leaving their mother, Lyn, devastated. Here, Sarah Heatley, 44, a nurse, whose GP husband killed himself after strangling their children, Jack, three, and Nina, four, 14 years ago, reveals her anger at how such men are often portrayed as victims, too

As told to: Lorna Martin

'When I heard about the Philcox family last week, I felt an enormous sense of sadness for the mother, Lyn. But more than that, I felt physically sick with anger. I'm furious that there are people out there who try to make excuses for Brian Philcox, and men like him. Lyn Philcox has been deprived of the most precious things in her life because of her own husband's hatred and desperation for control. That anyone could consider condoning their actions because their wives have challenged their access to their children seems incredible.

'Reports revealed that Philcox had been in touch with Fathers 4 Justice twice in recent months for advice, and there have been stories linking his actions to the breakdown of his marriage. Friends have spoken about him "snapping" over fears that his wife would find a new man, while some commentators have been quick to reinforce his image as "a loving father". It seems that despite all the shock and horror, there is an element of sympathy for a man who supposedly loved his children so much that he couldn't bear not to be with them.

'How dare these men get sympathy'

Photo posed by model

'But how can we keep justifying the actions of men whose sole purpose in life is the control and manipulation of their families? We must stop looking for excuses and "explanations" for violence against women and children. In many cases, men like Philcox had a history of violence against their wife and children already. I have spent a lot of time researching and speaking to experts about what makes men kill their children. As well as a history of domestic violence, there is usually an image of domestic bliss portrayed to the outside world, despite the horror going on behind closed doors. In my own case, I was scared of my husband and finally left for my own sake, and that of my children. But the horrible irony in these cases is that it is exactly when a woman finally finds the courage to leave a violent, controlling and possessive husband that she and her children are at the greatest risk. In the Philcox case, the couple had separated, and there were allegations of violence, when the tragedy occurred. Brian Philcox spent Father's Day with his children, then drove to a beauty spot, turned on the engine and coldly took their lives. That is not love. It is evil. These men are not victims of the custody system who deserve our sympathy, they are violent aggressors committing abhorrent child abuse.

'With every high-profile killing by a father, people ask me if it brings back the ordeal of losing my beloved children Nina and Jack. In truth, the pain has never left me and not a day goes by when I don't relive losing them again and again. Even after 14 years, there are still moments when I find myself shaking my head

'It seems that despite all the shock and horror, there is an element of sympathy for a man who supposedly loved his children so much that he couldn't bear not to be with them.'

in utter disbelief that my husband, a man I once loved so deeply, the father of my children, could do something like that.

'I was just getting ready to pop out to the shop when I heard what had happened to my children Nina, four, and Jack, three, on Sunday 6 February 1994. They were spending the day with their father – who I had left six months previously – and were due home later that afternoon, when the police knocked at the door. Just one sentence from the ashen-faced officer on my doorstep changed my life forever. "Your husband has killed your children," he said, tearing my heart in two. I remember only snapshots of the next few hours – the tears, hysteria, confusion and gut-wrenching guilt.

'All these years on, the emotions are too raw to put into words. But that afternoon, in a haze, I went to look at their little bodies in the mortuary and howled with pain. Their faces were still stained with my lipstick that they had been playing with just hours earlier at home. Their father had strangled them both with a pyjama cord, wrapped their bodies in duvets and placed them in the cellar. He then walked two miles to a block of flats and jumped to his death. Taking the most precious thing from me was his way of making me suffer for the rest of my life, and in this sense he has achieved his aim.

'When people read stories like mine and that of the Philcox family in the paper on their way to work, I think what they sometimes don't really grasp is that these little children are gone forever. The story is in the news for a day or two and then it is forgotten. But for me, it's a life sentence and every single day I am left to cope with the consequences. My children will never grow up. They have been deprived of the chance of life.

'If I see a little dark-haired three-year-old boy or a four-year-old girl I am often stopped in my tracks. It brings tears to my eyes. I dream about them – about trying to save them and about not being there to protect them. Every time I read these stories every emotion comes flooding back. Yes, I have gone on to meet another partner and have another baby and my new child has given me the joy and strength to start rebuilding my life. But when a stranger says, "Are you quite happy with just one child then?" I have to make the snap decision about whether to tell them what happened to my other little babies. I want to scream: "No, I'm not quite happy with one. I should have three."

'Today, I allow myself to daydream about Jack and Nina. Jack would have been a big lad. He would be 6ft tall. I fantasise about what they would be doing right now – whether they'd be working or at university. I think about them taking their mum to the pub every now and

What drives a father to kill?

'Children are more likely to be killed by their parents than a stranger – and in the majority of cases of children past infancy, by their father,' says Professor David Browne, who specialises in forensic and child psychology at the University of Liverpool. 'We call these men "family annihilators". To the outsider, he may appear to be a devoted father, but he is probably violent within the home – and sees violence as a way of control. Family annihilators do not tend to be psychotic (hearing voices in their head, for example) but they are more likely to be suffering from a personality disorder or mental illness brought on by a prolonged period of depression or anxiety. When he suffers a loss that he can't reverse – whether the breakdown of a relationship, financial difficulty or losing his job (as in the case of Brian Philcox) – he feels a profound sense of helplessness. Often the family courts will grant him only limited access to his children, or, if proven he is violent, he will have no access until he proves he has changed. His sense of powerlessness then escalates until he sees killing his children and himself as the only way of regaining control.'

again. I watch my niece and nephews getting older – who are the same ages as Jack and Nina – and it is utterly heartbreaking. Every family birthday, christening and wedding reminds me so much of what I haven't got.

'As a society we are letting our women and children down every time a case like this happens. Figures show that children are at a much greater danger in their own homes than on our streets, and it's time society woke up and addressed the fact that there are violent men out there. To try and stop more tragedies, we need to help women who

'My children will never grow up. It's a life sentence'

manage to escape violent relationships and there need to be support networks in place for both parties when a woman leaves a violent partner. I do believe that if my former husband had received support to help him cope with the loss of his self-worth, the loss of control over his marriage, and his own possessive and controlling behaviour, then this terrible event could have been prevented.

'Of course, I agree with equal rights for both fathers and mothers and, in an ideal world, both parents in a divorce should have equal access to their kids. But we don't live in that ideal, perfect world. It is a different breed who goes to the extreme lengths of killing their children. Men who have a history of domestic violence should not have unsupervised access to their children. Nothing can bring back my beautiful babies or those of Lyn Philcox. But, unless the system changes, more women like us will face the same agony and life sentence of suffering.'

Grazia Magazine June 2008

Religion
Issues to think about and discuss

I wanted to tell the inside story of Islam – Does this personal account help you understand why someone might join – and leave – an extremist organisation?

Religious beliefs can be tolerated at best – What happens when someone's sincere religious belief means they are opposed to someone else's civil rights? And when a change of job description brings those two areas into conflict, which should give way? A Christian registrar who refused to conduct same sex marriages was confronted with a choice between her faith and her job.

Graham Holter was agnostic, now he's atheist. His children, however, have quite different ideas... – "I didn't expect the religious lobby to get its claws into Happy Birthday to You" says this shocked dad, after it is revealed how much religious "indoctrination" his children are getting at school. Who should decide what children are taught? Does it matter if people in the same family have different religious beliefs?

Don't get creative with facts when it comes to evolution & **Religion in schools – Creating problems** – Two articles, which pose the question: can creationism sit alongside science? Should it be taught in schools?

Brown is the new black – and white – Multicultural, multifaith families are increasingly the norm, but will this 'browning' lead to opposition from both black and white?

Religion

Multiculturalism

Christianity

Islam

Religion

Science

Creationism

Tolerance

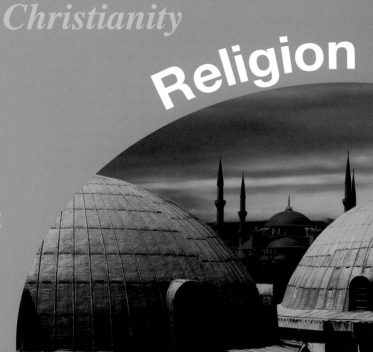

I wanted to tell the inside story of Islam

Ed Husain, 33, is the author of the controversial book The Islamist, an account of how he embraced extremist Islamism when he was 16. He is married to Faye and they have a one-year-old daughter, Camilla. Interview by **Ann McFerran**.

Me and my family always knew where we belonged — England. England was home. My father had come here from what was British India in his thirties and ran a small Indian takeaway in east London, in Limehouse. He liked to wear three-piece suits and was proud to be a subject of the Crown. We were a Muslim family, but my mother took us to see Santa Claus every year. My

We were a Muslim family, but my mother took us to see Santa Claus every year.

upbringing was warm, inclusive, genuinely multicultural and multi-faith. My primary school, a three- or four-minute walk from our house, felt like an extension of our home. My parents would help the head teacher and staff prepare for exhibitions or trips to places like the New Forest. Good days.

I got on really well at primary school. I used to write stories which were printed, laminated and distributed to the class as storybooks. Towards the end of my time there the headmistress said she felt I shouldn't go to Stepney Green secondary. But my father thought that going

I yearned for what I'd had in my primary school days — a mixed school with real expectations of its pupils and a strong sense of multiculturalism.

to this all-male, predominantly Muslim school was perfectly healthy. I was confused.

I did go to Stepney Green. Not only was it all-male and all-Muslim, but it was 90%

Bangladeshi. These kids were part of the new immigrant intake, whereas I was born and raised here. I, and people like me, ended up as unofficial English teachers. And then I did begin to feel like an outsider. I yearned for what I'd had in my primary school days — a mixed school with real expectations of its pupils and a strong sense of multiculturalism.

> **Islamism and Islamists, with their radical world agenda, seemed to make sense. After all, I was bookish, and they seemed bookish too.**

At Stepney Green all that went by the wayside. The headmaster was strict; the sports teachers would shout all the time. Most of the kids left at 16 to work in Indian restaurants, market stalls or garment factories. If I'm honest, being at this school totally destroyed me.

Worse was to come. I was horribly bullied because I wore glasses. To most of the kids, who were from Bangladeshi villages, glasses were worn by old people or people who'd lost their sight. The concept of someone my age having an eye test didn't exist. I was called "Glass Man", and after martial-arts

sessions I was kicked and bullied. But who would I tell? I didn't belong with the guys in my class. I didn't even belong to a gang.

Often guys played truant after assembly. They'd go to Oxford Street and steal things. The teachers just shrugged. Lessons weren't much better. I remember one science class run by a supply teacher which was mayhem. There was water everywhere, the Bunsen burners were on, chairs were thrown around. The teacher just stood back — he was getting his £25 an hour. "This is meant to be school," I thought. But I didn't say: "Don't do this, guys." One day — I was 15 — I was waiting for my father after school and he was late. A guy who'd left school for the day returned covered in blood — he'd just walked into the wrong area. That could so easily have been me. I wanted a cause. I was desperate for life to have meaning.

Islamism and Islamists, with their radical world agenda, seemed to make sense. After all, I was bookish, and they seemed bookish too. I'd met an Islamist born and raised here. He wore a Palestinian

> **Most of the kids left at 16 to work in Indian restaurants, market stalls or garment factories. If I'm honest, being at this school totally destroyed me.**

scarf and went to the local mosque. He gave me book after book to read — books I couldn't show my father. Islamism offered me not only an identity but rebellion. I joined the extremist group Hizb ut-Tahrir. Eventually, in 2005, I went to Saudi Arabia. I yearned to be close to Mecca and Medina. But during my time there I saw how Islamism was becoming the most dangerous force, wreaking havoc throughout the world.

I visited the Prophet's mosque in Medina just after dawn prayers, when there's a very spiritual feeling in the air.

A group of Shia were praying, chanting beautiful poetry in praise of the Prophet. But to the Saudi guards the Shia were dissenters, and they chased them away.

I thought: "I came here to be closer to the Prophet, but I'm witnessing extreme intolerance." I said to the guards in Arabic: "Why are you doing this?" The main guard said: "Do you know who they are?" I said: "They're Muslims." He just said: "They're Shia." I was bullied at school for being different. Now these Muslims were being bullied for being different Muslims. The incident led me to vow to fight those who had hijacked my faith. So I wrote The Islamist, to tell of what was going on from within the Muslim community, to right my own wrongs.

Not long after it was published, my daughter was born. We called her Camilla, an English and an Arabic name. I'd hate her to grow up in a world where guys judge her as a woman by Islamist scripture and see her as subhuman. Muslim men must stop their sisters and daughters being treated as subhuman.

Today work can be frustrating. There are parts of London and some mosques I wouldn't go to. There are entire blogs denouncing me. But someone has to speak out. Camilla is Arabic for completion. Being with her brings me such warmth, so for me Camilla really has to do with completion.

The Sunday Times Magazine 10 August 2008

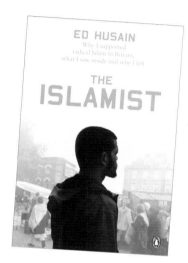

The Islamist by Ed Husain is now available

Photos courtesy of Caroline Davidson – Literary Agent

I thought: "I came here to be closer to the Prophet, but I'm witnessing extreme intolerance."

Religious beliefs can be tolerated at best

Sam Leith

How tolerant should we be of intolerance? This question is at the centre of the tricky case of Lillian Ladele

Miss Ladele is a registrar who - after being threatened with the sack by Islington council for refusing on religious grounds to preside over civil ceremonies for homosexuals - is now in line for a large payout on the grounds of religious discrimination.

It is easy to feel sorry for Miss Ladele. She finds herself in the position of a devout apprentice at a halal butchers which, under new management, starts up a thriving sideline in pork charcuterie. She signed up, in good faith, for a job that involved marrying men to women.

Rather than throw her toys from the pram when her job description changed, she attempted to come to an accommodation. For 15 months, she swapped shifts with colleagues to avoid presiding over civil partnerships for gay couples.

It sounds to me as if Islington council could have been more delicate in its dealings with her, and perhaps have found a compromise. I am well prepared to believe that Miss Ladele's life was not much fun as she was presented with a choice between her faith and her job.

But Islington received formal complaints about her refusals.

And regardless of her personal convictions, the job of a registrar does now involve presiding over civil ceremonies for gay couples.

So you can well see why the council, which needs to make the best use of the tax money contributed by residents of all sexual and religious stripes, was exasperated by having a registrar on full pay who refused to do part of her job.

Miss Ladele is not simply in the position of a private citizen who, since 1950, has had a sign in the window of her boarding house saying "No Dogs, No Blacks, No Irish", and then falls foul of liberal legislation. She is,

Bigotry is bigotry, whether or not it hides behind the skirts of the Almighty

as a registrar, a representative of the British state.

In 1967, that state took the decision that it was no longer any of its business what two adult men or two adult women do with their private parts in the privacy of their own home. In the past couple of years, and not before time, it took the decision that devoted homosexual couples were entitled to the same legal status that married heterosexuals enjoy.

There is a problem there, of course. In some ways, the introduction of civil partnerships for gay couples - since their tax breaks and privileges are extended exclusively to couples in a sexual or at least romantic relationship - can be argued to be

retrograde: it makes what we do with our private parts, once again, the business of the state.

But that is no more than a debating point. Nobody sensible wants or expects the institution of marriage to be disestablished - and as long as it exists and is recognised by the town hall, and as long as gay people pay the same taxes as the rest of us, there is no case for making it the exclusive preserve of heterosexuals.

And, it's worth remembering, the change in the law to establish civil partnerships did not presume on the prerogatives of religion. If your faith forbids you to see man and man joined in matrimony, you're under no obligation to marry them in your church.

But, equally, your church has no right to presume on secular rights and privileges extended to those two men by the commonwealth in which you have an equal share. This is a case of rendering unto God what is God's, and unto Islington council what is Islington council's.

That is why I am uneasy about the tribunal's complaint that Islington council "took no notice of the rights of Miss Ladele by virtue of her orthodox Christian beliefs".

The suggestion seems to be that rights in law are conferred on her

This is a case of rendering unto God what is God's, and unto Islington council what is Islington council's.

"by virtue" of her Christianity - that a special protection should be extended to her prejudice because it is superstitious in character.

That's rubbish, and pernicious rubbish. Bigotry is bigotry, whether or not it hides behind the skirts of the Almighty.

If I decide that I won't have black people in my house because I think they smell, that is no more or less admirable - and deserves no more or less protection in civil law - than refusing to register a homosexual union because I think God disapproves.

This nonsense lies behind the cant notion that religious belief should be "respected". It should not. It should be tolerated. You're entitled to believe whatever you damn well like about the disposition of the universe.

But you should not expect a pat on the head because the conclusion you reach is religious in character. This exact understanding of the term "respect" is what gives us the political party of that name - and the respect it extends to illiberal clerics under the flag of anti-imperialism.

So, as much as your sympathy goes out to Miss Ladele, it is worth bearing in mind that there are some much uglier and nastier people - with similar feelings about the relationship between church and state - who will look on the finding of this tribunal with a smile.

The Daily Telegraph July 2008
© Telegraph Group Ltd 2008

Lilian Ladele told the council she could not reconcile her faith with the union of homosexuals

You're entitled to believe whatever you damn well like about the disposition of the universe. But you should not expect a pat on the head because the conclusion you reach is religious in character.

It is worth bearing in mind that there are some much uglier and nastier people - with similar feelings about the relationship between church and state - who will look on the finding of this tribunal with a smile.

Graham Holter was agnostic, now he's an atheist. His children, however, have quite different ideas. Linus, four, has embraced the Lord and his brother, Max, may be going the same way

In common with all the other parents in our social circle, I had no idea there was a second verse to Happy Birthday to You. At the point of the song when kids from the 1970s would traditionally extinguish the candles with a mixture of hot breath and spittle, my six-year-old son was only halfway through his intonation.

"We're glad God made you," he chimed. "We're glad God made you. We're so glad God made you... we're glad God made you."

"Where does that come from?" asked Max's baffled parents (us).

He shrugged. "It's what we sing at school."

As a non-believer (I recently upgraded from "agnostic" to "atheist" after turning the final page of Richard Dawkins' The God Delusion), I am developing a deep unease about the guiding voices Max, and now his younger brother, Linus, have started hearing. I'm not naive enough to expect them to get through primary school without encountering Noah, the baby Jesus and a plague or two of locusts. But I didn't expect the religious lobby to get its claws into Happy Birthday to You.

I could, of course, make a stand. I could issue the school with an opt-out lyric sheet just for my sons: "We're so glad you evolved from hominids" is scientifically sound but hard for Year 1 kids to sing or to comprehend. But perhaps I should relax - after all, what's so dangerous about my children being assured that they're treasured creations of a benevolent super-being?

The point is, parents have virtually no say about the religious messages their children receive. It's almost impossible to run a non-faith state school without providing "daily collective worship". The education system in this country subscribes to the principle that, while it doesn't necessarily matter which set of supernatural beliefs your child is indoctrinated with, it's important that they're taught to believe something.

This creates some bizarre situations at home. For example, I've invested a lot of effort in explaining to my kids why I hate guns and why I refuse to buy toy weapons. "Shooting someone is a terrible thing," I explain. "Killing someone is horrible. Imagine one of us dying because we were shot by a gun."

"Well, you would just get up again afterwards."

"I'm afraid not. When you're dead, you're dead. You can't get up again."

"Jesus did."

Ah yes ... Him. The uninvited guest.

Dawkins argues that there is no such thing as a Christian, Muslim or Hindu child, merely children with Christian, Muslim or Hindu parents. It's one of the few aspects of his book I dispute: what about kids with religious teachers? Linus, aged four, has recently announced that he is a committed Christian, is happy to embrace the Lord, and is absolutely confident that his body was lovingly crafted by an omnipotent creator. It's been quite a month for the little fellow. This milestone has been reached within weeks of finally learning which way the tail goes on the lower-case letter Y, managing to swim almost a whole width of the local pool, and deciding, for reasons he can't quite articulate, that he no longer enjoys hummus.

I may find his beliefs bizarre and objectionable - I mean, what's to dislike about hummus? - but I don't feel it's my job as a parent to impose my credo on anyone. Mine certainly didn't on me. I was one of the few children in my peer group not to be christened - partly as a result of my

"I'm afraid not. When you're dead, you're dead. You can't get up again."

"Jesus did."

Ah yes... Him.

mother's Roman Catholic baptism and my father's supposed but highly questionable loyalty to the Anglicans. I don't recall my dad ever uttering a word on the subject of religion; my mum was occasionally uncomfortable at her children's casual use of the phrase "oh God", but would have been even more so at the thought of dragging us to church of a Sunday.

I grew up with the vague sensation that God was in some way responsible for what was going on in the world. I guess I saw him as the slightly bored chairman of a committee whose members numbered Father Christmas, the Tooth Fairy, Mother Nature and the Angel Gabriel.

Like every kid before and since, if I could have, I would have asked God the inevitable question: if you exist, how come you let so many bad things happen? The traditional response offered by parents and the clergy is that "well, he moves in mysterious ways - we can't expect to understand". Frankly, I despair of anyone who's prepared to respond to such an intelligent question with such an unsatisfactory and unthinking answer.

I'm getting prepared for all manner of Bible-generated questions as my kids get older. If the animals went in two by two on the Ark, what did the anteaters survive on? Is the Holy Ghost like the ones in Scooby Doo (in my view, yes)? Does God use a deluxe version of Google Earth to keep an eye on everyone and if so, can we get a similar edition at PC World?

If the animals went in two by two on the Ark, what did the anteaters survive on? Is the Holy Ghost like the ones on Scooby Doo (in my view, yes)?

I have no objection to my children learning about the planet's multi-faceted religions, but what gives my local primary school - excellent in every other respect - the right to assume that my son has signed trainee papers for the Church of England? Especially when there is every likelihood that the teachers spouting claptrap about snakes in the Garden of Eden are just as unbelieving as I am. Things must get particularly tricky when the syllabus requires those same staff members to deal with fossil records or the voyage of the Beagle.

Yes, I can request that my children are excluded from religious education. But why should they be forced to feel different, when a recent survey by the religious charity Tearfund showed that 47% of the population

does not consider itself Christian?

The strange thing is that most parents we know share our lack of religious belief and our incredulity at the sudden holy spoutings of our offspring. (Admittedly, a few have suddenly "found" Catholicism because the church school five miles away is housed in an actual building, not just a swarm of prefabs like their local junior.) But we don't march on the headmaster's office with placards or threaten to burn teachers who don't share our moral code. We sit back and tolerate a situation in which Jesus feeding 5,000 people with

If Bible stories are presented simply as inspirational parables, as defenders of the system might attest, I'm afraid the metaphors are largely wasted on the CBeebies generation.

a loaf of bread and a couple of fish is presented as immutable fact, along with two plus two equalling four and water flowing downhill. If Bible stories are presented simply as inspirational parables, as defenders of the system might attest, I'm afraid the metaphors are largely wasted on the CBeebies generation.

The Campaign for Secular Education provides reassurance that we're not alone in our concerns. "We believe that morals are rooted in our human experience and that to teach opinion

1 CORINTHIANS 13:13

as fact to children is an abuse of their trust, and their rights," its website declares. "Instruction in religion should be the province of parents and their religions, in homes and churches if they insist on indoctrinating their children in their particular faith. It should be not be the business of the state education system to do other than educate, or to condone indoctrination."

I wasn't planning to get metaphysical on my kids at the tender age of four and six, but I have been forced into a series of "little chats" purely to counter some of what they have been lapping up at school. Playing on their love of all things scientific, I encourage them to search for proof of what people teach them. Look - by holding up the fingers on our hands, we can see for a fact that two and two makes four. We can observe geese flying south for the winter, we can kick a ball into the air and watch gravity force it down again, we can use momentum to balance on two wheels and then throw our stabilisers into a skip. All of it is wonderful in its own way, but none of it is magic.

I wouldn't want my sons' secular fervour to go too far - my aim is for them to respect other people's beliefs, and to give serious thought to their own. The idea is not for them to hate religion, but to question it. Society has moved on and we have new religious issues to contend with. The demands of the national curriculum. Suicide bombers. And, of all things, a second verse to Happy Birthday to You.

The Guardian 8 March 2008
© Guardian News and Media Ltd 2008

Graham Holter

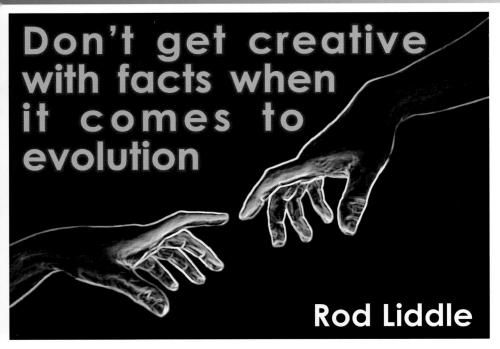

Don't get creative with facts when it comes to evolution

Rod Liddle

It's been a damned good week for God, all things considered. Not only have those scientists been trying to find His very own particle in a large bicycle inner tube near Geneva, but the traditional view of Him forming the Earth in a week, resting only to take out a cable subscription to Setanta on the last day, has received a sort of official endorsement from the most unlikely of places – the Royal Society. Normally when you mention God to scientists they blush and start surreptitiously sniggering. Not any more. At last, He has tenure.

The biologist Michael Reiss, from the Institute of Education, has told the Royal Society that creationism should not be written off by scientists as a fantastically stupid notion, at odds with everything we know about the Earth and the universe, but allowed in the classroom as an "alternative world view". Reiss is worried that some 10% of pupils might be put off science at an early age if they are told that creationism is a belief system which can be adhered to only if you have a vat of tomato soup between the ears or very thick parents, or both. Instead, he argued, it should coexist alongside the accepted scientific discoveries – Darwinism, natural selection and so on.

Creationists believe that the world was conjured into existence in 4004BC, something which would come as a grave shock to the Sumerians, for example. They – the creationists, not the Sumerians – think that dinosaurs roamed the Earth at the same time as mankind; there was no big bang, no amoeba turning into fish, then turning into apes, then turning into Jade Goody. Instead it's Adam and Eve; snake, apple, quick shag, bob's your uncle. They believe this because a book

These two things – creationism and science – cannot coexist in the schoolroom. Education should still be about the imparting of knowledge and the expunging of crass ignorance, even if it is crass ignorance which has been around for quite a while

they like – way too much – has told them it is true. Insofar as we can be certain of anything, it is very much not true; indeed, it is a ludicrous suggestion, believable only by the blank-minded and terminally credulous.

Michael Reiss, who is – not coincidentally – an ordained Church of England minister, thinks creationism is rubbish as well, so far as I can gather. Two years ago he argued against the consideration of creationism in school science classes but he has since changed his mind. Perhaps he has received a Visitation, or something. Or his bishop has been on the phone. Who knows?

These two things – creationism and science – cannot coexist in the schoolroom. Education should still be about the imparting of knowledge and the expunging of crass ignorance, even if it is crass ignorance which has been around for quite a while. The world is not precisely how we might want it to be – reality sometimes intervenes. If a child balked at the suggestion of his maths teacher that five plus five equals 10 and argued, instead, that it was 342, because his parents thought that to be the case and therefore it was, for him, an article of faith, he would not be entertained in his delusion. He would be told that he was wrong and that his parents were idiots.

Reiss will have caused some consternation with his address, some of it mitigated by the fact that his chosen discipline is biology. For the physicist, biology is virtually a branch of the arts, a half-science at best.

However, some people have found succour in Reiss's consensual, if not Panglossian, approach. Science, they argue, should not be too dogmatic, and they refer slightingly to Richard Dawkins's silly and dangerous suggestion that parents who bring their kids up with a Christian or Muslim doctrine are "child abusers". We could all do without such certainty and arrogance. Well yes, indeed.

But equally, it is iniquitous to shoehorn science into the present zeitgeist where things can be exactly what you want them to be, and that one view is as correct as any other. Where teachers explain natural selection to their classroom and add, as a horrible 21st-century postscript, "Unless you think otherwise, in which case that's okay."

The Sunday Times 14 September 2008

Religion in schools – Creating problems

The education director of the Royal Society has called for creationism to be discussed in school science lessons. But many scientists vehemently disagree writes Jonathan Leake, Science Editor

CHALLENGE TO DARWIN

Call to debate creation myths alongside science

The director of education at the Royal Society, the UK's most venerable scientific body, last week suggested that creationism – the view that life and the universe were created by God rather than natural evolution – could be discussed in school science lessons. Professor Michael Reiss, who is also a Church of England clergyman, was not arguing that creationist views as set out in the Bible or Koran are correct. However, he said science teachers should acknowledge that they form a view of the world held by about 10% of students – and be ready to discuss it. Reiss told a scientific conference last week: "Just because something lacks scientific support doesn't seem to me a sufficient reason to omit it from a science lesson." [The Royal Society claimed his comments had damaged its reputation and Professor Reiss resigned on 16 September 2008.]

EVOLVING CREATIONISM

Traditional views turn to intelligent design

In its original form, creationism suggested the universe and living things were made by God, with the Bible saying it was done in six days. This was later taken further by "Young Earth" Christian fundamentalists who believed the universe was created by God a few thousand years ago – making the Darwinian theory of natural evolution over millions of years a heresy. Some creationists have now reformulated their beliefs as "intelligent design", asserting that the evolution of the universe is so complex it can have been caused only by God. Creationism is gaining ground in the US. Sarah Palin, the Republican vice-presidential candidate, has spoken out in support of the subject being debated in schools.

SPREADING TO THE UK

More schools adopt controversial stance

Creationism and intelligent design are now creeping into British schools' curricula. Research earlier this year suggested that at least 40 schools in the UK included creationism on their syllabus. This has developed partly because of the government's programme for new city academies, under which independent organisations, including churches, can run schools and determine their curricula. The Emmanuel Schools Foundation, sponsored by Peter Vardy, a businessman and evangelical Christian, was one of the first to introduce intelligent design into science lessons. The government has said that creationism and intelligent design are not supported by scientific evidence and should not be taught as part of the national science curriculum.

DEEPENING DIVISIONS

Scientific community is split on the issue

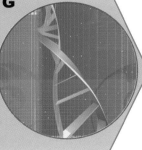

Senior scientists reacted strongly against Reiss's suggestion. Professor Lewis Wolpert, of University College London, said: "Creationism is based on faith and has nothing to do with science, and it should not be taught in science classes." However, Reverend Tim Hastie-Smith, new chairman of an organisation representing 250 leading independent schools, said creationism should at least be discussed. His school teaches it as a hypothesis some people believe in, but not a fact. The divisions and confusion run deep in the scientific community. Reiss's views hint at tensions within the Royal Society. Last year the society wrote a letter saying that creationism had no place in schools.

The Sunday Times 14 September 2008

Brown is the new black – and white

The number of mixed-race children is increasing rapidly in the UK, and clear-cut racial groups could disappear. America has led the way, its status as a 'brown nation' confirmed by Obama's election. But will it mean new confidence or conflict caused by fundamentalism? **Richard Rodriguez**

Despite deadly hatred in the world – despite religious wars and tribal massacres and weapons that even a teenager can detonate to destroy a city like London – we are embarked on a great erotic age, an age of such extravagant love-making and unlikely marriages that old notions of race are being threatened. Threatened, too, is religious distinction.

According to a report by Lucinda Platt at Essex University, one in 10 children currently in the United Kingdom belongs to a mixed-race family. Most dramatically, half of all men who are of Caribbean ancestry have sexual partners outside their race. This leads Ms Platt to suppose that we may already be seeing the disappearance of certain racial minorities in the UK. By the same logic, we may be seeing the disappearance of "whiteness" in the British Isles.

Racial mix

In the United States, in the age of Barack Obama – our first brown president – there is new public attention being given to racial intermarriage. When Barack Obama was born in 1961, 16 states in America had laws prohibiting miscegenation. On the day of his inauguration, The New York Times published an admiring article on the new president's lushly complicated family. Along with his African relatives, there was also in attendance the president's half-sister, Maya, along with her husband, a Chinese Canadian.

Although he is the child of miscegenation, President Obama was in some ways the most racially conservative member of his family. Born and raised in Hawaii,

he spent much of his adult life trying to recover his "blackness" by working as an activist and academic in south Chicago. By contrast, a generation earlier, his mother and father – she from white Kansas, he from black Kenya – married and transcended their own racial identities. Before their divorce, they had settled in Hawaii. After their divorce, Barack Obama's mother moved on to Jakarta and married an Indonesian. The couple gave birth to Maya.

> Obama's sister is Buddhist. His African relatives are Muslim (his middle name is Hussein – something his detractors used against him during his presidential campaign to suggest a sinister Middle Eastern connection). There is also a rabbi in his extended family

One hears young people in the United States who are part-Asian and part something else refer to themselves as hapa. Once Hawaiian slang and derogatory, hapa has become a boast. I do not know whether Maya Obama uses the term to describe herself, but to many young Americans she is a hapa.

Religious mix

While The New York Times stressed the racial variety of the Obama family, it only slightly referred to what I find is the family's more interesting religious variety.

At Christmas, before my mother's 'grace before meals', my uncle's sister would chant a Hindu hymn over the turkey

Obama's sister is Buddhist. His African relatives are Muslim (his middle name is Hussein – something his detractors used against him during the presidential campaign to suggest a sinister Middle Eastern connection). There is also a rabbi in his extended family.

More than a generation ago, I grew up, the son of Mexican immigrants, in an Irish-Catholic parish in California. I remember from those years the warnings in catechism class against "mixed marriages". The term had nothing to do with black-white marriage; the term was meant to alert us to the dangers of marrying a non-Catholic. Most of my schoolmates probably imagined the dangerous romantic suitor as a Methodist or a Baptist. But in my own Catholic family, my Mexican aunt Lola had married a Hindu from Bombay with the magical name of Krishna. At Christmas, before my mother's "grace before meals", my uncle's sister would chant a Hindu hymn over the turkey.

Nowadays, of course, many other Catholics are, like my aunt before them, marrying across oceans. Which is why I routinely end up at weddings where a Protestant minister will co-officiate with a priest. Or a Buddhist monk appears, or a Mohican medicine man or a rabbi is in attendance, official or otherwise.

If in the UK there is speculation that the Afro-Caribbean may be disappearing as a result of intermarriage, there is concern in American Judaism that religious intermarriage (Jewish marriage to Christians) may lead to the disappearance of Jews.

But assimilation is a mutual process. In their meeting, both parties are changed, though never equally or evenly. So, while it is easier to notice that the Caribbean lover is disappearing in England and the Jew is disappearing in the embrace of Christian America, it may also be true that the Jewishness of Christians will increase from intermarriage, just as whiteness is being "Caribbeanised" in the UK.

Age of mixture

This is my optimism in our new age of mixture – not loss but some growth from connection with the stranger. My pessimism is that our browning – the end of black and white distinctions – may lead to a resurgence of black and white fundamentalism of various sorts, racial and theological among them. In the United States, there is growing expectation that the national census of 2020 will be the last federal census that will ask Americans to indicate our racial or ethnic identity. By that time, many of us will have two or three or four racial identities.

Curiously, two very different groups of Americans are alarmed at this brown prospect. On the one hand, racist skinheads are angered by the possible end of whiteness. But besides white separatists, the people in America who seem most troubled by the mixed future are the administrators of major non-white civil rights organisations who depend, for example, on a stable notion of "black" to define their mission.

My expectation is that, even as middle-aged Americans happily line up at clinics to pay several hundred dollars to have their DNA scrutinised and their complicated racial histories revealed, and as young people take

> This is my optimism in our new age of mixture – not loss but some growth from connection with the stranger. My pessimism is that our browning – the end of black and white distinctions – may lead to a resurgence of black and white fundamentalism

pleasure in multiple identities, we may see the end of racial distinction and the rebirth of new categories of separation, like gender and age and class.

What about religion?

But what about religion? I live in San Francisco, not far from an Episcopal church where a Jewish friend of mine attends the daily yoga class in the church social hall every afternoon. The question for religion in families like the Obamas is how they will live – with what sense of difference or lack of difference will Muslim and Hindu and Jewish relatives show up for Christmas dinner?

I do not expect much guidance from the Vatican, which has managed lately to offend Jews and Muslims alike, about how we should conduct ourselves within our own families of so many colours and faiths. But as a Catholic, I recall the Spanish Church in the Americas and the syncretism that enabled Catholicism to thrive in Mexico in the sixteenth century. There is no more modern image in Catholicism that forecasts our brown future than the image of the Virgin of Guadalupe – the image of Mary, as she appeared to a Mexican Indian in 1531, dressed as an Aztec princess and speaking Nahuatl, the language of the Aztecs.

Richard Rodriguez is the author of *Brown: the last discovery of America*, published in the UK by Penguin.

The Tablet January 2009
http://www.the tablet.co.uk

Sport & leisure

Issues to think about and discuss

I fear the Wii folk are playing a dangerous game – Can the electronic version be better than playing the real sport? Why might people be missing out on real life if they play too much Wii? Shouldn't children be climbing trees?

Young talent discover gruel world – Meagre rations and strict discipline – is this the best way to develop athletes? At this camp for young Olympic hopefuls, determination is being put to the test.

Rugby in the 'hood – What does rugby have to offer potential gang members in Los Angeles? Perhaps it holds out the hope of a way off the streets?

Can freerunning stay free? – Does it matter if freerunning becomes commercialised? Doesn't that conflict with the essence of what the sport is? Once commercial interests are involved, will it still be urban and cool?

Sport & leisure

Freerunning

Olympics

Rugby

Discipline

Nintendo Wii

I fear the Wii folk are playing a dangerous game

Nigel Farndale

'Don't see what all the fuss is about," I said. "Mmm?" my colleague said, without looking up.

"These Nintendo Wii games consoles. Says here, one in four homes now have them. I don't see what all the fuss is about."

"Mm."

"Apart from anything else they rob people of their dignity. It's those movements the players have to make. They are so, well, undignified."

My colleague agreed that people do look odd when waving their remote handsets around. Indeed, when he saw his brother-in-law trying to play baseball with one over Christmas he thought he was having a seizure.

But he disagreed with the general thrust of my argument, that the Wii is the work of the devil. After all, he said, it's a harmless activity the whole family can enjoy together.

I'm not so sure. Just because the embarrassment is collective doesn't make it any less embarrassing. And a child could be scarred for life by the sight of his father attempting a back swing with a plastic golf club that is 18 inches long. Also, have you seen the gormless trance that Wii players go into? Spectators too.

But my main problem with the Wii is that it bears so little relation to the real experience. That jerky little flick you have to do is not a proper backhand, it's a bad habit stored for when you next pick up a real racquet. Assuming, that is, that the Wii generation will one day be inspired to pick up a racquet. Why would they want to when the virtual version of tennis requires little effort, less skill and doesn't involve the inconvenience of leaving the house and breathing fresh air?

I know, I know. It's only a game and it's probably better than watching television. But one activity is always at the expense of another. My heart sinks when my sons come back from friends' houses and say they played on the Wii all afternoon. What happened to climbing trees and building dens? What, for that matter, happened to playing actual tennis or picking up a real guitar? What will they have to look back on? A virtual childhood.

This was when my colleague punched below the belt. You're showing your age, he said. Perhaps I am. Perhaps I'm turning into Roger Scruton.

His first child was born the same year as mine, 1998. I remember he declared that, like John Stuart Mill, his son would be learning Greek and Latin by the age of six. He wouldn't enjoy his childhood much, he added. But he wanted people to find his son not only interesting but also well-mannered and likeable and this was the price that had to be paid.

As things turned out, four years later Scruton admitted that what his son was most interested in was playing with cement. But even that, I think, makes him more interesting, and less scary, than a Wii child whose eyes are glazed and whose wrist muscles are in permanent spasm.

The Sunday Telegraph 17 January 2009
© Telegraph Group Ltd 2009

Young talent discover a gruel world

Ashling O'Connor

Boiled cabbage and rice for breakfast may have been stretching the point, but at boot camp for wannabe Olympians and Paralympians, nothing is sugar-coated. Presumably, once you have won three Olympic gold medals like Chris Hoy, you are allowed to start your day with a bowl of Bran Flakes.

For the 80 British teenagers handpicked from six sports — canoeing, cycling, hockey, rowing, sailing and wheelchair basketball — the meagre rations are part of a process to discover whether they have what it takes to become the best in the world. After four days at the annual National Talent Orientation Camp at Loughborough University, organised by the Youth Sport Trust, many will arrive at an unpalatable truth: despite talent, they just don't want that medal badly enough if it means years of pain, disappointment and sacrifice.

"The greatest athletes are not necessarily the ones with the greatest innate talent, but the ones with the greatest desire," said Sue Campbell, who chairs the trust and UK Sport, the Government's funding agency for Olympic athletes. "The sexy bit is standing on the podium, waving from the top of a bus and winning BBC Sports Personality of the Year. The unsexy bit is the blood, sweat and tears."

The camp, funded by the Department for Children, Schools and Families, poses the difficult questions that young athletes may not have asked: what is my dream? What will I give up to achieve it? Can I perform when it counts? What if I fail?

As most of the participants have finished or are approaching their GCSEs, it is not unreasonable to think that they have not mapped out their careers. "I don't think many people know what they want to be doing in ten years," Patrick Galbraith, 15, an endurance cyclist from Edinburgh, said. "I prefer thinking season to season. After that, it's a blank patch."

However, he insists that he does know he wants to be an Olympian. By virtue of being at the camp at all, British Cycling officials think that he has the talent. The rest is up to him.

Nine out of ten participants are more positive in training after the camp and 94 per cent are hungrier for success

Jason Gardener, part of the men's 4 x 100 metres relay team that won gold in the Athens Olympics in 2004, is one of seven athlete tutors sharing their highs and lows. "I wish I had something like this when I was young," he said. "I was just stumbling in the dark. These kids stand ahead of the rest but they need to know what the Hoys have gone through. If you turn on the TV and see people winning all the time, you think it's easy. Nothing is easy in this world and this kind of life is not for everyone. Better to recognise that now than on the start line, realising you are not as good as you thought you were."

All sports are packed with cautionary tales of the most talented individuals falling by the wayside because they did not want to do the hard yards. This would not be a boot camp without the 6am wake-up call for circuit training and night-time army command tasks but the most important aspects relate to mental attitude.

'Well, the gruel certainly yielded results!'

There is the "reaching the summit" analogy from Jake Meyer, who, at 21, became the youngest Briton to climb Everest, and tips on how to "train your chimp" by Steve Peters, British Cycling's elite team psychiatrist who helped Victoria Pendleton.

Their determination is measured by how long they can hold a litre bottle of water with straight arms at 90 degrees — a canoeist proved the most dogged, ignoring the pain for more than 12 minutes to break the camp record and impressing Ian Wynne, who won a bronze medal in the 1,500 metres flatwater canoe in Athens.

The camp organisers hope to prepare potential Olympians for the slog ahead while helping them to keep other education and career options open. "These are the ones with the extra spark pushing for the Olympic development squad but do they really understand what it takes?" Simon Wergan, the youth racing manager for British Sailing, asked. "They have to make that choice. The last thing we want is an athlete investing the years between 16 and 25 and then finding out they wished they had done something else."

They probably do not yet know whether they have the stomach for it. An easier life beckons for some but the hungry ones would eat gruel every day for an Olympic medal. Pain? Please, sir, can I have some more?

Generation building

- 14- to 18-year-olds are selected from six sports not part of the UK School Games

- There are seven athletes' tutors: Jason Gardener (athletics), Miriam Batten (rowing), James McCallum (cycling), Clare Strange (wheelchair basketball), John Bleby (hockey), Ian Wynne (canoeing), Joe Glanfield (sailing)

- There are four themes: talent and ability; attitude and ambition; knowledge and understanding; education and lifestyle support

- Nine out of ten participants are more positive in training after the camp and 94 per cent are hungrier for success

The Times 12 January 2009

Rugby in the 'hood

Picture courtesy of Nick Stern, http://www.nickstern.com/nickstern.com.html

In some of the toughest neighbourhoods in America, where wearing the wrong colour can get you killed, the oval-shaped ball is offering a passport to a better future. *Guy Adams reports from Los Angeles*

Jesse Owens Park is a world away from the playing fields of Rugby School where William Webb-Ellis first picked up the ball and ran with it, in a famous act of teenage rebellion which spawned the sport that now bears his alma mater's name.

Situated in Crenshaw, one of the grittiest neighbourhoods in Los Angeles, the muddy expanse of grass sits a stone's throw away from Slauson Avenue, a busy road that marks an informal dividing line between the territories of the Crips and the Bloods, the city's two most notorious gangs.

On a normal day, as one of the few bits of greenery in a concrete jungle, the park provides a haven to the local homeless community, who put up with the 24-hour din from police sirens and overhead flights into nearby LAX airport.

This week, however, it bore witness to a more orderly scene that would perhaps be better suited to the English Home Counties: 100 teenage boys and girls passing oval-shaped balls backwards and forwards, during the gruelling first training session of their new rugby season.

The players, all aged between 14 and 17, are part of an

The muddy expanse of grass sits a stone's throw away from Slauson Avenue, a busy road that marks an informal dividing line between the territories of the Crips and the Bloods, the city's two most notorious gangs.

extraordinary sporting and social experiment. They are among thousands of youngsters, from some of America's most gang-ridden areas, who are being taught to play rugby – in an attempt to turn them away from a life of crime.

Few Americans have heard of the game, but it was introduced to the View Park Charter School, which most of the children attend, by players from Santa Monica Rugby Club, on LA's prosperous Westside, a few years ago.

Today, dozens of schools compete in the Inner City Rugby League, one of several competitions that have sprung up across America to cater for teams made up of children from the country's toughest urban areas.

"At first, a lot of them found the sport confusing, but pretty soon they grew to love it," says Dave Hughes, View Park's English-born PE teacher and rugby coach. "They have tons of ability. Some are just incredible athletes, kids who can run 40 yards in 4.7 seconds, and hurdle as high as their own shoulder."

Learning rugby, which teaches values like hard work and team-building, can help improve the students' self esteem, says Mr Hughes, and prevent them ending up on the wrong side of the tracks. At View Park, its benefits are also being keenly felt in the classroom. "We've got kids here who were totally uncontrollable," he says. "They used to make me want to quit my job

The players, all aged between 14 and 17, are part of an extraordinary sporting and social experiment. They are among thousands of youngsters, from some of America's most gang-ridden areas, who are being taught to play rugby – in an attempt to turn them away from a life of crime.

every day. Now, you should see what rugby has done for them. It's incredible, like something has just clicked. Suddenly they want to help out, be part of a team, and have a future.

"Some are even getting into universities like Berkeley and UCLA on the back of their potential, because although it's only a minor sport, the coaches of the teams there are able to make sure they get offered a place."

View Park hasn't been alone in advocating the positive values of rugby. At Hyde School, in one of the most

"I hope to benefit from the trip by learning better rugby skills, but my community and family will also benefit from it by knowing that something good has come off these streets,"

disadvantaged suburbs of Washington, coaches of the rugby team made headlines this year when, in defiance of expectations, every one of the 15 players in their team secured a place at university.

In LA's Hawaiian Gardens, an undefeated youth side which won the regional championships is credited with breaking down inter-racial tension, which led to an unprecedented drop in violence between black and Latino high-school students, together with a decline in graffiti in the local area.

Now inner-city rugby is starting to be taken seriously at the very highest levels of the sport. Next month, View Park's team will travel to Twickenham for England's game against Italy, as guests of the RFU.

The trip will form part of a week-long tour for the players – most of whom have never left California, let alone travelled overseas. They will stay at Wellington College, the Berkshire public school, play alongside the first XV and be coached by James Haskell, the England player and Old Wellingtonian.

Watching the children prepare for their trip provides frequent reminders of sport's potential to break down barriers. In normal circumstances, gang allegiance is demonstrated by the colour of clothing they and their contemporaries wear: red for the Bloods, blue for Crips.

But on the field many of View Park's players wear outfits that symbolise their rejection of old divides. Some have one red sock, and one blue. Others wear blue shorts with red socks, or vice versa.

Speaking to them also reminds you how far they have come. "I hope to benefit from the trip by learning better rugby skills, but my community and family will also benefit from it by knowing that something good has come off these streets," says View Park's soft-spoken 15-year-old scrum half, Darius Dawkins. "When I get older, it will hopefully help me become a big-time rugby player and go to a big-time rugby school."

Players in the NFL, the professional league, were recently banned from celebrating touchdowns and other on-field successes by making gangland gestures.

The growth of inner-city rugby comes as American Football, which evolved from it and is now the USA's most watched sport, struggles to distance itself from associations with gang culture.

Players in the NFL, the professional league, were recently banned from celebrating touchdowns and other on-field successes by making gangland gestures.

Rugby also makes solid commercial sense for schools in deprived neighbourhoods, which can struggle to raise sufficient funding to provide the equipment and team of coaches necessary to run an American football programme. View Park's entire league gets by on a small sponsorship deal with Evolution Capital, a finance firm in Santa Monica.

USA Rugby, the sport's governing body, says the number of schools offering the sport, particularly in disadvantaged urban areas, is increasing exponentially "Traditionally, only a tiny number of high schools have played rugby, a lot of them Irish Catholic schools on the East Coast. But that has roughly doubled in the last five years, and now we know of roughly 750 schools," says Mark Griffin, the organisation's youth director. "Plenty of that increase has been happening in the cities."

The USA's national rugby team, which achieved prominence at the last World Cup when it scored what was later voted the try of the tournament against South Africa, is hoping to eventually benefit from the influx of young talent from the inner cities.

Yet the most immediate benefits are on the streets. "Rugby is a full contact extreme sport, and like all extreme sports, it's a release," says Stuart Krohns, the founder of the Inner City Rugby League. "All teenagers have angst, and rugby gives them a sense of emotional balance.

"It's helping these children look at life differently because they are playing a sport that originated overseas, and to start seeing themselves as part of a global community. And in this day and age that has to be a very valuable thing."

The Independent 20 January 2009
© 2009 Independent News & Media Limited

To see more pictures from the 'Rugby in the 'hood' collection and other interesting photographs go to:
http://www.nickstern.com/nickstern.com.html

War & conflict
Issues to think about and discuss

Could ecoterrorists let slip the bugs of war? – Could insects be the next, and most effective, terrorist weapon? According to this writer they are "cheap, simple and wickedly effective." Is this a realistic threat?

Destitute and confused: bleak future of refugees caught in the crossfire – Displaced and bewildered, is it any wonder that some Afghan refugees long for the certainties of Taliban rule? What can be done to help those caught between the British army and the Taliban?

"I'm a conscientious objector" – In Israel, army service is compulsory and this writer's early ambition was to be a soldier. But seeing the reality of her country's actions in Palestine changed her mind. Was she right to go to jail rather than fight for her country?

War & conflict

Objectors

Refugees

Afghanistan

Tradition

Ecoterrorism

War & conflict

Threat

Could ecoterrorists let slip the bugs of war?

Insects can spread disease and destroy crops with devastating speed. Do not underestimate their potential as weapons

Jeffrey A. Lockwood

The terrorists' letter arrived at the Mayor of Los Angeles's office on November 30, 1989. A group calling itself "the Breeders" claimed to have released the Mediterranean fruit fly in Los Angeles and Orange counties, and threatened to expand their attack to the San Joaquin Valley, an important centre of Californian agriculture.

With perverse logic, they said that unless the Government stopped using pesticides they would assure a cataclysmic infestation that would lead to the quarantining of California produce, costing 132,000 jobs and $13.4 billion in lost trade.

The infestation was real enough. It was ended by heavy spraying. It is still not known if ecoterrorists were behind it, but the panic it engendered shows that "the Breeders" were flirting with a powerful weapon.

The history and future of insects as weapons are explored in my new book, *Six-Legged Soldiers*. As an entomologist, I was initially interested in how human beings have conscripted insects and twisted science for use in war, terrorism and torture. It soon became apparent that the weaponisation of insects was not some quirky military footnote but a recurring theme in human strife, and quite possibly the next chapter in modern conflicts.

Insects are one of the cheapest and most destructive weapons available to terrorists today, and one of the most widely ignored: they are easy to sneak across borders, reproduce quickly and can spread disease and destroy crops with devastating speed.

A great strategic lesson of 9/11 has been overlooked. Terrorists need only a little ingenuity, not sophisticated weapons, to cause enormous damage. Armed only with box-cutters, terrorists hijacked aircraft and brought down the World Trade Centre. Insects are the box-cutters of biological warfare - cheap, simple and wickedly effective.

Am I being an alarmist? I wish I knew. But I do know that few people have an inkling of how insects can - and have - been used to inflict human suffering and economic destruction. And I know that government officials admit that entomological attacks are, "not something that is yet on our radar". So my goal in *Six-Legged Soldiers* is to find a measured concern that lies between complacency and panic.

Yet insects have shaped human history. In the 14th century, 75 million people succumbed to flea-borne bubonic plague. But few people realise that the Black Death arrived in Europe after the Mongols catapulted flea-ridden corpses into the port of Kaffa. People fled, carrying bacteria, rats and fleas throughout the Mediterranean.

And it was lice, not enemy armies, that nearly broke the back of the Soviet Union when typhus made 30 million people ill and killed 5 million after the First World War.

caused miscarriages in livestock while young animals suffered 10 to 70 per cent mortality rates. Mosquitoes spread the virus from Kenya. In 1997 a virulent strain appeared, able to infect the human nervous system. About 200,000 Egyptians fell ill, of whom 2,000 lost their sight and 598 died of encephalitis. Every region of the US has a mosquito species that is capable of carrying the disease.

Nor would it be difficult to introduce. According to biodefence experts, a terrorist with $100 worth of supplies, simple instructions and a plane

What would be the cost of an insect-borne disease? If it destroyed enough orchards to cut the sale of orange juice by 50 per cent for five years, the US economy would lose $9.5 billion - approximately the cost of building the World Trade Centre from scratch.

Stacking a nation's defences along its borders is a strategic error. The better model is that of public health. Rather than hoping to stop every sick traveller entering a country, a wise government would stockpile vaccines, train health professionals and educate the public.

> And it was lice, not enemy armies, that nearly broke the back of the Soviet Union when typhus made 30 million people ill and killed 5 million after the First World War.

Military strategists have seen the potential for warfare in all this. In the Second World War, the French and Germans pursued the mass production and dispersal of Colorado beetles to destroy enemy food supplies, and the Japanese military killed more than 400,000 Chinese by dropping plague-infected fleas and cholera-coated flies.

During the Cold War, the US military planned to produce 100 million yellow fever-infected mosquitoes a month, and produced an "entomological warfare target analysis" of vulnerable sites in the Soviet Union and its allies' territories. The dispersal and biting capacity of (uninfected) mosquitoes was tested by secretly dropping them over US cities.

America believed that insect-borne diseases were the bane only of underdeveloped nations until the summer of 1999, when West Nile virus arrived. A natural experiment in entomological warfare unfolded. Over the next seven years, the technological might of the US could not stop mosquitoes carrying the disease across the nation, infecting nearly 7,000 people and killing 654.

Many insect-borne pathogens could afflict Western nations. But given the losing battle against West Nile virus, the greatest concern is its African cousin, Rift Valley fever. Originally discovered in 1931, this viral disease

ticket could introduce Rift Valley fever to the US or another target country with almost no chance of being caught. Western societies are understandably worried about disease, and terrorists would relish the opportunity to introduce deadly pathogens. But they are aware that we take our wealth as seriously as our health. The World Trade Centre was an icon of US economic prosperity. And agriculture accounts for a trillion dollars in economic activity as well as one in every six jobs in the US.

The best "homeland defence" is flourishing human and agricultural health systems that can detect and deal with whatever comes in. Such an infrastructure would pay for itself. Even without terrorists, new diseases and insect pests will continue to arrive.

Western societies tend to think in terms of the short-term spectacle and heroic saviours of Hollywood action movies. Our disconnection from the natural world makes us believe that risk and benefit unfold at a blistering pace. For a terrorist group with patience, a slow-motion disaster in ecological time would be a perfect tactic against an enemy that thinks in terms of days or months, but would suffer across the generations.

> In the Second World War, the French and Germans pursued the mass production and dispersal of Colorado beetles to destroy enemy food supplies, and the Japanese military killed more than 400,000 Chinese by dropping plague-infected fleas and cholera-coated flies.

An entomological attack would not empty America's larders completely but it could go a long way to emptying its wallets.

In economic terms, the 9/11 attacks resulted in direct losses of $27.2 billion. The Asian longhorned beetle, which arrived in 1996, with the emerald ash borer, found in 2002, together have the potential to destroy more than $700 billion worth of forests, according to the US Department of Agriculture.

Jeffrey A. Lockwood is the author of Six-Legged Soldiers: Using Insects as Weapons of War (OUP). Educated as an entomologist, he is a professor of philosophy and creative writing at the University of Wyoming

The Times 2 February 2009

Photo: Emilio Morenatti/AP/Press Association Images

Destitute and confused: bleak future for refugees caught in the crossfire

Residents of grim camp tell of clashes between coalition forces and the Taliban

Jason Burke, Kabul

In the evening the temperature falls at last and light slants across the camp, throwing long shadows across the stagnant puddles and shining through the kites, made from plastic bags, that the children fly.

It shines, too, through the thin walls of the makeshift tents that cover a patch of wasteland in the west of Kabul. The 3,500 refugees who live in them are a long way from their homes in the badlands

of the south where the British are fighting. Most of the refugees are from districts such as Sangin, Nawazad, Kajaki or Gereshk in the southern province of Helmand, sites of fierce battles between British troops and the Taliban.

Their stories reveal a different side of the conflict. Few understand who is fighting, even fewer distinguish between British troops and those of other nationalities, all tell stories of civilians killed by coalition air strikes. There is little sign of progress in the campaign to win hearts and minds.

Rozi Khan, a day labourer from Kajaki, said he had no idea which soldiers were fighting around his village when he left two months ago. In fact, securing Kajaki with its strategically important reservoir and dam has been a British

objective since the initial days of the deployment in 2006. Last week British soldiers successfully transported a huge turbine to the dam, which could eventually supply nearly 2 million people with electricity. Coalition spokesmen claimed to have killed more than 250 Taliban during the operation.

But there is little evidence of material improvement on the ground, according to the refugees. "They say they have come to help us but they have come for fighting," Khan, 25, said. "But instead of killing one person who has attacked them they kill 50 people in the village. Is this a help?"

Bismatullah, who like many Afghans uses only one name, said "the Americans" and the Taliban were fighting around his home in Sangin, again in the British zone of operations. He too spoke of how large numbers of civilians had been killed and buildings destroyed. Independent confirmation of the claim was unavailable.

Bismatullah, 32, was nostalgic for the days when the Taliban were in power. "There was peace and security and no real fighting. The Taliban were following the path of the Qur'an," he said.

Such sentiments appear widespread. Many refugees interviewed said that the insurgents had not bothered them; others said that, as they had nothing, the Taliban had accepted their refusal to provide food. "They came asking but I showed them my children who are hungry and have no clothes and they left me alone. They get food from the richer people," said one farmer from Sangin.

Elsewhere, however, the refugees said the Taliban demanded food, lodging or even volunteers. "If you have nothing else to give them you have to go with them and they give you a gun and you have to fight. They haven't committed any atrocities but people are afraid of them," said another Sangin resident.

Often, villagers made a distinction between local Taliban they knew personally, such as those apparently operating in Kajaki district, and those who came from elsewhere, sometimes Pakistan, with whom they had more trouble. The real problem, most said, was not the Taliban or the "Amriki", as western troops are universally known, but the combination of the two.

"We had to leave because the Taliban were coming to our village and firing once or twice and there would be a big bombardment and some civilians would die," Ahmed Shah, from Nawazad district, said. The word bombardment has been integrated into local languages.

Nato spokesmen frequently allege that the Taliban deliberately invite attacks that will kill civilians in order to turn local populations against the international forces and the Afghan government they support. Taliban spokesmen deny the charge. The situation is muddied further as local officials and tribal elders often inflate the number of civilian casualties for political gain or more compensation.

But that the villagers are caught in the crossfire is without doubt. Nor is their extreme poverty. Most are landless labourers forced to travel to

---

'Instead of killing one person who has attacked them they kill 50 in the village. Is this a help?'

---

seek work. For them the war brings particular problems.

"If I went out of my village I risked being shot by the government as a Taliban spy or shot by the Taliban as a government spy," said one refugee from the central Oruzgan province, where Dutch and US soldiers are deployed. "The government holds the district centres, the Taliban run everything outside."

'If you have nothing to give the Taliban you have to go with them and you have to fight'

Most of the refugees are destitute, often having borrowed money or sold their last possessions to travel by truck to Kabul. The unauthorised camp has been established on unused government land. There is no sanitation and summer temperatures reach 40C (104F). They live on scraps of stale bread scavenged from rubbish piles across the city.

As a widow with four young children, Gul Pari is in a worse situation than many. She said her husband, a labourer, was killed a year ago in Helmand in a "bombardment" but is unsure which side was to blame. "When there was fighting, we did not know what was going on. But I think it was the fault of the Taliban because they were shooting and then there was an attack afterwards. Now we have nothing except the 50 Afghani [65p] each day that my son gets from selling ice creams."

The refugees have received blankets and plastic sheets from the United Nations Refugee Agency (UNHCR), and an initial ration of food from the government, and are helped by local businessmen.

"They are in a poor situation but are better off than many other such communities around the country who are less visible," said Mohammed Nader Farhad of the UNHCR. "Especially in the south and east there are problems with displacement due to military operations. Most people want to go home but can't due to the fighting."

Government estimates place the number of internally displaced by the conflict at 10,000, though aid agencies believe the true total is seven times greater.

Said Ali, who last month fled the Helmand town of Gereshk, where British troops have struggled for two years to stabilise a secure zone, said: "There was fighting with the Taliban and local people shooting at the soldiers and then the planes were coming. My house was destroyed, my animals were killed, my brother injured. We have nothing there and we have nothing here."

Ali was unsure of the future. "When there is peace we will go home but now there is war," he said.

For a few autumn months at least the temperatures will be relatively pleasant and the dust storms will end. But then the vicious Kabul winter will come.

The Guardian 3 October 2008
© Guardian News and Media Ltd 2008

"I'm a conscientious objector"

Omer Goldman

I first went to prison on September 23 of this year and served 35 days. By the time you read this, I will be back inside for another 21. This is going to be my life for the next two years: in for three weeks, out for one. I am 19 years old now and by the time the authorities give up hounding me, I will be 21. The reason? I refused to do my military service for the Israeli army.

I grew up with the army. My father was deputy head of Mossad and I saw my sister, who is eight years older than me, do her military service. As a young girl, I wanted to be a soldier. The military was such a part of my life that I never even questioned it.

Earlier this year, I went to a peace demonstration in Palestine. I had always been told that the Israeli army was there to defend me, but during that demonstration Israeli soldiers opened fire on me and my friends with rubber bullets and tear-gas grenades. I was shocked and scared. I saw the truth. I saw the reality. I saw for the first time that the most dangerous thing in Palestine is the Israeli soldiers, the very people who are supposed to be on my side.

When I came back to Israel, I knew I had changed. I told my dad what had happened. He was angry that I had been over to the occupied territories and told me I had endangered my life. I have always discussed history and politics with my father but on this subject – my rejection of the military and my conscientious objecting – we can't speak.

My parents divorced when I was three and my father has a new family. My mother is an artist and she is very supportive of me. But my father has been horrified by my decision. I think he thought that I was going through a stage that I would grow out of. But it hasn't happened.

> ## "The most dangerous thing in Palestine is the Israeli soldiers, the very people who are supposed to be on my side"

In prison, I wake up at five and clean all day, inside and out. It's a military prison so we are made to do ridiculous stuff. They painted a white stripe across the floor, and I have to keep the stripe glowing white and clean. I have to wear a US army uniform. The uniforms were given as a present to the Israeli army by the US Marines. I feel stupid. I am anti-military. I am against the whole idea of wearing the uniform.

The other prisoners are women from the army. They are in for silly things such as playing with their guns, smoking dope, running away from the army. None of them is really a criminal. And then there are five girls like me who are conscientious objectors.

We talk to the other girls, tell them things they have never heard about before. Like that everyone is a human, no matter what religion they are. Some of them are really ignorant. They have never heard of evolution theory, or Gandhi or Mandela, or the Armenian holocaust. I try to tell them that there have been a lot of genocides.

Of course I get scared when I am in prison. Three times a week, I have to help guard the prison at night. But also, it's frightening that my country is the way that it is, locking up young people who are against violence and war. And I worry that what I am doing may damage my future. The worst part is that I have a taste of freedom and then I am back inside, back to my mundane prison life. It's hard to go from being a free girl who can decide things for herself – what to wear, who to see, what to eat – and then go back to having every minute of the day timetabled.

Last time I was out of prison, I went to see my dad. We tried not to talk politics. He cares about me as his daughter, that I am suffering, but he doesn't want to hear my views. He hasn't come to visit me in prison. I think it would be too hard for him to see me in there. He is an army man.

I suppose, actually, we have similar characters. We both fight for what we believe in. It's just that our views are diametrically opposed.

As told to Sarah Duguid

Financial Times
22 November 2008

Wider world

Issues to think about and discuss

Women's rights are human rights – Women's rights are violated in many parts of the world. Is Amnesty right that women should continue to campaign for equal rights, earnings and power?

Dignity and the decent facility – Decent toilets are more than a health issue for women – they actually make a difference to their safety, education and prospects. Shouldn't aid organisations be prioritising this essential but unglamorous need?

An ordinary Zimbabwean is laid to rest wrapped in plastic. He died of cholera – Why does a president party in luxury while people in his country are dying? Zimbabwe has astronomical inflation, a worthless currency and at least five million people going hungry. Why does the rest of the world allow this to happen?

Lost mothers, lost children – 99% of maternal deaths occur in developing countries – with devastating effects on the children and communities left behind. We know that there are simple solutions. These heart-rending pictures and stories beg the question: where is the political will to put this right?

Grow your own – BIKE! – An inventive solution to the transport problems in Africa. But will people really use them?

Wider world

Abuse

Poverty

Water aid

Violence

Wider world

Human trafficking

Transport

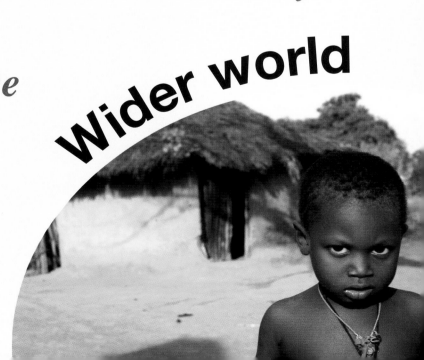

Women's rights are human rights

Women's rights are violated all over the world: wherever women are subjected to violence, wherever they face discrimination in access to land and employment, or are barred from participating in decisions that affect their lives. In some countries women are prevented from going to school or attaining health care, or are subject to harmful traditional practices. In some, the legal system subordinates them to the men in the family.

But the story of women's human rights is not only a tale of abuse and inequality. It is also the story of struggles by women the world over to claim the rights set out 60 years ago in the Universal Declaration of Human Rights. By challenging impunity for sexual violence, campaigning for equality before the law, or demanding equal pay for work of equal value, they are asserting that human rights are universal: they are for women as well as for men.

ARTICLE 3 EVERYONE HAS THE RIGHT TO LIFE, LIBERTY AND SECURITY OF THE PERSON

Women and girls suffer disproportionately from violence, both in peace and war, at the hands of the state, the community and the family. Violence against women is reported in every war-zone: in Sudan, Iraq, Colombia, DR Congo, Sierra Leone, Rwanda and the former Yugoslavia. But women are at greatest risk of violence in their own homes, from a husband or partner. According to a study by the World Health Organisation in 2005, more than half of women in Bangladesh, Ethiopia, Peru and Tanzania reported they had been subjected to physical or sexual violence by intimate partners; the figure for rural Ethiopia was 71%.

ARTICLE 4 NO ONE SHALL BE HELD IN SLAVERY OR SERVITUDE

Trafficking, the modern day form of slavery, affects all regions of the world. According to a 2006 UN global report on trafficking, 127 countries have been documented as countries of origin, and 137 as countries of destination. Although women, men, girls and boys can become victims of trafficking, the majority of victims are female. Poverty, resulting from gender discrimination, puts women and girls at higher risk of being targeted by traffickers, who use false promises of jobs and educational opportunities to recruit their victims.

ARTICLE 7 ALL ARE EQUAL BEFORE THE LAW AND ARE ENTITLED WITHOUT ANY DISCRIMINATION TO EQUAL PROTECTION BEFORE THE LAW

In many countries, the law fails to protect women from discrimination and violence, or discriminates against them directly. In Sierra Leone the constitutional guarantee of equal protection under the law does not cover 'adoption, marriage, divorce, burial, devolution of property on death or other interests of personal law'. These areas are regulated by customary law, which treats women as minors, subordinate to a father, brother or husband. In Iran, laws are weighted heavily against women.

ARTICLE 13 EVERYONE HAS THE RIGHT TO FREEDOM OF MOVEMENT AND RESIDENCE WITHIN EACH STATE AND THE RIGHT TO LEAVE OR RETURN TO THEIR COUNTRY

In much of the Middle East, women's freedom of movement is restricted. Even in Algeria, relatively more liberal on women's rights than other countries in the region, policemen and court officials consider it acceptable for a husband to forbid his wife to travel. In Saudi Arabia, a woman needs permission from a male relative to travel abroad. She is not allowed to drive a car, and if she walks unaccompanied or in the company of a man who is not her husband nor a close relative, she is as risk of arrest on suspicion of prostitution or other 'moral' offences.

Amnesty International Magazine
March/April 2008
http://www.amnesty.org.uk

ARTICLE 16 MEN AND WOMEN OF FULL AGE HAVE THE RIGHT TO MARRY AND FOUND A FAMILY, WITH FREE AND FULL CONSENT, AND EQUAL RIGHTS DURING AND AFTER MARRIAGE

Women of all ages may become victims of forced marriage, but free and full consent is most likely to be lacking when one or both of the spouses is under 18. Research studies indicate that half of Ethiopian girls marry before the age of 15; in Nepal 40% of girls are married by age 15 and 7% by the age of 10; and in the state of Kebbi in northern Nigeria, the average age of marriage is just under 11. In the UK, the FCO handles 300 cases a year (85% of them women and girls) of British nationals taken abroad for forced marriages.

ARTICLE 21 EVERYONE HAS THE RIGHT TO TAKE PART IN THE GOVERNMENT OF HIS OR HER COUNTRY

Throughout the world women face barriers to participation in politics, often rooted in social and economic systems. On 2 May 2003 the Welsh Assembly became the world's first legislative body with equal numbers of men and women. National parliaments with high proportions of women members include Rwanda (48.8%), Sweden (47%) and Argentina (40%). The global average is 17.9%. (Figures are for lower or single house.) Saudi Arabia remains the only country in the world where only males can vote.

ARTICLE 23 EVERYONE HAS THE RIGHT TO WORK, TO FREE CHOICE OF EMPLOYMENT, TO FAIR AND EQUAL PAY, AND TO FORM AND JOIN TRADE UNIONS

In all parts of the world, women generally have fewer job opportunities than men and earn less. The employment rates of women are on average only 50% those of men (in South Asia 29% and in Arab States only 16%). In the European Union, women earn on average 15% less than men. In South Asia, two-thirds of all employed women work without pay, usually in a family business or farm. Gender-based discrimination and sexual harassment severely limit women's job opportunities and the ability to make choices about work. Job advertisements in Ukraine regularly specify a man, and in parts of Central America companies routinely demand that female applicants have a pregnancy test.

ARTICLE 24 EVERYONE HAS THE RIGHT TO REST AND LEISURE

Women tend to work much longer hours than men, performing about two-thirds of the world's working hours. In most countries in the world, men tend to work longer hours than women in paid employment, but women work more hours in unpaid activities – housework and caring for children and elderly parents. This gender stereotype extends to domestic workers who are expected to work extremely long hours.

ARTICLE 25 EVERYONE HAS THE RIGHT TO A STANDARD OF LIVING AND HEALTH CARE ADEQUATE FOR THEIR HEALTH AND WELL-BEING, ESPECIALLY MOTHERS AND CHILDREN

Globally, experts estimate that women are 70% of the world's poor. They lag behind men in control over essential resources including cash, credit, property, land and wealth and often also in access to education, job opportunities and political representation. For these reasons, women are often poorer relative to men of the same household and social group. In Macedonia 39% of Romani women have had no education, or an incomplete primary education, compared to 22% of Romani men and 8% of non-Roma; 83% of Romani women and 65% of Romani men have never been employed in the formal economy, compared to 50% of non-Roma; and 31% of Romani women suffer from chronic illness, compared to 27% of Romani men and 23% of non-Roma.

ARTICLE 26 EVERYONE HAS THE RIGHT TO EDUCATION, INCLUDING FREE AND COMPULSORY PRIMARY EDUCATION

In every region of the world, women are much less likely than men to be literate. Schools around the world commonly impose charges for primary education. School fees are an insurmountable obstacle for many children, and girls are more likely to be excluded from school than boys when there isn't enough money to go round. Another obstacle is the threat of violence against girls in and around many educational institutions all over the world, inflicted by teachers, other school employees, fellow students and outsiders.

Photo: WaterAid/Suzanne Porter.

DIGNITY AND THE DECENT FACILITY

Sanitary engineers regard a toilet as a health aid. But women paint a very different picture, as *Libby Plumb* explains.

'We didn't have anywhere to defecate as there is nowhere private. When we went outside, the boys used to follow us and we felt shy and afraid. We used to end up going inside our houses, on the floor, just like children, and then cleaning it up.' It took guts for 15-year-old Baby from the Indian city of Gwalior to describe how she dealt with having no toilet in her home. The personal and sensitive nature of excretion renders it taboo, a topic that many grown women in developing countries, let alone adolescent girls, are uncomfortable discussing in public.

Women want and need toilets, but are profoundly inhibited from saying so. Access to a toilet is essential for female dignity, especially in cultures that demand high standards of modesty. But lack of discussion means that their provision is given very low priority, especially by those with the financial and political power to correct the situation – predominantly men. This paradox results in women living in a state of constant discomfort and anxiety. While men and boys can be seen squatting by Indian roadsides in broad daylight, similar behaviour for women and girls is unthinkable.

The sense of degradation is almost universal among the millions of women without facilities. 'During the day we must walk far into the bush if we do not want to be seen. At night there is a danger from snakes and scorpions. Sometimes men follow us and that also makes us afraid,' says Januta Buniya, a 30-year-old Nigerian mother. Women 'prisoners of daylight' – those obliged by custom to wait until nightfall to venture outside to relieve themselves – often face increased chances of urinary tract infection and chronic constipation. The stress and pain can be acute, especially for pregnant, elderly or disabled women.

Sexual exposure – and possible harassment – forms part of the embarrassment. Discussing the benefits of a WaterAid toilet-building programme in the city of Tamale in Ghana, 40-year-old Fatimata liked the idea of less disease and filth and fewer encounters with snakes and pigs in the forest, but top of her list was privacy. 'This will save me from exposing myself to the public. It is a serious worry when men other than my husband see me naked. Now we will have a room where we can go and do whatever we want.' Her neighbour Ashetu concurs: 'In the forest men, women and children clash. Sometimes when I am squatting there a man comes and squats behind me. I can't tell him to go away because it's a public place, but people see things they shouldn't see.'

Women also have to deal with their children's bodily expulsions. In Tamale, this means extra trips to the forest to dispose of excreta, as Ashetu described: 'Younger children defecate in chamber pots and we empty them in the forest. Older children who can cross the road come with us. But if they need to go in the night we take them outside, and then in the morning we dig a hole and bury it.'

'Flying toilets'

In dense urban slums, high population density often means there is nowhere secluded outside or in. Women and girls often resort to 'flying toilets' – plastic bags that are thrown on to a dump – or, as in Baby's case, the floor. People also resort to buckets, which are poured into open drains at night, creating serious public nuisance and adding to the risks of diarrhoeal infection.

Lack of sanitation can destroy girls' education. As they hit puberty, many parents withdraw daughters from school out of concern for their modesty. Or the girls themselves choose to stay away when menstruating or suffering from diarrhoea. 'Before the school had toilets we used to hide under the bamboo when we had to go,' recounted Sabina Roka from Simle, Nepal. 'During menstruation it was really difficult, and we used to stay at home instead.' For millions of girls, lack of attention to their adolescent needs leads to their leaving school altogether – and thus, very often, to early marriage. Providing separate toilet blocks for girls – and inculcating a culture of respect towards all students and for personal and school cleanliness – helps retain them.

Women and girls also miss work and school due to their responsibility to care for relatives who are sick – often with diseases exacerbated by poor sanitation, indicating the compounding nature of the problem. In many children under five, diarrhoeal diseases prove fatal. Honufa, a 20-year-old mother from Dhaka, Bangladesh, laments: 'Life is very hard here. The sanitation conditions everywhere are foul. Every day there is disease in this slum. I lost a two-year-old son to diarrhoea.' Thus where health risks are understood, the impulse to adopt sanitary practices and hygiene can be strong. The difficulties are the crowded nature of the living space, lack of community organization, and expense. But where the will is there, these difficulties can be overcome.

Toilets aren't the only sanitary improvement that women need. Private showers or washrooms are another female concern. A study by WaterAid in Tanzania cited how women from the village of Songambele who were able to bathe regularly during menstruation reported improved personal hygiene and with this, increased confidence. Mdala Rhoda Senduwu recalled the previous embarrassing situation where: 'Women who had problems with their menstrual hygiene were taken to the elders for consultation so that they could improve their cleanliness.' Some sanitation programmes offer a closet with toilet and bathroom tap or simple shower combined, with waste water used for flushing.

Waste-water disposal is also a problem – stagnant pools attract mosquitoes, and rotting garbage brings vermin and flies. In Ouakam, a poor urban community on the outskirts of arid and drainless Dakar, Senegal, women without their own soakpits have to pay other women 50 cents a time to carry their bowlfuls of dirty water away. This makes household laundry, washing-up and personal hygiene an extremely expensive affair.

Plenty of women customers

Better understanding of the misery and indignity that women endure is gradually emerging as genuine discussion and exchange become the basis of sanitation programmes – instead of the 'build and lecture' model too often deployed by public health engineers in the past. Most women without toilets and water taps live in serious poverty and have barely been to school. Even if they could summon the courage to talk frankly about their personal needs, they lack the time, skills, connections and knowledge to petition their governments, community leaders or even husbands for change. But now

SANITATION: WHAT WOMEN NEED

The following are female sanitation priorities – mostly connected to dignity and convenience rather than health.

Privacy: no-one witnessing you going to the toilet or bathing.

Security: separate Male and Female facilities, in public and school toilets.

Soap and water: to wash hands, bodies, clothes, utensils, nappies/diapers and pads.

Disposal facilities: for sanitary cloths, wastewater and garbage.

Potties: to help deal with infants' excreta.

Proximity to home: so that visiting the toilet doesn't mean leaving children unaccompanied and there is easier access for the sick, elderly and disabled (all cared for by women).

Easily cleanable designs: women are invariably responsible for toilet maintenance.

that more of them are being asked sensitively to identify their personal needs, and are being offered facilities they can afford, the myth that there are few customers for sanitation in poor communities is gradually being dispelled.

Consultations with women have led to various innovations. For example, children may fear a dark hole, and need to be reassured into using the toilet by special open-plan child-friendly design. In Mali, one programme adapted designs to make it easier for people blind from trachoma to use the toilet without the assistance of a caregiver – usually a woman. Teenage girls have been taught how to make reusable sanitary napkins. In a recent revamp of government-approved school toilet designs in India, a UNICEF sanitation officer managed to ensure that incinerators for menstrual cloths would automatically be included in the girls' blocks. All the evidence suggests that women are effective leaders of sanitary change, in both rural and urban settings, where they are given encouragement. But they need to be given the chance to express themselves without fear of ridicule and humiliation. Until the subject of human waste is removed from the closet and the silence surrounding it broken, poor sanitation will remain one of the most pressing concerns for women around the world; and by far the most politically neglected.

Libby Plumb is a British writer living in Seattle. She worked for international development organisation WaterAid in London for eight years and now works as a communications consultant for WaterAid America.

New Internationalist August 2008

For further information visit:
http://www.wateraid.org/uk

An ordinary Zimbabwean is laid to rest, wrapped in plastic. He died of cholera

As Robert Mugabe's cronies prepare a lavish 85th birthday party, the people wait in vain for a 'unity' government to rescue them. Daniel Howden reports

Richard Mutoti was not celebrating Robert Mugabe's 85th birthday yesterday. Neither were his friends and family. Instead, they were lowering his body into the ground at Granville Cemetery outside Harare. The 59-year-old was wrapped in a plastic bag to prevent the mourners from contracting the cholera that had emaciated his body and killed him.

Mr Mutoti was put to rest amid earth mounds, evidence of the appalling legacy of Mr Mugabe's misrule, which Zimbabweans will be coerced into celebrating this week. The cholera victim, from Harare's impoverished Budiriro 4 district, had been discharged from a cholera isolation camp on

Friday and sent to die at home. He was lucky to have lived so long; Rectar Musapingo, in the grave next to him, died on 22 January, eight months short of his 40th birthday.

Twisted blue and white flowers, fashioned from shreds of plastic, lie about between black metal name-plates offering a roll-call of the dead, few of whom had survived for even one-third of their President's lifetime. Some of the mourners may have seen yesterday's Herald newspaper on their way to the funeral, proclaiming that "Comrade Mugabe has been in the trenches slaving so that you and me could live a life of dignity". The only dignity left to the Mutoti family was

a white cloth, used to conceal the cholera bag in which their loved one was interred.

The state mouthpiece had over five pages of gushing praise for the President, a former schoolteacher born at a Jesuit mission station in Kutama in 1921. "Like a mighty crocodile, you have remained resilient, focused and resolute against all odds," said an advertisement from the Defence Ministry, in an unintentional echo of the title of author Peter Godwin's scathing indictment of Mugabe, When a Crocodile Eats the Sun. It gushed on: "If everyone gives just a fraction of what comrade Mugabe has given this country, we will be up there with

Children collect stagnant water for use at home in Glen View, Harare. Cholera is easily prevented and cured, but Zimbabwe's medical and water-treatment systems have all but disappeared.

Photo: TSVANGIRAYI MUKWAZHI/AP/Press Association Images

The inflation rate is astronomical, the currency worthless – but the youth wing of Mr Mugabe's Zanu-PF party has been raising money for a lavish celebration. Their target is $250,000

the most advanced countries in the world."

There was no mention in the Herald's editorial that during his stewardship, Zimbabwe's life expectancy has been slashed from over 60 to the lowest in the world, at 34 for women and 37 for men. Like so many of the incomprehensible statistics that haunt this southern African nation, these figures are woefully out of date. They were based on data collected four years ago – before the cholera epidemic, before the ranks of the hungry swelled from three million to more than five million.

The number of cholera deaths similarly trails events. According to the World Health Organisation the death toll from the five-month epidemic stands at 3,759, with 70,000 reported infections. Experts say these figures, which have already surpassed the UN's worst-case scenario, are a fortnight out of date.

The inflation rate is astronomical, the currency worthless – the government long abandoned the Zimbabwe dollar for the US dollar or the South African rand. And the difficulty Mr Mugabe's Zanu-PF party has been experiencing in raising money for a lavish party, planned for 28 February, seems set to disprove the African proverb that "you can never finish eating an elephant". The scale of this economic meltdown has left the party's February 21st youth organisation – set up for the annual drive to pay for the birthday party – short of their $250,000 fundraising target. It will have to stage extra events this week to secure the money.

Zimbabwe's new Prime Minister, Morgan Tsvangirai, was due back in Harare last night after a fundraising mission of his own. He has visited Cape Town in search of the first instalments of what he claimed would be the $5bn needed to rescue Zimbabwe's economy. He was not expected to be invited to a private celebration hosted by Mr Mugabe's notoriously extravagant wife, Grace, at their lavish mansion in Harare's affluent suburb of Borrowdale last night.

*The Independent on Sunday
22 February 2009 © 2009 Independent
News and Media Limited*

Photo: AP/Press Association Images

A man suffering from cholera is taken in a cart to a nearby clinic in the high density suburb of Budiriro, Harare. The lack of clean water and poorly maintained sewage systems have seen the waterborne disease thrive.

Every day in Zimbabwe:

34 people die as a result of the country's cholera epidemic.

6,328,767 is the percentage increase in the real rate of inflation.

40 political prisoners still wait for release under the "unity" government.

600 people flee to neighbouring South Africa.

600 Zimbabweans are infected with the virus that leads to AIDS.

20 grammes of maize is the UN daily ration after recent cutbacks.

Lost mothers, lost children

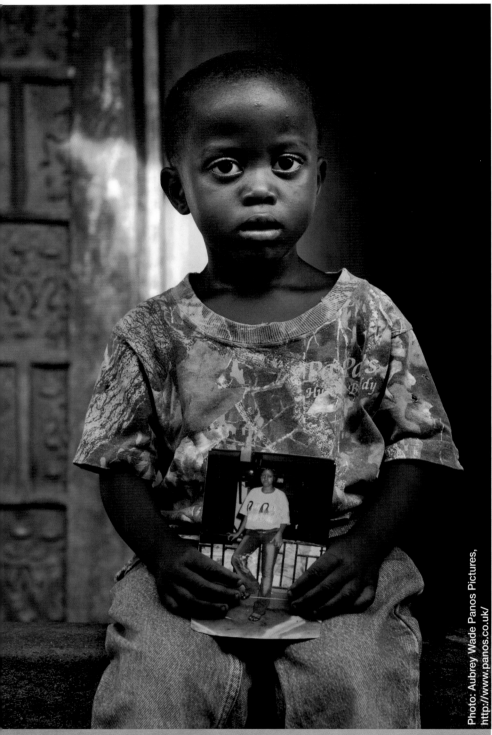

Photo: Aubrey Wade Panos Pictures, http://www.panos.co.uk/

SIERRA LEONE Freetown

Three year old orphan Suleiman holds a photograph of his 26 year old mother, Kadiatu Kamara, who died shortly after giving birth to him. Suleiman's father died from malaria soon after his wife became pregnant. He is now cared for by his aunt. Sierra Leone has the highest maternal mortality rate in the world, with one in every eight women dying in childbirth.

In words and pictures, the tragic – and preventable – loss of life

Every minute of every day a woman dies during pregnancy and childbirth. Each year more than 536,000 women die due to complications during pregnancy and childbirth and 10 million more suffer illnesses and lifelong disabilities as a result. The vast majority of these deaths could be prevented if women had access to vital health care.

In general, women in towns and cities fare better than those in more rural areas as they are more likely to have access to skilled birth attendants. Similarly, educated women are less at risk than uneducated. The major difference, though, is wealth. Within any country the rich face fewer risks than the poor and it is the difference between rich and poor countries on this issue that is the biggest health inequality in the world.

99% of maternal deaths occur in developing countries. In the developing world the lifetime risk of dying in pregnancy and childbirth is 1 in 76. In the developed world, where we assume that skilled helpers will always be available during births, this risk is only 1 in 8,000.

While the situation has improved in many parts of the developing world, on average only 61% of births are attended by skilled personnel. In Southern Asia coverage is only 40% and in sub-Saharan Africa 47%. It is not surprising that these are the two regions with the greatest number of maternal deaths.

In 2000 the United Nations set a series of Millennium Development

Goals - intended to improve key areas of human life. Goal 5 – to reduce maternal mortality and to give everyone access to reproductive health services has made the least progress of all MDGs. At the current rate of progress, Goal 5 will not be met in Asia until 2076 and later still in Africa.

When mothers do not receive adequate care, this fuels a vicious cycle of poverty. Families take on the expense of medical intervention that is often too late. When mothers die the bereaved family becomes still more impoverished and a financial burden then falls on the community and ultimately on the whole country.

When a woman dies in childbirth, the survival of all her children is threatened. The baby she delivers is more likely to die within two years. Any of her children below 10 years of age are three to 10 times more likely to die within two years than children with a living mother.

When a mother dies, younger children start school later and older children often have to leave school to support their family. Children without a mother are less likely to be immunised, and are more likely to suffer from malnutrition and stunted growth.

Graça Machel, a renowned international advocate for women's and children's rights recently wrote "We are more knowledgeable than ever. We have more resources than ever. We have and share more information than ever. So we should be more aware than we have ever been of the millions of people, especially women and children, left behind. We should realise that in my home country of Mozambique, as in much of Africa, a mother who gets sick will have older children who miss school to assume her responsibilities. It is very likely that the youngest children will not get enough to eat, and will get sick as well."

But something can be done to break the cycle. Cost-effective interventions, including family planning, skilled health worker attendance and emergency medical services, would prevent 80 percent of maternal deaths.

More skilled health workers would mean more living mothers, which in turn would mean more children living through early infancy. This has been demonstrated in Sri Lanka which now

Photo: Aubrey Wade Panos Pictures, http://www.panos.co.uk/

SIERRA LEONE Freetown

12 year old Ibrahim Kamara helps to take care of his three year old cousin Ibrahim Tarawallie, after his mother died in childbirth.

Photo: Aubrey Wade Panos Pictures, http://www.panos.co.uk/

SIERRA LEONE Freetown

50 year old Mabinty Conteh holds a photograph of her daughter and her one and a half year old granddaughter Isatu Conteh, who was named after her late mother Isatu Conteh who died in childbirth at the age of 20.

has a trained midwife for every 1,800 people compared to one midwife for every 33,500 people in Niger. While Sri Lanka now suffers a total of 190 maternal deaths per year, Niger, which has a smaller population, loses 14,000 during pregnancy and childbirth every year.

Professor Anthony Costello who is head of the Centre for International Health and Development at University College London, has highlighted an even more immediate and cheap way to reduce these deaths. If traditional birthing attendants and health volunteers were supplied with just two critical drugs – one to treat infection and one to stop bleeding after birth – lives would be saved immediately.

Sarah Brown, wife of the British Prime Minister and patron of The White Ribbon Alliance for Safe Motherhood, gave a speech to the United Nations in September 2008 in which she summed up the situation:

"If you save mothers, you improve the chances of children. To be able to save mothers and children, you need to invest in education, fill the health worker gap and make health care accessible to even the most vulnerable.

The ingredient needed to unlock progress is political will. We know how to save the lives of mothers and children; we do not need to invent a cure. We simply need to decide to follow in the steps of those who have already succeeded."

At about the same time, Margaret Chan, director-general of the World Health Organisation, was asking for more money and more effort. "Despite two decades of efforts," she said, "the world failed to make a dent. We still have time, but just barely, to make up for this failure."

The faces of that failure are the faces in the photographs here – the people for whom time ran out.

Sources: Various

**For more information visit:
http://www.whiteribbonalliance.org/**

Grow your own – BIKE!

The problem? The lack of accessible transport throughout Africa. The solution – bamboo bikes!

What's the problem?

In Africa, very few people can own cars or motorcycles and most have to rely on inadequate and relatively expensive buses. Without good transport local trades and services that need to develop cannot, job options are limited and health care workers find it impossible to reach people in remote areas. The bicycle – flexible, easy to maintain and relatively inexpensive – would seem to be the answer. But while the number of bikes being used across the continent is growing, bicycles currently used in Africa are generally unsuitable for the terrain they are used on. They are manufactured outside Africa, in China and India, and shipped complete. Despite the desperate need for bicycles in Africa, there are no local bicycle building businesses anywhere in sub-Saharan Africa.

What's the solution?

This is where the bamboo bike project comes in. In Asia, bamboo, which is strong and plentiful, is used routinely as material for scaffolding on high-rise buildings and even to build load-bearing structures such as bridges. Africa has bamboo too – which could be used to build a better bike for poor Africans in rural areas and to stimulate a bicycle building industry that could meet local needs. When designer Craig Calfee came up with the bamboo bike idea, and the Earth Institute at Columbia University got involved, a solution seemed possible.

Where did the idea come from?

Over a decade ago Craig Calfee was watching his dog chew on a piece of bamboo behind his bicycle shop in Santa Cruz, California. Luna, the dog, was normally able to turn a log into splinters in a very short space of time, yet after gnawing the bamboo for a fair while, only managed to leave a few teeth marks. And that got Calfee to wondering: If bamboo was strong enough to withstand Luna, why couldn't it be a bicycle frame? Craig Calfee is no ordinary bicycle-shop owner. He's considered one of the country's elite bike builders, someone who creates machines for the likes of Greg LeMond, the first American to win the Tour de France.

How easy are they to make?

The bamboo bike is easier to build than any other bike. It is possible to build a bike in a shack in an African village without electricity. This means that little infrastructure is needed, and so the scheme is relatively easy to get up and running in countries where immediate solutions are needed. The bamboo bike project will demonstrate the building of bamboo bikes and also teach those in the village how to build and service them. The plan is to build a small fleet of bamboo bicycles to be used as community property and kept in a central location.

But will people want them?

There were worries that the bikes wouldn't be taken seriously but people thought they were really useful and inexpensive. The project's long-term plan is to establish more than just one or two bike shops in Africa making bamboo bikes. They aim to get a proper workshop going where people can share skills and tools to make the bikes on a larger scale. Once it has found an investor who's interested in sponsoring it, the bamboo bike project could make a significant contribution to the UN Millennium Development Goals of reducing extreme poverty and improving health care.

http://www.bamboobike.org

Work

Issues to think about and discuss

A hair-raising price for being too honest – A hairdresser refuses to give a candidate wearing a hijab a job – because it will give the wrong message to customers. The candidate goes to court and wins £4,000 for hurt feelings. Who is right here? Was the hairdresser guilty of religious discrimination or was the candidate applying for the wrong sort of job?

No wonder bullied call centre workers are off sick the most – A look at an undervalued and stressed out workforce.

I've tried working beside a pool – and it sucks – Can you work and relax at the same time? Or do you ruin both by attempting to mix them?

Prejudice isn't what keeps men out of nurseries – There are no young men under 25 currently working in state-run nurseries. Why not? Does it matter? Why do certain jobs attract certain sexes?

Work

Work

Gender

Relaxation

Internet

Call centre

Compensation

Depressio

A hair-raising price for being too honest

Janet Street-Porter

Just over a year ago, Bushra Noah applied for a job as a junior hairstylist at a funky salon in London's King's Cross. The interview lasted less than ten minutes. The owner, Sarah Desrosiers, was unimpressed that Miss Noah was unwilling to remove her Muslim headscarf when working.

As far as she was concerned, the staff at Wedge hair salon were advertisements for the shop, and if one of them covered their head completely it would send out the wrong message to potential customers. The decision was tough on Miss Noah, who had previously worked as a junior in a salon before leaving Britain to get married in Syria in 2006.

But Ms Desrosiers could never have predicted the impact of her decision not to offer the girl a job that day. The unsuccessful applicant sued her for religious discrimination, seeking £34,000 in damages. This week, Miss Noah was awarded £4,000 for "injury to feelings" and is working as a shop assistant while studying travel and tourism at college. Ms Desrosiers reckons she has lost £40,000 in income while fighting the case. Is this political correctness gone mad? Are hurt feelings just part and parcel of not getting the job you desperately wanted?

This is a modern story of two single-minded, highly principled young women. Ms Desrosiers, 32, started as a junior at 17, just like Miss Noah, sweeping the floor where she worked, practising on friends and fellow staff. Over the years, she had come up with a business plan and eventually invested £5,000 of her hard-earned savings to secure a lease on premises in an up-and-coming area near King's Cross,

offering adventurous hairstyles to a local clientele. Miss Noah obviously had ambitions as a hairdresser too. Over the years, she unsuccessfully applied for jobs in 25 salons.

But was Ms Desrosiers guilty of

Islamaphobia, or too brutally honest for her own good? Unfortunately, the laws relating to discrimination are so woolly, so open to misinterpretation, that this ruling neither helps devout youngsters like Miss Noah get the jobs they want, nor does it protect employers like Ms Desrosiers, who

claim they can be exploited in the name of religion.

Ms Desrosiers' defence was that how her staff did their own hair was integral to the atmosphere in her salon and to the business of

> This week, Miss Noah was awarded £4,000 for "injury to feelings"... Is this political correctness gone mad? Are hurt feelings just part and parcel of not getting the job you desperately wanted?

attracting customers. Of course this is spurious rubbish. My own hairdresser shaves his head, so I certainly don't get any ideas there! Look at top hairdressers (generally male) like Nicky Clarke (weird horse's mane haircut I wouldn't be seen dead in), Sam McKnight (not very much hair at all) and colourist to the stars Daniel Galvin (boring layer cut). Great hairdressers exude confidence – and that's about it.

Visiting a salon for the first time, I ask for the youngest person to do my hair. At least they'll have an inkling of what is happening at street-level. The person I want fiddling around with my hair is not some bitchy, middle-aged queen who thinks I'm too old and too chubby to bother with. If Miss Noah was the youngest person at Wedge, I would probably have been perfectly happy for her to attend to my needs.

Ms Desrosiers' other claim – that she could not understand why anyone would be working in hairdressing if they were against the display of women's hair on religious grounds – has much more validity.

The case should never have come to court. Ms Desrosiers was too honest to Miss Noah and has paid a high price. On the other hand, I don't believe that hurt feelings are worth 4p, let alone £4,000.

The Independent 19 June 2008
© 2008 Independent News and Media Limited

No wonder bullied call centre workers are off sick the most

Sylvia Patterson

A friend of mine once worked in a call centre. It was for a home energy company and she loathed it so much she was signed off, after two years, with borderline clinical depression.

"If only it was just boring," she muses, now with a decent-ish job as a manager in a coffee shop chain. "But you're treated like a robot - in fact, trained like a robot - spied on, told you're failing your 'personal targets', threatened with the sack and blamed by the public for everything, including their children possibly dying of hypothermia if they've been cut off for not paying the bills.

> "You're treated like a robot - in fact, trained like a robot - spied on, told you're failing your 'personal targets', threatened with the sack and blamed by the public for everything"

"You would," she added, "be better off being a beagle in a cancer research laboratory, forced to smoke loads of fags in a cage, because at least you'd be doing some good - and you'd probably be a lot more healthy!"

Harsh words, perhaps, but the Office for National Statistics agrees, telling us this week the conditions inside the country's call centres are making the employees sick. Call centre workers in general, and call centre workers in customer services specifically, are twice as likely to take a day off sick than any other employee in the country, at 4.8% on any given week. And some of this sickness is physically real as well as "merely" sick in spirit.

Commenting on these figures, Karen Darby, a call centre veteran and now founder of a price comparison website was not surprised. "It's a reflection of the type of people who work in call centres," she says. "They are notoriously underpaid and, you know, if you pay peanuts... Absenteeism and attrition are the two biggest issues you face and some call centres go through 100% staff turnover every year."

Meanwhile, Claudia Hathaway, editor of an intriguing gazette called Call Centre Focus Magazine, attempts to stick up for the beleaguered staff. "It's an incredibly stressful job," she notes. "They're dealing with complex problems and people who are not happy to be calling you up." The people who take the fewest sick days off, meanwhile, at an almost negligible 0.8%, are transport workers, including train drivers, pilots and air traffic controllers.

Which is almost certainly nothing to do with unhealthy lifestyles or even considerably greater salaries and everything to do with having the kind of job which not only requires great responsibility for people other than yourself but inspires a genuine universal respect from both public and employers, and perhaps most importantly, in the employees themselves.

On the very day the call centre sickness news arrived, so did news of rising unemployment, estimated at hitting two million by Christmas. One TV news team went straight to a job centre in Leicester, filming a young adviser attempting to help a middle-aged man.

"There is one job," she chirped, brightly, "it's for a customer services adviser." We couldn't see his face, but relief, excitement and fabulous pension opportunities were possibly not visibly registered. But he might, like so many in the coming months, have no choice but to apply, other than the choice between the call centre drudge or watching Deal Or No Deal in poverty on the dole. And many, definitely, would prefer poverty on the dole to a minimum-wage working environment which runs on fear, paranoia and bullying from employers coupled with anger, frustration and rudeness from the public. None of which would be happening, perhaps, if we weren't so stressed out in the first place, in this stupefyingly frenetic world where the self-respecting working class has long been replaced by the never-satisfied consumer class, while the spectres of profits and corporate greed still rule. Which is what got us into this mess in the first place.

The only person who has ever benefited from the call centre, in fact (other than their owners) is comedian Alan Carr, whose years working in a call centre dealing with issues to do with lost

and stolen credit cards gave him his very first stand-up material after wearily regaling chums with stressed-out tales of continual grief from both employers and strangers.

"The number of weirdos and freaks who would ring up was incredible," he once told us. "People would say stupid things like: 'I bought a DVD player at this bazaar in Morocco and when I got home it didn't play. Can I get a refund?' I'd be thinking: A bit of common sense please! You don't buy a DVD player from a bloody nomad!" The call centre made him sick, his skin erupting in continual bouts of psoriasis.

And many, definitely, would prefer poverty on the dole to a minimum-wage working environment which runs on fear, paranoia and bullying from employers coupled with anger, frustration and rudeness from the public.

"When I was in the call centre, I really looked like the Singing Detective," he added. "I remember when it started happening. My face went all red. And this guy said, 'what's up with yer face?' and I just said, 'I feel all funny and itchy' and scabs were coming up. I just burst into tears and thought, I've got a crap job, I look ugly, I'm covered in scabs'. But after I left, I never had it so bad."

Which makes working in a call centre, officially, more stressful than the hitherto universally-acknowledged most stressful job - a stand-up comedian. And many comedians, as we know, end up so acutely stressed out they're paralysed with neuroses in a mental hospital for years and, in some cases, actually end up dead, due to suicide. It's enough to make you call-centre sick all right.

The Sunday Herald 16 November 2008

The only person who has ever benefited from the call centre, in fact (other than their owners) is comedian Alan Carr

I've tried working beside a swimming pool - and it sucks

Sun, sea, sand...laptop?

Ravi Somaiya

You hear it all the time: wireless internet, mobile phones and laptops mean there really is no reason to stay in the office. You can work from anywhere. It's the future, you know.

No it's not: it's a barefaced lie. It's along the same lines as the untruths we tell children about farmyard animals. It would be nice if cows went "moo" and looked clean, but in reality they bellow "meuuuuuuuuuurghhhhhh" and are encrusted in filth. It would be lovely if pigs were pink and happy, instead of huge, smelly and angry. It would be fantastic if I could work effortlessly on a beach or on a mountain top. But I can't.

> **I defy anyone to be comfortable lying on the floor and working on a computer for more than seven minutes**

Without wishing to make this too zoological - have you ever read that children's book in which an insomniac bear tries to find somewhere to sleep? After trying what I remember to be the kitchen, the car and the bathtub, he returns to his bed with a happy sigh. That's exactly how I feel when, having tried to work somewhere glamorous and cool, I return to the convenient confines of an office complete with computers, phones, tea-making facilities and a photocopier.

Let's examine a variety of likely wireless-world working locations, part of the much-vaunted future office. Firstly, the cafe. It sounds perfect - catch up on your emails while enjoying a pain au chocolat, a cafe au lait and other foods with "au" in their names. In reality? You get a keyboard full of croissant flakes and a laptop liberally smeared in pastry grease. Furthermore, unless you have a secret military-grade battery, you'll need to sit by a plug. And, of course, there will be only one table in the whole place with such an extravagant accessory, so you'll have to weave an elaborate web of cabling to get some power. You'll also, if you want to get anything serious done, have to spend about £57 and continuously consume snack foods for the duration of your stay.

I defy anyone to be comfortable lying on the floor and working on a computer for more than seven minutes. As this prone position is the default in the park, I fail to see how it's possible to do more than open some documents before needing to roll over. The lack of toilet facilities and exposure to the elements also makes the park deeply impractical for being productive.

You wouldn't take a project you had to finish with you to the cinema...

I've recently tried being a giant cliché by writing next to a pool. On a sun lounger no less, while sipping various (soft) drinks. It's how I imagine Don Johnson might have worked if Miami Vice had been about an office job. The problem being that I panic wildly every time anyone splashes nearby, and am risking sunburn, skin cancer and that crinkly lifeguard look if I do it regularly. Also, I can't get the sleeves of my suit jackets to roll up properly.

I'm not trying to spread misery here - I'm just pointing out that leisure activities and dull research on a computer are often incompatible, and you ruin both by attempting to mix them. You wouldn't take a project you had to finish with you to the cinema, or on a kayaking trip, because it would lead only to frustration and disaster. We should start seeing more sanguine pastimes in a similar light.

And it's about time we started to appreciate the joy of offices. You don't have to hoick around essential items such as staplers, plants, half-eaten chocolate and leftover napkins. Your chair will be a suitable height for sitting and working at. All the amenities we need are on hand. The internet connection is fast and free, and IT support is a mere phone call and a three-day wait away. There are toilets - and if there aren't you should seriously consider putting a note in the suggestion box.

For the most part we're warm in the winter, cool in the summer and don't have those odd marks from lying on grass. I, for one, think the future of working away from the office is, well, the past. I'll be at my desk if you need me.

The Guardian 21 July 2008
© Guardian News & Media Ltd

Prejudice isn't what keeps men out of nurseries

Barbara Ellen

If one was ever in any doubt that men have rigid ideas about what types of employment they're prepared to sully their lily-white hands for, one only has to think back to Arnold Schwarzenegger in Kindergarten Cop: a movie entirely dedicated to the premise that the job of nursery teacher was intrinsically demeaning for a red-blooded male, even if the actor playing him did resemble Stretch Armstrong nervously arriving at his first gay disco.

Almost 20 years on, and it's not that guys are just as picky - they're getting worse. According to the General Teaching Council, there are no young (under 25) males currently working in state-run nurseries. Elsewhere in the state sector, female teachers still outnumber men three to one, and it remains rare for a man to teach in primary school. One of the reasons given for this centres on men saying they find it hard to counter the gender stereotypes inherent in working with young children - that it has become such a female stronghold, males are put off by the thought of being perceived as 'unmanly', out of place, even 'suspicious'.

Reading this, one might surmise that there is a barrier unfairly stopping men from making genuine headway in such careers. That, in this professional area, it's men who have become the oppressed minority - quivering in the corners on parents' evening, holding placards reading: 'I'm not a paedophile.' Really? Or could it be that the real reason there are so few men in nursery and primary teaching, arenas where strong male role models are sorely needed, is that the money isn't great, while the work is demanding, but low-status - all hallmarks of that widespread, though still barely acknowledged, phenomenon, 'chick-work'.

> One of the most screamingly funny sights of recent years has been the way men have muscled in on cooking - sorry chef-ing - since it started to look profitable and fun.

What is chick-work? It is many things, but basically it is any field of employment in which men don't fancy participating, and therefore allow women to dominate. In this way, classic chick-work would be anything low-paid, gruelling, most probably relating to cleaning, small children or 'the caring professions': hence the comparative rarity of 'mannies', male nurses, or guy-cleaners. My brother, a male rarity, has managed state care facilities for the elderly and the homeless, and, by his account, women willing to work in this twilight sphere generally outnumber men by at least five to one.

Isn't this the real reason men shy away from teaching small children? That it falls into the category of jobs they don't feel 'become' them? Nothing to do with some bizarre borderline sci-fi concern about how their penis-decked persons are not welcome on Planet of the Female Nursery Teachers. After all, since when did that ever bother them? One of the most screamingly funny sights of recent years has been the way men have muscled in on cooking - sorry chef-ing - since it started to look profitable and fun. Amazing how, with a few rings of Gordon and Jamie's cash tills, scrambling an egg went from something sissy and domestic your mum and Delia did, to an act of high-grade machismo.

What happened to worrying about looking 'unmanly' then? See also the astonishing number of males prepared to wriggle their booty on The X Factor, or even enter model shows. Just a few examples of how when men want to pursue a profession, even change its 'gender', as it were, they're generally not shy about doing it. And good luck to them, so long as they don't try to pass off their lack of interest in areas such as nursery education with cries of sexist-'wolf'.

In truth, men in female-dominated fields have little in common with women in male-dominated fields. Only last week the Chartered Management Institute reported that, at the current rate, women in management positions should achieve equal pay by 2195. (Wow. Only 187 years to wait - should we feel spoiled?) By contrast, education continues to fall over itself to attract men. Just a wild guess, but I'm thinking it was never going to take 187 years to get men paid equally in the female-dominated profession of teaching.

Indeed, maybe Kindergarten Cop said it all. After all, it wasn't the children raising objections to the new guy, or the mainly female staff, or the parents, it was Arnie's character himself who seemed to fear that his very maleness came under threat the more he got his hands dirty with chick-work. The only difference being that at the end of Kindergarten Cop, Arnie tearfully realised he'd 'learned something'. In real life, what's the betting he'd have been tearing open his wage packet, and sneering: 'Is this all you dopey bitches get paid?'

The Observer, 21 September 2008
© Guardian News & Media Ltd

For up-to-date statistics on:

Alcohol
Animals
Britain & its citizens
Consumers
Disability
Drugs
Eating disorders
Environmental iss
Financial issues
Food
Health
Internet & media
Law & order
Religion
Sport & leisure
War & conflict
Young people

as well as many other topics in Essential Articles see:

Fact File

NEW

Online Quicksearch for Essential Articles and Fact File

Quicksearch will instantly generate a list of articles and statistics on a topic, searching current and previous volumes of both Fact File and Essential Articles.

Just type the word you want to find into the search box:

http://www.carelpress.co.uk/quicksearch